Building Victorian Boston

Building Victorian Boston

The Architecture of Gridley J. F. Bryant

Roger G. Reed

University of Massachusetts Press
Amherst and Boston

LC 2006033405
ISBN 10: 1-55849-555-X
ISBN 13: 978-1-55849-555-5

Designed by Dennis Anderson
Set in New Baskerville by dix! Digital Prepress, Inc.
Printed and bound by Sheridan Books, Inc.

Library of Congress Cataloging-in-Publication Data

Reed, Roger G., 1950–
    Building Victorian Boston : the architecture of Gridley J. F. Bryant /
Roger G. Reed.
        p.   cm.
    Includes bibliographical references and index.
    ISBN-13: 978-1-55849-555-5 (cloth : alk. paper)
    ISBN-10: 1-55849-555-X (cloth : alk. paper)
 1. Bryant, Gridley James Fox, 1816–1899.
 2. Architects—Massachusetts—Biography.
 3. Public architecture—Massachusetts—Boston—History—19th century.
 4. Public architecture—New England—History—19th century.
 I. Bryant, Gridley James Fox, 1816–1899.   II. Title.
    NA737.B743R44 2007
    720.92—dc22
    [B]
                                2006033405

British Library Cataloguing in Publication data are available.

This book has been published with the support of a generous
grant from the Graham Foundation for Advanced Studies in the Fine Arts.

Cover illustration: Franklin Street with Arch Street entering at left,
circa 1870. (Courtesy Earle G. Shettleworth, Jr.)

To Earle G. Shettleworth, Jr., scholar, colleague, and friend

CONTENTS

ILLUSTRATIONS

ACKNOWLEDGMENTS

MY RESEARCH has benefited from the assistance of many kind scholars. Foremost among them is Earle G. Shettleworth, Jr., without whose assistance and encouragement this book would not have been written. Moreover, a good deal of information, particularly about the Maine projects, was made available to me through the extensive files of the Maine Historic Preservation Commission, where he has long served as the State Historic Preservation Officer. Support and encouragement were also provided by Keith Morgan of Boston University. Many others have also been generous with their assistance. As Bryant left no single repository of documents, I have depended on many individuals who have contributed important pieces of evidence and information. They include Lorna Condon, archivist at Historic New England (formerly Society for the Preservation of New England Antiquities); James Garvin, architectural historian for the New Hampshire State Historic Preservation Office; Lyman Holmes, attorney and historian in Machias, Maine; Arthur Krim, architectural historian in Cambridge, Massachusetts; James O'Gorman, professor emeritus of art history at Wellesley College; Pamela Scott, architectural historian in Washington, D.C.; Catharina Slautterback of the Prints and Photographs Collections at the Boston Athenaeum; Darrin Von Stein, architectural historian in New York City; Sara E. Wermiel, architectural historian in Boston; and Bernard Zirnheld, architectural historian pursuing a degree at Yale.

Introduction

LOOKING BACK at the life of Gridley J. F. Bryant (1816–1899) in 1901, his friend Henry Bailey characterized him as "An Architect of the Old School."[1] What Bailey referred to as "old school" was an era of unregulated building, when traditions of craftsmanship were being replaced by products of the machine age. Bryant's career began in the early nineteenth century, when there were few professional architects. By the time of his death, well-established schools, both in the United States and abroad, provided formal training and offered degrees in architecture. The American Institute of Architects was working to establish professional standards that included fee schedules, regulated competitions, and the licensing of architects. By contrast, Bryant typified the unregulated, aggressive practitioner who advanced his career and profession by his own high standards and work ethic in an age of intense competition.

Although Bryant was a product of his times, he played a lasting role in shaping the architecture of Boston and New England. Following his death, all six leading Boston dailies featured accounts of his life and career under such headlines as "Great Builder," "Famed Bostonian," and "Work Lives"—this despite the fact that much of his architecture was no longer in fashion and he died penniless in an old men's home.[2]

For a young man of Bryant's era the best option available for training was to work in an architect's office. Typically, young men started out having to pay as students, only later receiving compensation as draftsmen. Alternatively, an aspiring architect might apprentice with a carpenter, housewright, or mason. After learning a trade in the construction industry, anyone could teach himself the rudiments of drafting and declare himself an architect.

As far as is known, Bryant never traveled to Europe. He learned his architectural history from books and from better-educated colleagues, applying ideas to buildings through his grounding in neoclassical design learned from Boston architect Alexander Parris, the city's leading practitioner after Charles Bulfinch departed for Washington, D.C., in 1818. Parris, who worked in both the Federal and Greek Revival styles, also owned one of the best architectural libraries in Boston. Bryant's training under Parris was grounded in the traditions of neoclassical architecture, and that influence would always be strongly reflected in his work. But Bryant also learned about building construction from his father, who not only was a mason but also possessed remarkable innovative skills related to his work as a masonry contractor. Gridley J. F. Bryant grew up watching his father work as a builder and could have chosen to continue in that line of employment. Being more ambitious, young Gridley attended the Gardiner Lyceum in Gardiner, Maine, where he received an elementary education in mathematics and engineering before joining Parris. He also took lessons from a Boston artist and lithographer. At age twenty-one, at a time when the country was in an economic depression, Bryant established his own architectural practice in Boston.

For Bryant, architecture was above all a business. In his understanding of the commercial aspects of the profession, he was one of the first truly modern architects.[3] He recognized that as an advocate for his client, an architect should seek to obtain the best expertise available in the preparation of design solutions and should complete the building as economically as possible, using sound construction practices. Bryant understood that he could best serve a client by ensuring that a building was constructed efficiently and durably. At the same time, Bryant frequently tried to persuade a client to spend more than he might have planned, in the interests of erecting a structure with greater aesthetic value to the community.

Much of Bryant's work was done in collaboration with others. In the early nineteenth century, it was not economical to maintain a large office of draftsmen. The small number of drawings an architect was required to produce did not warrant keeping many paid employees on hand; nor did the uncertainty of being retained for the more time-consuming work of construction supervision. Yet if the architect was to provide a more useful service than simply drawing pretty buildings, it was important to be able to offer a client assurances that his project would be properly constructed according to budget. This was particularly important in an age when new building materials were frequently being introduced as the construction industry become more industrialized. One solution Bryant devised was to avoid the time-consuming process of making drawings by instead preparing lengthy and detailed written specifications. Another was to collaborate with other designers as needed. Although the specifics of Bryant's arrangements with other architects are not known, it is clear that temporary agreements with colleagues enabled him to turn out an astonishing number of projects. By the time of Bryant's death, a typical architect's office maintained a large staff of draftsmen producing multiple sheets of detailed drawings to document the work to be done, at least for major building projects. That Bryant was able to provide efficient construction supervision without maintaining a large office of draftsmen is part of the explanation for his success.

Being a "modern" architect also meant being skilled at advancing one's own reputation in a competitive profession. Bryant's single-minded determination to become the foremost architect in the city is evident in his use of lithography for self-promotion. There was certainly a precedent for this among earlier architects, but Bryant proved particularly adept at making an investment in the promotion of his work. He produced printed views of many important projects in colored renderings. It is especially remarkable that with no American professional journal to feature an architect's work, by 1856 the London journal *The Builder* had featured designs for three of Bryant's finished projects. No other American architect could make that claim. Knowing, however, that it was the public, not other architects, he had to impress, Bryant also made heavy use of popular journals, such as *Ballou's Pictorial Drawing Room Companion,* which frequently featured illustrations of his projects during the 1850s.

Many of Bryant's largest commissions were either for public buildings or for commercial blocks involving building committees or multiple clients. This was not like designing a house, where the architect could establish a relationship with a single client and obtain a great deal of artistic freedom. As an architect who specialized in the design of public buildings, Bryant often had to bring groups of clients to the table and get them to agree on a design. His skills in this regard may not always have been admired by some of his colleagues. John Hubbard Sturgis, an architect with whom Bryant worked on a few projects in the 1860s, reflected the attitude of a typical upper-class architect when, in 1868, shortly after Bryant established a formal partnership with Louis P. Rogers, Sturgis wrote, "What with Rogers to do the designing & drawing & you the letter-writing, wire-pulling & '*bunkum*' I should say you made a very promising firm."[4]

Given Sturgis's wealthy English background, it is doubtful that this sarcasm was meant good-naturedly. He was writing at a time when Bryant dominated the architectural profession in Boston, having obtained most of the major commissions for large public buildings and many of the commercial blocks built in the city. It is not unreasonable to suspect that a mixture of envy and resentment colored the attitudes of other architects as well. It is no accident that his opinionated and acerbic colleague Arthur Gilman never achieved the same success alone that he did when working with Bryant. Artistic temperament could produce innovative designs but not necessarily buildings that got constructed.

Bryant often worked in small towns and rural areas of New England as well, where "bunkum" meant an ability to persuade trustees and building committees to spend more money for a building that used the best materials and was designed in the latest style. New England is notorious for its miserly ways when it comes to public spending, but Bryant was particularly successful in appealing to the sense of public pride in many communities. There is circumstantial evidence that his building projects often turned out to be more lavish than was originally intended.

Toward the end of his life, Bryant lamented that he had lived long enough to see much of his work demolished. Yet what survives has ensured that his importance as a nineteenth-century architect continues to be recognized. In 1946, at a time when mid-nineteenth-century architecture was commonly consigned to the trash heap of history, an early admirer and fellow architect, Walter H. Kilham, offered measured praise: "Bryant's work was always well balanced, sane, and practical, and carried out with materials at hand rather than with materials which had to be imported. He was a stabilizing force in an architecturally uncertain age."[5]

Bryant left no office records or collections of letters and drawings. Or rather, the collection he left with his friend Henry Bailey has long since disappeared. In 1890 Bailey compiled an inventory of what had been lost, but this list of drawings and specifications cannot be considered comprehensive. Not only are important projects missing from the list, but also it includes projects never built that are not identified as such. A large number of Bryant's drawings do survive in widely scattered locations. These form a good representation of most phases of the architect's career. My own research has relied heavily on the newspapers of the day. Given Bryant's unfailing skills as a self-promoter, it has been possible to compile an extensive record of his life's work. It is my hope that this interpretation of Bryant's career will result in a greater appreciation of his architectural legacy.

1

Granite Bred in the Bone

GRIDLEY J. F. BRYANT (fig. 1.1) grew up in a world of granite construction. Although brick was the predominant building material used in Boston, major architectural landmarks erected after Bryant's birth in 1816 were often built of granite derived from regional quarries. The architect's father, also named Gridley (fig. 1.2), worked as a mason and constructed many of these buildings. Indeed, the elder Bryant was best known as the inventor of mechanisms and devices to transport and manipulate the heavy stone used in construction. His most famous accomplishment, the "Granite Railroad" in Quincy, was designed and built when his son was a young boy.[1] Throughout his childhood, Gridley J. F. Bryant witnessed his father's work as a contractor, both in the procurement of stone and in the actual construction of these granite buildings.

One of the elder Bryant's most important projects was the Suffolk County Courthouse, begun in 1833 and completed in 1836, just as young Gridley was coming of age. In Boston's dense urban center, monumental public buildings typically occupied sites between rows of urban blocks on narrow streets. Such was the case with the massive granite courthouse, constructed in the Greek Revival style. This imposing structure stood on Court Street between Washington and Tremont streets. Dwarfing its neighbors, the building was a long, two-story rectangular barn with massive Doric porticos at either end (fig. 1.3). The great Doric columns, each weighing sixty-four tons in the rough, were quarried out of Quincy granite at a location four miles from the nearest waterway, the Neponset River, south of the city. Gridley Bryant's responsibilities included transporting the columns from the quarry to the building site on sleds. Because of an early thaw, however, Bryant quickly had to construct special wagons capable of carrying the

Figure 1.1. Gridley James Fox Bryant, age sixty-five. *New England Magazine*, November 1901. (Courtesy Trustees of the Brookline Public Library)

Figure 1.2. Gridley Bryant. This image of the architect's father in old age does little to suggest his intrepid nature as an inventor and builder. From Stuart's *Lives and Works of Civil and Military Engineers of America.* (Courtesy Earle G. Shettleworth, Jr.)

load. The wagons were drawn by sixty-five oxen and twelve horses.[2] The procession of animals and granite, as it snaked its way through Boston, provided dramatic evidence of the elder Gridley's ability to take on ambitious construction projects, and to develop innovative solutions when difficulties arose. There can be little doubt that young Gridley's self-confidence as an architect derived in large part from his firsthand experience of these accomplishments.

Although Gridley J. F. Bryant grew up in Boston and Quincy, his parents were from the south shore farming community of Scituate. It was there

Figure 1.3. Second Suffolk County Courthouse, Court Street, Boston, Solomon Willard, architect. Supervised by Alexander Parris and built by Gridley Bryant, senior, this granite structure was completed in 1836. A year later, Gridley J. F. Bryant opened his Court Street office nearby. (Courtesy Earle G. Shettleworth, Jr.)

that his father was born in 1790. Having lost his own father when he was still a boy, Gridley senior received only a few months' education each year in a local school before, at age fifteen, apprenticing with an unidentified builder in Boston. According to biographical accounts, within a few years he took charge of his employer's business before, at age twenty-one in 1811, establishing himself as an independent masonry contractor.

Boston's architecture in 1811 consisted mostly of brick buildings, and much of his early work was presumably as a brick mason. Charles Bulfinch's designs dominated the city at that time, just as they do today when one thinks of Boston at the turn of the eighteenth century.[3] A variety of well-known structures survive as testimony to Bulfinch's skills, including the Massachusetts State House (1795–97), the three Harrison Gray Otis houses (1795–96, 1800–1802, 1805–8), and the enlargement of Faneuil Hall (1805–6). In Gridley Bryant's day, there were many more distinctive landmarks, now gone, such as the Boston Theater (1793–94), the Tontine Crescent (1793–94), Park Row (1803–5), India Wharf (1803–7), and the Colonnade (1810–12). This Bulfinch legacy of elegant Federal-style brick buildings gives a somewhat misleading image of a city where granite buildings, including many designed by Bulfinch, also figured prominently in the early nineteenth century. Since granite, unlike brick, had to be quarried and transported to a given site, its popularity offered Gridley Bryant opportunities to work as more than just one of many bricklayers in Boston at that time.

Within a year of starting his own business as a brick mason, he was employed to rebuild the Boston Harbor defenses under the supervision of Loammi Baldwin. This large-scale construction project involved working with masonry in difficult locations. Loammi Baldwin (1780–1838) earned great renown as an engineer. A graduate of Harvard in 1800, he began his adult life practicing law. Within a few years, Baldwin's interest in the mechanical arts took him to Europe to study public works. His career as the "Father of American Civil Engineering" sent him around the country and back to Europe again, either working on or studying public works projects such milldams, canals, and naval dry docks.[4]

It was probably fortunate for Gridley senior that he obtained work rebuilding harbor fortifications, as the early nineteenth century was not a good time to enter the construction business in Boston. In 1807 President Jefferson imposed an embargo on trade with war-torn Europe. Commerce had only just begun to recover from the effects of the embargo when the War of 1812 began. It was not until 1815 that revenue duties in Boston regained their prewar levels. Bulfinch's warehouse complex known as India Wharf was completed the year of the embargo. Significantly, Central Wharf, a four-story brick block consisting of fifty-four stores, a major construction project, was not begun until 1816.

Gridley Bryant's success as a stone contractor for major buildings benefited from his close working relationships with the leading architects and engineers who rose to prominence in the city after Bulfinch's departure from Boston in 1818. Bryant had gained the confidence of Loammi Baldwin early in his career. He also worked closely with three other remarkable individuals who came to dominate the architecture of Boston in the 1820s and 1830s: Alexander Parris, Isaiah Rogers, and Solomon Willard. Like Bryant, two of these men also grew up in south shore farming communities and had little formal education. Alexander Parris (1780–1852) was raised in Pembroke and apprenticed to a local carpenter, Noah Bonney, at age sixteen. He worked as an architect in Portland, Maine, and Richmond, Virginia, before settling in Boston in 1815. Isaiah Rogers (1800–1869) grew up in Marshfield and also apprenticed to a local carpenter, Jesse Shaw. His training as an architect was acquired under Solomon Willard (1783–1862) between 1822 and 1826.[5] Willard, who grew up west of Boston, combined the skills of carpenter, engineer, mason, and architect, though he too began as a carpenter. His talents enabled him to work as a carver and builder of architectural models, as well as a sculptor. He later acquired architectural training in a school taught by Asher Benjamin, the author of many important early builders' guides. Willard gained lasting fame for his work supervising the Bunker Hill Monument, a long-drawn-out project that also required engineering skills and expertise as a mason. Although there were other architects practicing in the city at this time, Parris, Rogers, and Willard dominated the construction of most of the prominent granite buildings erected during Bryant's youth.

Within a few years of establishing his own business as a mason, Gridley Bryant married Maria Winship Fox of Boston on December 3, 1815. The couple had ten children, of whom Gridley James Fox was the eldest, born on August 29, 1816. Although the family was large, and all of the siblings lived into maturity, only the eldest achieved any prominence. Following Gridley's birth, there were three more boys and six girls. All apparently lived unremarkable lives in Plymouth County and never left the working class from which their father originated.[6]

Except for his work with Loammi Baldwin on the Boston Harbor defenses, little is known about Gridley Bryant's early projects as a mason.

Presumably he constructed many of the brick building erected in Boston after the War of 1812. A building contract in 1822 for the house of Henry Gassett on Summer Street (for which Solomon Willard was the architect) provides a rare record of Bryant's work as a brick mason. He also worked as the stone mason (with John Redman) on St. Paul's Church in 1819–20 and the Leverett Street Jail in 1822–23, both built of granite and designed by Alexander Parris. In 1823 Bryant was the contractor for the United States Bank building, a granite structure designed by Solomon Willard. The bank is said to have had the first cornice fabricated of granite in the country. In the course of this project Bryant designed a portable derrick for moving stone on site which apparently became a model of its type in building projects. He was one of the masons for the Faneuil Hall Market (Quincy Market) in 1824–26, another of Parris's designs. These projects were important buildings with high public visibility, and they brought Bryant into contact with many prominent citizens.

His involvement with the Quincy granite quarry and the invention of the "Granite Railroad" began with the planning for the Bunker Hill Monument. Many leading citizens were involved in raising funds to construct a granite obelisk near the site of the famous Revolutionary War battle in Charlestown. Lack of funds caused frequent work stoppages, so even though it was begun in 1826, the monument was not dedicated until 1843. No man played a greater role than Solomon Willard, the supervising architect for the project for the entire duration of its construction. To ensure a dependable supply of granite, it was decided that the Bunker Hill Association would purchase a quarry. Willard personally inspected granite quarries all over New England to find the best stone, settling on a quarry in Quincy, south of Boston. With funds supplied by Dr. John C. Warren, Bryant purchased the quarry on behalf of the association. During these years before much of the landfill around the Boston peninsula had been completed, the land route to Charlestown was very circuitous and required crossing the Charles River. Bryant's contribution in the earliest stages of construction was to devise a practical method of transporting the stone to the building site.[7] In the fall of 1825 Bryant obtained the backing of several prominent Bostonians who petitioned the Massachusetts legislature to obtain a charter for a "railroad" to transport the stone, the first such means of conveyance in the country. With several wealthy merchants as backers, including Thomas H. Perkins, William Sullivan, Amos A. Lawrence, Isaac T. Davis, and David Moody, the success of the railroad was assured. Without the support of these men, Gridley Bryant's innovative idea for transporting stone might not have overcome the skepticism of the legislature. That he was able to enlist such sagacious businessmen as Perkins and Lawrence is evidence of his skills of persuasion, which his son inherited.

Bryant began the survey for the railroad in April 1826. His idea was to build a line consisting of a three-mile track from the quarry down to the landing on the Neponset River. From there the stone would be loaded on flatboats and taken by water to Charlestown, where it would be unloaded and hauled up the hill to the site of the monument. The three-mile-long track consisted of stone sleepers laid eight feet apart, upon which were set wooden rails (later replaced by stone) six inches thick and twelve inches high. On top were spiked three-inch iron plates one quarter of an inch thick. From the beginning, stone rails were used at road crossings with thicker plates four inches wide and half an inch thick. Stone was used instead of iron because for that short distance, it was more economical to use material that was readily available. No steam engines were involved. Cars hauled by teams of horses pulled the loads. The cars were moved on an endless chain that returned them after unloading. Bryant designed a platform balanced by weights and operated by gears which allowed the cars to be tipped for unloading and then returned to the horizontal position. He also invented the turntable, which was positioned at the foot of the quarry. Switches and turnouts were also developed for the railroad. Bryant's achievement was more than simply constructing railroad tracks from the quarry to the wharf, or even being the first to experiment with this new means of transportation. One of his most important inventions was the four-wheel car, later an eight-wheel car, to carry the heavy stone needed for the Charlestown Navy Yard dry dock built by Laommi Baldwin in 1828. This eight-wheel car operated under the same principle as the later passenger cars and locomotives on railroad lines throughout the country.[8]

Notwithstanding the technical accomplishment of Bryant's railroad, it was not a success in regard to its intended purpose. Stone hauled by the Granite Railway and actually used for the Bunker Hill Monument made up only the foundation and the lower forty feet of the obelisk. Owing to the amount of loading and unloading of the stone, and the concomitant damage resulting from frequent handling, it turned out to be more cost-effective to revert to the land routes. Where the railroad did prove economical was in the transportation of larger stones, such as the columns for the Suffolk County Courthouse and the stone for the naval yard dry docks. Bryant, however, never patented his inventions and thus missed an opportunity to derive significant financial benefit from his work.

His career as a building contractor included some exceptionally difficult projects late in his life. In the 1840s he contracted to build lighthouses and beacons in remote locations off the coast of Maine under the direction of Alexander Parris, who was then working for the United State government. Bryant built the granite lighthouses at Saddleback Ledge and Mantinicus Island, both hazardous sites well out in the Atlantic. An example of this exceptional man's willingness to undertake challenging and dangerous work was the York Ledge Monument (1840–41).[9]

At age fifty, Bryant assembled the cast iron beacon off Portsmouth and York harbors, designed by Parris. The hazardous conditions involved in this project make this project a particularly remarkable story. The site consisted of a maximum of two hundred square feet of buildable rock no more than two feet above sea level. Even in calm weather the sea swells broke in every direction. Over a period of five hundred days, Bryant and his crew were able to work only ninety-nine, often for less than two hours at a time. A lighthouse was not a practical option for these dangerous shoals, so it was decided to erect an iron spar beacon. This structure was to consist of six hollow cast iron pillars, each twenty-two and a half feet tall and ten to twelve inches in diameter, to be filled with hydraulic cement. They were erected in the form of a pyramid by drilling holes in the rock. The apex formed by these columns supported a tubular iron cap eight feet high. Supporting the pillars were an iron plate and six diagonal braces.

The first phase of the project involved erecting a staging area at Godrey's Cove five miles away. In addition to temporary houses, Bryant had his crew construct three boats he designed specifically for landing at the site in heavy seas. The second phase was to construct the drilling machines, permanently affixed to the rock, that would make the holes for the pillars. Although the first phase was supposed to run from February 8 to April 15, 1840, it was not until May 19 that the first successful landing was made, and frequent landings were not possible until July. Work was suspended and the crew dismissed in late November, but mild winter weather encouraged Bryant to begin again in late January 1841. By June all the pillars were set in place, though this work was often done with the men standing in the water and holding onto the structure to keep from being washed away. The beacon was finally completed on July 20.

Gridley Bryant's career came to a close around the time that Alexander Parris completed his work for the government. Toward the end of his life Bryant was listed in the Boston city directories as a builder and engineer, or simply an engineer. In that capacity, shortly before his retirement,

Bryant formed a partnership with Albert Blaisdell in 1850–51. He died in 1867, having lived out his final years in an old family homestead in North Scituate.

ALTHOUGH YOUNG Gridley J. F. Bryant acquired a firsthand familiarity with the world of architecture through his father, this period produced little in the way of design that was innovative or remarkable other than the monumental structures built of granite. The Boston of Bryant's youth was a city where wealthy residential neighborhoods existed not only on Beacon Hill, but also on streets such as Park, Tremont, Franklin, and Summer. Often these included freestanding houses with gardens within a few blocks of the city's wharfs. One visitor's description in 1834 is particularly evocative: "Another pleasant feature of Boston is the many green and shady front yards which relieve and refresh the eye, as you wander through its winding streets. More or less of these are met with in every part of the city; but Summer street, on both sides, is lined with them from one end to the other. This, to my taste, is decidedly the handsomest street in Boston. Town and country seem here married to each other, and there is no jar between the husband and the wife. It is a harmonious union, and the source of many pleasures." With what is now known as Federal period architecture no longer fashionable, however, other observers had a more critical view of what was being newly built in the city. Henry Russell Cleveland, for example, observed in 1836 that although Boston was known as the Athens of America, "the days of Pericles have not yet come, if we judge from the architecture of the city, which is singularly bad."[10]

If there were few noteworthy examples of modern architecture in Boston during the 1820s and 1830s it was in part due to the city's declining situation as a major center of trade and commerce. Architectural innovation tends to come with economic prosperity, or at least a willingness to expend money on prestigious buildings. The construction of the Erie Canal in 1826 had provided New York City with direct access to the new markets opening up in the midwestern states. Not only was Boston farther from these new markets, but it had the additional disadvantage of a barrier created by the mountains along the western border of the state. It is for this reason that the city would later make concerted efforts to promote the construction of railroad lines to the southwest, west, and northwest of Boston. The stagnation of Boston's economy in relation to New York explains the importance of Mayor Joshua Quincy's Faneuil Hall Marketplace, a redevelopment project to invigorate the city's waterfront facilities, built in 1824–26.

As noted, Charles Bulfinch had dominated the architecture of Boston up to his departure for Washington, D.C., in 1818.[11] Today his work is popularly associated with surviving brick buildings. Consequently, the role this architect played in making granite a popular building material has not been given adequate attention. Indeed, any examination of granite architecture in Boston and environs must include a survey of the large variety of stone buildings by Bulfinch if we are to appreciate fully the later popularity of this native stone. Much of the granite used by Bulfinch derived from Tyngsboro and Westford, near Lowell. Transported by the Middlesex Canal (completed in 1803) and known as "Chelmsford" granite, this stone had a light hue commonly referred to as white. It is likely that the stone appealed to Bulfinch for the same reason he used marble. Light-colored granite and marble were similar in appearance to the limestone found in the neoclassical structures in Britain that provided models for the architect's work.

The state prison in Charlestown, erected in 1804–5, is the first example of a Bulfinch design in granite. Convict labor was used to work the stone shipped in along the canal, making it more economical to use than other materials. The austere Bulfinch design for the Charlestown prison was followed by a long list of notable successors by the same architect: the Massachusetts Bank on State Street (1809), the first Suffolk County Courthouse on School Street (1810–12; fig. 1.4), the New England Marine Insurance Office on State Street (ca. 1811), the Third Latin School on School Street (1812), University Hall at Harvard College (1813–14), the New South Church at Summer and Bedford streets (1814), the Blake-Tuckerman houses on Bowdoin Square (1814–15), the Manufacturers and Mechanics Bank on State Street (1814–15), the Massachusetts Fire and Marine Insurance Office on State Street (1814–15), the Middlesex County Jail in Cambridge (1815–16), and the Massachusetts General Hospital (1818–23). Where a more pronounced architectural effect than plain ashlar blocks was desired, the principal story was typically distinguished by the use of round-arched windows or blind arches. In exceptional cases, such as University Hall and the Massachusetts General Hospital, further embellishments such as pilasters and porticos were added.

After Bulfinch left Boston, the three architects known so well to Gridley Bryant senior were responsible for most of the important examples of granite architecture. Indeed, Bulfinch's last major local building, the

Massachusetts General Hospital, was erected under the supervision of Alexander Parris. It was Parris who took up Bulfinch's mantle as the pre-eminent architect in the city. Parris's major Boston projects in this post-Bulfinch period included St. Paul's Church (1819–20), the David Sears House (1819–22), and the Faneuil Hall Market buildings (Quincy Market) of 1824–26 (fig. 1.5). To this list should be added the First Parish Church in Quincy, built in 1827–28. These buildings are all in the Greek Revival style. The Sears House, built for David Sears, the wealthiest man in Boston, was originally a freestanding structure with its entrance on the east side. Just as the nearby Hancock House was the most remarkable residence in Boston in the late eighteenth century, so the Sears House was one of the most outstanding examples of residential architecture in the early nineteenth century. It was built of Chelmsford granite with carved ornamental panels by Solomon Willard.[12]

The granite architecture of Alexander Parris survives as among the most enduring architectural landmarks in Boston. After Parris, Solomon

Figure 1.4. First Suffolk County Courthouse, School Street, Boston, 1810–12, Charles Bulfinch, architect. This building was one of several structures Bulfinch designed using Chelmsford granite. It was converted for the Boston City Hall in 1840 by Gridley J. F. Bryant and Jonathan Preston with only minor changes. (Author's collection)

Figure 1.5. Quincy Market development, Boston, 1824–26, Alexander Parris, architect. Gridley Bryant, senior, was one of the principal masons. This drawing by Abel Bowen from 1828 conveys the importance of this project in the redevelopment of Boston's waterfront shortly before the advent of the railroad. (Courtesy Historic New England)

Willard was the second-most prominent designer of Boston's granite architecture in the second quarter of the nineteenth century. His three major known designs of the 1820s (apart from the Bunker Hill Monument) were the Central Universalist Church of 1822–23, the branch bank of the United States Bank, built in 1824, and the Norfolk County Courthouse in Dedham, erected in 1826. These structures exhibited Willard's skills as a model maker and sculptor more than as an architect, for they were more impressive as monumentally carved objects than as buildings with fully integrated designs. All three supported façades with monumental porticos (the Norfolk Courthouse had two, one on either end). Willard's limited skills as an architect did not show improvement with the Suffolk County Courthouse of 1833–36. Henry Russell Cleveland, writing about the building as it was nearing completion, observed that the Doric columns (again supporting two porticos, one at either end) were beautiful in their own right. "But they do not belong to the building; they would look just as well, and would seem as appropriate, if they stood on the opposite side of the street; they add nothing to the beauty of the edifice, because it has no beauty to add to, and they certainly do not constitute its beauty, because no one thinks of viewing them as parts of it."[13] Though harsh, such criticism was not unwarranted for that massive structure.

Isaiah Rogers, the third major Boston architect who worked with the elder Bryant, had a more successful career than either Parris or Willard, though few of his buildings survive. Having begun independent practice in 1826, the year Parris completed his Faneuil Hall Market buildings, Rogers achieved rapid success with the designs for two granite buildings facing each other on Tremont Street. The Tremont Theater of 1827 provided the city with its most elegant neoclassical design. With its rusticated first story supporting pilasters and a full pediment, the theater avoided the heavy temple-front treatment associated with the Greek Revival style. Three entrances on the ground floor and two niches for sculpture at the colonnade level were round-arched in the neoclassical tradition of Bulfinch. Even the city's severest critics of the architectural scene admired this building before the façade underwent a major alteration in 1843. Henry Cleveland, the scourge of Solomon Willard's courthouse, praised the building in 1836, as would the even more acerbic critic Arthur Gilman in his controversial piece published in 1844.[14]

In 1828–29 Rogers designed the famous Tremont House across the street, perhaps the first palatial hotel to be built in this country. The Tremont House responded to the refined elegance of the theater with a monumental portico in the Doric order. Yet even the severe geometric lines of this Greek Revival–style edifice were modified by the bow-shaped granite end looking out over the adjoining cemetery. With this success, Rogers went on to design the conversion of the Old State House for the Boston City Hall in 1830. This work included a Greek Revival portico that has since been removed. In the same year Rogers began the Masonic Temple on Tremont Street opposite the Boston Common (fig. 1.6). Completed in 1832, this granite structure was a Gothic Revival design that fared less well with critic Henry Cleveland. That merciless observer of Boston architecture viewed it as a crude interpretation of the style. He savaged the design by making an analogy to a jackass with corner pinnacles representing the ears.[15] However intemperate his remarks, they did point to the unsophisticated simplicity of Boston's early efforts in the Gothic Revival style. Criticism notwithstanding, Rogers's work with the Tremont Temple and the Tremont House provided Boston with exceptional examples of modern architecture and led to major commissions for the architect in New York City.

Gentleman architect George W. Brimmer had earlier introduced the granite Gothic Revival in Boston with Trinity Church in 1828 (fig. 1.7).[16]

This structure established a pattern for stone churches with a central tower and crenellated parapets. In fact, this was the traditional New England meetinghouse, embellished with Gothic trim. Perhaps only the expense of carving Gothic detail in stone discouraged more embellishments. At any rate, that is certainly suggested by Brimmer's 1831 design for a wooden essay in the Gothic Revival, the remarkably ostentatious First Parish Church of Plymouth, Massachusetts. In Boston the granite design for Trinity Church was followed, in 1830–31, by the Bowdoin Street Church, attributed to Solomon Willard. Isaiah Rogers produced another variation of this granite design for St. Peter's Episcopal Church in Salem, in 1833–34. Like

Figure 1.6. Painting of Tremont Street, Boston, circa 1843, by Philip Harry. On the right is the Tremont Temple (1827) and on the left is the Tremont House (1828–29). Both structures were designed by Isaiah Rogers and represented two outstanding examples of modern granite architecture completed during Bryant's youth. (Museum of Fine Arts, Boston. Gift of Maxim Karolik for the M. and M. Karolik Collection of American Paintings, 1815–1865)

Figure 1.7. Trinity Church, Summer Street, Boston, 1828, George W. Brimmer, designer. This 1829 Gothic Revival–style church served as a prototype for many of the earliest New England churches in the Gothic Revival style. (Author's collection)

Brimmer, Rogers also produced a more elaborate essay in wood with the First Parish Church in Cambridge, erected in 1833.

It was another young architect, William Washburn, who introduced the first Boston example of a Gothic Revival design patterned after the cathedrals of Europe rather than the country parish churches of England. Grace Church on Temple Place, built of granite in 1835–36, featured aisles flanking a nave, as well as spires embellished with finials and crockets. Washburn had arrived from northern New Hampshire and worked in Boston with his brothers, Theodore and Jeremiah, as housewrights. The Washburns also operated a planing mill. William soon emerged as the architect of the family and eventually practiced on his own. Its not known where he acquired the training to construct such an ambitious granite structure, nor is anything known about the origins of the design.[17]

Houses of granite construction were also built during Gridley J. F. Bryant's youth. Preeminent among these was the already mentioned David Sears House by Alexander Parris. At the same time, in 1821–23, three granite structures were built as country houses in the adjoining rural town of Brookline. John Tappan, his brother Lewis, and their partner Arthur Sewall all erected houses of ashlar granite. The source of granite for these rather plain but substantial inland houses is not known, although it may have derived from Parker Hill in Roxbury. That location provided the stone for the Mill Dam in the Back Bay, erected at the same time and, like Brookline, in close proximity to Roxbury.[18] In any case, it is remarkable that these three merchants would choose to build stone houses in a community where most of their wealthy colleagues constructed their country homes with wood. In Boston, Samuel Cabot erected a plain granite house in 1823 on Temple Place, where a masonry residence seems less out of place. Other examples may have existed, as there clearly was a fashion developing in the 1820s for granite houses. In some respects, these houses were more directly related to the early commercial warehouses, for the plain granite block construction had none of the stylistic elegance of the David Sears House. The construction of these houses must have played a role in the popularity of granite-fronted commercial blocks built by members of the same merchant class.

For commercial architecture, granite was first used to frame door and window openings in shop fronts, the upper floors being brick.[19] The first known use of this type of granite shop front is the Custom House, erected in 1810 and said to have been designed by Uriah Cotting. Cotting was also responsible, as least as the builder, for a row of brick commercial buildings with granite shop fronts on Cornhill Street in 1816. The rationale for choosing granite instead of brick is not known for certain, but it seems likely that, as with the houses, the use of stone conveyed a sense of durability, as well as projecting an appearance of a uniform neoclassical elegance not as evident with brick. The Brattle Block, built in 1819, the same year the Sears House was begun, was the first commercial building with an entire façade of granite.

Alexander Parris's twin North and South Market buildings (1825) flanking Quincy Market provided a major example of granite commercial architecture, although only the façades are stone. With these structures, Parris followed the tradition established by Charles Bulfinch, contributing to the popularization of granite as a material to grace entire façades as opposed to just shop fronts. The granite work of Parris prior to the 1830s had a smooth finish in the tradition of neoclassical design. A change came with early granite warehouse buildings, such as Commercial Wharf (84 Atlantic Avenue) built in 1832–34 and designed by Isaiah Rogers. The stone for the walls is unfinished rock-faced granite. Only the stone that frames the windows and doors, and the first-story lintels, the cornice, and frieze were given a smooth finish. This was no doubt a economical decision in terms of saving the cost of even providing margins for the stone, but it contributed to popularizing an aesthetic for rock-faced granite, which historians later praised as the "Boston Granite style."

At the same time that Rogers was working on his Commercial Wharf block in the early 1830s, Alexander Parris was designing granite buildings for the Charlestown Navy Yard. Parris had overseen the construction of several granite structures at the navy yard when young Gridley Bryant began his apprenticeship. Thus, the aspiring architect would have considered granite the material of choice for all types of buildings throughout the city.

GRIDLEY J. F. BRYANT received his public school education, first in Boston, and then in Quincy, where his father had moved to manage the granite quarry, from April 1, 1827, until April 15, 1830. Upon graduation, the fourteen-year-old Gridley did something extraordinary for the son of a stone mason. On April 29 he booked passage by stage to Hallowell, Maine, on the Kennebec River above the river town of Gardiner, where he took up studies at the Gardiner Lyceum. Established by Benjamin Hale in 1822 with the assistance of Robert Hallowell Gardiner, this institution (located in a granite building) has been called the first engineering school in

America. It offered courses in civil architecture and carpentry.[20] Young Gridley was ambitious enough to look beyond the traditional sources of education to learn the profession of architecture at a time when programs for formal training scarcely existed. His father, who must have understood the benefits of a formal education through his Harvard-educated friend Loammi Baldwin, presumably supported his son's ambitions. The boy, however, attended the school for barely a year, his last tuition bill being dated February 1, 1831. The reason for his departure is not known. Perhaps young Bryant's restless energy, which kept him on the move throughout his career, made classroom studies difficult to abide. Perhaps also the emphasis on engineering rather than architectural design at the Gardiner Lyceum reflected his father's preferences, not the architectural ambitions of the son.

Whatever the reason, it was not his intention to return to Boston and work with his father as a mason-contractor. Bryant himself said that he "left home to commence the study of architecture" on November 1, 1831. As far as is known, his first position, presumably as a student, was at the Charlestown Navy Yard, working for Loammi Baldwin and Alexander Parris. His friend and biographer Henry Bailey, who had access to Bryant's records, noted representative facts and figures from early account books. The record he provides us with indicates that Bryant took twenty-four drawing lessons from Thomas Edwards in 1833, but does not mention any other formal schooling in architecture. This reference is in itself significant, for it establishes that at a very young age, when he could not easily afford lessons at seventy-five cents each, Bryant was intent on improving his rendering skills. That Thomas Edwards was his teacher is also significant in that Edwards was known for his early work as a lithographer of landscape views. Lithographic renderings of architectural designs would play an important role in Bryant's career.[21]

By this point Gridley Bryant was working for Parris in the capacity of a student. This typically involved a payment to the employer for the training received. It was not until September 13, 1836, that the twenty-year-old Bryant began to be paid—two dollars a day. Parris's career at that time mostly involved work for the government at the naval shipyard. In his capacity as an apprentice, Bryant would have gained close familiarity with the granite structures designed by Parris. In particular, the storehouse (Building 34) and the great Ropewalk were built while Bryant was learning to design under Parris's guidance (fig. 1.8). The Ropewalk was significant for its early use of fireproof brick with iron floors.[22] Parris had other

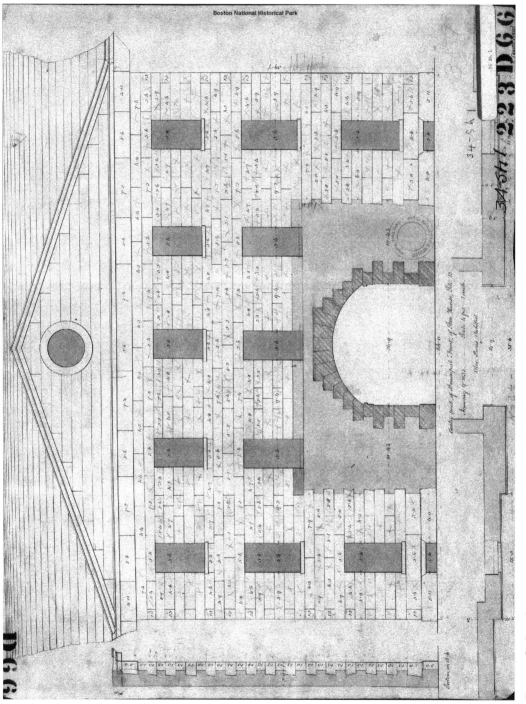

Figure 1.8. Storehouse (Building 34), Charlestown Navy Yard, Alexander Parris, architect. This drawing, dated January 7, 1835, illustrates the type of training Bryant received working for Parris. The drawings for Building 34 are not signed, but the building was under construction during Bryant's employment at the shipyard. (Courtesy Boston National Historical Park)

nongovernmental work, such as the Mechanics Bank building in South Boston (1837), which Bryant considered his "first triumph" in terms of architectural design. Unfortunately, no view has been located of this long-demolished building.

Parris was sufficiently impressed with Bryant to recommend him for the position of assistant draftsman at the Charlestown Navy Yard early in 1837 at the rate of three dollars a day. Parris had a large project in the offing and was prepared to limit his work to supervising Bryant two or three times a week. The government did not accept this arrangement, however, and the large unidentified project (probably the United States Custom House in Boston) did not go to Parris. This setback coincided with a worsening of economic conditions, and Parris wound up continuing with his work at the shipyard under his existing arrangements with the government.[23] With Parris having failed to improve his own situation, Bryant chose to set out on his own. In the summer of 1837 he took a job as a clerk for the Frankfort Granite Company of Frankfort, Maine, a concern in which his father had had an interest. Then, that fall, Bryant established his own architectural practice. On September 20, 1837, just past his twenty-first birthday, he received his first independent commission: five dollars for the plan of a cottage for a Mr. Abbott.

That Alexander Parris remained at the Charlestown Navy Yard was not surprising, for the national economy was entering a difficult period. Indeed, it was a particularly inauspicious time for Bryant to start a practice. The 1830s had begun with the newly established City of Boston taking significant actions to improve its commercial situation. Although the city was at a distinct disadvantage compared to New York, efforts were made to provide increased economic incentive for the city to grow. A major concern was the lack of land to build housing for an increasing population. The last portion of Beacon Hill to be reduced for landfill enabled developers to lay out Pemberton Square in 1835. Other landfills along the periphery of Boston's peninsula provided breathing room. Yet real growth for middle-class housing required a more substantial expansion of land. At the same time, the search for ways to foster financial growth led to a widespread interest in the railroads as an essential component of the growing city. The need to establish terminals in the center of the city also added to the pressure for more land.[24]

It is easily forgotten today how important the railroad was considered for sustaining the lifeblood of the city. After the innovation of Gridley Bryant senior's Granite Railway in 1826, a group of influential citizens took up the scheme for rail lines to connect Boston with other cities in New England. Abner Phelps, Nathan Hale, P. P. F. Degrand, Josiah Quincy, and Thomas Handasyd Perkins led this initial effort. But they had to convince people that the concept was even practical, let alone financially feasible. After having surveyed various routes, railroad advocates reported to the state legislature in 1829 that no city could compete without this means of transporting goods. Economic centers required markets, and markets required a ready means of transportation. In 1830 the state incorporated three lines, the Boston and Lowell, the Boston and Providence, and the Boston and Worcester. The Eastern Railroad through Salem to Portland, Maine, followed a few years later.

All four lines required a railroad terminus in the city, as well as a network of bridges and causeways linked on filled land. In 1830 East Boston was platted for development, and a year later capitalists began planning to fill the South Cove between Boston, South Boston, and Dorchester. An agreement was made with the Boston and Worcester Railroad to establish a terminus on the new land there in 1833. With additional salt flats purchased in 1836 and a large hotel begun near the railroad terminus, the new "South End" promised to play a major role in fueling the city's growth.

Unfortunately it was in 1837, the year Gridley J. F. Bryant went into business on his own, that the economy, inflated by land speculation in the western states, began to contract. President Jackson had ordered the Treasury Department to refuse to accept paper money (this was before there were Federal greenbacks) as payment for land sales. This induced an economic crisis when many investors, including banks, found they lacked the hard currency to pay their debts. In early 1837 banks in Boston and New York followed the lead of the United States Treasury and suspended specie payments in which paper money could be redeemed for gold or silver coins. One local newspaper reported that since November of the previous year, seventy-eight large mercantile houses and sixty retail stores had failed.[25] The economy briefly recovered in the summer of 1838 but contracted again a year later and entered a three-year depression.

This drag on the economy made conditions for architects, which had already not been easy, even more difficult. As early as 1833, Alexander Parris had lamented that there were too many architects competing in Boston. By 1837 there were even more men to compete with. Some, like Solomon Willard, Thomas Sumner, Asher Benjamin, and Cornelius Coolidge, were nearing the end of their careers. Among the most active young architects in 1837, several were already well established: Isaiah Rogers, William Washburn, Richard Bond, Richard Upjohn, Edward Shaw, Charles G. Hall, William Sparrell, Ammi B. Young, and Charles Roath. The unsettled economic situation under which these men sought work is illustrated in a letter written by Richard Upjohn from Boston in October 1837 to a client who had not been prompt in his payments: "We have nothing to do here, nor is there any means that I know of to meet rents and all the other expenses attending the keeping of a family etc. etc. etc. these nothing to do times."[26]

Under conditions such as these, it is remarkable that Bryant prospered from the very beginning. According to Henry Bailey, Bryant secured work on a variety of projects in his first full year in practice, 1838. He made drawings for his father, many apparently for patent applications, and surveyed land. Civil engineering was not an uncommon source of work for architects at this time. Indeed, there was little distinction as yet between the professions of architecture and engineering. The several architectural projects recounted by Bailey for 1838 remain unidentified. There was a boarding school for Noah Brooks, a mechanics' hall for George Darracott, a depot house for George M. Dexter (who later became an architect), a ship house for Alexander Parris, and a market house for J. W. Pinckney.[27] Initially Bryant evidently shared an office with Parris at 51 Court Street, but by 1840 Bryant had relocated to 4 Court Street, an office he would occupy for almost thirty years.

According to Bailey, the largest single project in 1838 was a house for Abbott Lawrence costing $42,000. This is the earliest surviving commission that can be linked to Bryant. The Abbott Lawrence House can be identified with reasonable certainty (fig. 1.9). Lawrence had purchased a brick house at 8 Park Street, built in 1809, opposite the Boston Common. The listing in Bryant's account book very likely refers to his having extensively remodeled this Federal period house in the Greek Revival style. The house at 8 Park Street later became the Union Club and was further remodeled on at least two occasions. Although a fifth floor was added in the 1880s, the lower stories of the Park Street exterior date from the acquisition of the house by Lawrence. Bryant, if he was the architect, took a simple brick façade and embellished it with sandstone and cast iron, also adding a square cupola on the roof and four dormers. The use of brown sandstone, particularly for the recessed entryway with its pilasters, entablature, and coffered soffit panels, is surprising. Dark-colored stone is not normally associated with classical Greek design, yet the suitability of this stone for carving Greek ornament made it attractive for such embellishments. The façade also features Greek Revival–style cast iron balconies.[28]

The interior of the house is more difficult to date, as the house underwent several major alterations. In 1863 Bryant and John Hubbard Sturgis were hired to remodel the house for the Union Club. The kitchen wing was removed and replaced with an extension that filled the rear portion of the lot. The stair hall and much of the first, third, and fourth floors also seem to date from this 1863 renovation. In the 1880s the architectural firm of Peabody and Stearns added the fifth floor. Finally, a new house built next door in 1896, designed by Ball and Dabney, joined the two structures. In all of this work, exterior changes were designed to be sympathetic

Figure 1.9. Abbott Lawrence House, 8 Park Street, Boston. Substantially remodeled and enlarged in 1838, this house (with iron balconies) is believed to have been Gridley J. F. Bryant's first major project, although perhaps not as a designer. (Author's collection)

to the 1838 design, with its iron balconies and sandstone trim. It is the front rooms on the second floor—the original "best rooms" belonging to the Lawrence family—that retain the most integrity from 1838. These rooms are among the finest surviving examples of the Greek Revival style in Boston.

The question remains: Does the Lawrence House reflect a major work by a precocious young architect? We have only Henry Bailey's recordation of Bryant's first year of commissions to link the architect to this project, and it is worth exploring for its potential ramifications for his career. As we have seen, according to Bailey, Bryant was paid $42,000 for his work, a very large sum for that period. The lavishness and extent of the surviving Greek Revival features strongly suggest that Lawrence did indeed spend a considerable amount on this house. That Bryant actually drew the plans has not been established. Even if his role were supervising the construction designed by an unknown architect, this project would have provided him with an important learning experience as a young man just establishing his practice. Indeed, Bryant's willingness to work in association with other, more artistic architects may have had its origins in this project.

Bryant's work for Abbott Lawrence must have contributed to his self-confidence in a difficult economy. It would certainly have provided him with an important business contact, especially since Abbott's father had worked with Bryant's father on the Bunker Hill Monument. At any rate, Bryant did not hesitate to compete with other prominent architects such as Isaiah Rogers and Richard Upjohn to design a new Boston City Hall. The Boston Common Council had solicited cost estimates for a new building in April 1837, just prior to the suspension of specie payments by the city's banks. A year later, by which time Bryant had begun his practice, a second call went out for proposals. In June 1839 the committee established to consider the various proposals recommended that Rogers's plan for a city hall be accepted and that Bryant's plans for probate and registry of deeds offices also be chosen.

It is likely that Bryant was selected to design the registry portion because of his expertise in fire-resistant construction techniques gained under Alexander Parris in the design of buildings at the Charlestown Navy Yard. In any event, it appears that the depression fatally hindered this project. The decision was made not to build a new city hall but instead to remodel the old Suffolk County Courthouse. In 1840, Jonathan Preston's plans for converting the old courthouse were selected. For reasons not known, Bryant was hired as an associate architect to execute Preston's plans.

Though not a major project in terms of work that needed to be done, the city hall renovation demonstrates Bryant's ability to work with competing architects, as well as a bulldog-like determination to persist in obtaining a highly visible commission.[29]

Who, then, was this ambitious young architect who was in such a hurry to succeed? There are two surviving photographs, one showing him at sixty-five and the other taken shortly before his death. Neither image suggests a dominating figure who, by his physical presence and force of personality, could intimidate clients. His friend Henry Bryant provides the only description:

> We remember Mr. Bryant as a man of commanding presence. He was not tall, but rather stout, with broad shoulders and a large strongly modeled head. His hands and feet were small and delicately formed. His habit of standing always with his hands behind, his feet rather far apart, and his head thrust forward, gave him a noticeable likeness to Napoleon . . . [of] which Mr. Bryant was not unconscious. He admired Napoleon! When he moved it was with the quick nervous step indicative of haste and unbounded energy. When he spoke, incisive words, enunciated distinctly and grouped in short epigrammatic sentences, held the attention of every person within ear-shot. He dressed faultlessly.[30]

One aspect of this description that is particularly relevant is the mention of Bryant's "unbounded energy." Bryant himself described how little sleep he needed and, consequently, how he was able to accomplish so much work. In a letter to Bailey, Bryant noted that he never had the time or inclination to travel for pleasure, but was constantly on the go:

> I carry in my mind a single day's work performed in a very hot day in the month of August. Left Worcester for Boston at 3:30 a.m., Norwich boat train. In Boston, from 5:30 a.m. to 11 a.m., visiting four buildings in progress. At 11 a.m., took train for Haverhill, Mass., examined progress of a church and a dwelling house, visited top of spire of the church. At 3 p.m. took train for Boston. At 5:30 p.m., visited Park Street Church and made measurements and sketches of inside alterations. Walked to Fitchburg Depot and took train for Waltham, where we were living through the summer. Drank two cups of tea and rolled back on to bed, Mrs. Bryant pulling off boots and clothes. Asleep in about four minutes "like a log." Up at 5:30 next morning and took six o'clock train for Boston only to repeat the misery of the previous day, or something equally exacting.[31]

Bailey's description of Bryant also includes reference to his great intellectual curiosity, and to the fact that he was an avid reader. Bailey obviously greatly admired his friend, but there is no reason to doubt his description. Unbounded energy and intellectual curiosity go a long way toward explaining how a man of Bryant's humble background could become the most prolific architect in Boston, if not New England, for so many years.

2

Mastering His Profession

By the beginning of the new decade, the economy had still not improved. Indeed, the economic depression had grown more serious over the summer of 1839. There continued to be new construction to meet the needs of the growing population, but as late as 1843 a local newspaper cautioned those in the building trades against coming to Boston in search of work: "We would not hold out . . . an encouragement for mechanics to come to the city—there is a sufficient number who have wintered with us, who have found it hard to get along, and to these belong the work there may be to be done." Bryant expressed a discouraging tone in a letter to Richard Upjohn, who had quit Boston for a more lucrative practice in New York. Dated April 21, 1841, Bryant's letter reports on the lack of major building in the city and inquires if he, Upjohn, might need "some assistance in drawing or writing." Bryant closes, "I have managed to get a very good living so far, since I commenced for myself, but as you are well aware, it has been all plain work, & I wish for some opportunity, to be employed upon some large work, although I might receive less emolument for my services." Upjohn's reply has not survived, but records exist of one exceptionally unusual project that is evidence of Bryant's efforts to find interesting work outside New England.[1]

In the early 1840s the architect was hired to prepare designs for a plantation house in Northampton County, North Carolina. Henry K. Burgwyn, member of an old North Carolina family, had married Anna Greenough of Jamaica Plain, then a suburb of Boston, in 1838. It was probably through his wife's family that Burgwyn met Bryant and hired the young architect to prepare designs for his house, Thornbury Plantation. What survives to document this project are detailed handwritten specifications for the construction of the house. Thornbury Plantation no longer survives, and it is not known if Bryant's plans were used, or even if the construction date associated with the house (ca. 1843–45) is accurate. From the description in the specifications, the house was intended to be a brick Palladian villa, similar to a plan published by Asher Benjamin in his *American Builder's Companion,* first printed in 1806.[2]

The specifications do not suggest an inexpensive house. The main block of the two-story structure, measuring fifty-two by ninety-four feet, was to be brick with sandstone trim and a hipped roof of leaded charcoal tin with a cupola. In addition to the flanking single-story wings, the specifications called for piazzas, bay windows, and woodwork consisting of "cornice, brackets, fascias, arches, bases and capitals." In addition to providing evidence of Bryant's involvement in the design of an elegant plantation house, the specifications are important in establishing how early in his career the architect was preparing such detailed construction documents. That this attention to detail was not an aberration is supported by the surviving specifications for the residential work that occupied much of the architect's time in the early 1840s.

Although, back in Boston, development was slowed by economic conditions, the filling of South Cove for the new South End neighborhood was completed, as was construction of the new United States Hotel opposite the Boston and Worcester Railroad Depot. With emigrants still pouring into the city—the population increased from 78,603 in 1835 to 114,366 in 1845—there was need for housing on the newly filled land. The houses built in this area, today bounded by Essex Street, Washington Street, Interstate 93, and the Massachusetts Turnpike, were modest brick dwellings occupied by tradesmen and clerks. The names of the architects of these relatively unpretentious structures generally do not survive. Indeed, the common belief is that architects were not involved in this type of construction, although one source contradicts that assumption and documents construction activity in this period by providing names of architects and tradesmen: the building contracts in the Suffolk County Registry of Deeds.[3]

Massachusetts, like many states, passed legislation to protect the rights of men in the building trades, called "mechanics," who often worked for speculative developers. It was not uncommon in the early nineteenth century for people to invest in speculative houses and commercial blocks and become financially overextended. This could result in tradesmen, particularly masons and carpenters, not receiving compensation for work performed and materials supplied. The Massachusetts Lien Law, approved on February 29, 1820, enabled mechanics to place a lien on a property in lieu of unpaid wages. To take advantage of this protection, the original contract for the work had to have been recorded in the Registry of Deeds for a given county. The detail and information in these contracts varied greatly. Often the names of architects who prepared plans were included. In some instances, a complete set of specifications for a particular trade was recorded as well.

Through these building contracts a large number of Bryant's early projects can be documented. In some instances, contracts were recorded even if the client was wealthy and there was presumably less fear of economic loss. In most cases, however, the recorded projects involved construction in newly developing neighborhoods for the middle class. For example, in 1843 Bryant was hired to provide plans and specifications for fourteen houses on Tyler and Hudson streets in the new South End. The client was Eli Fernald, a house painter. Although it was not uncommon for mechanics themselves to engage in real estate speculation at the time, in this case Fernald was the agent of John Thorndike, who often listed himself as an architect but in fact was an early real estate developer (to use a term not current until the twentieth century). These two groups of seven row houses built back-to-back still survive, but they have been so extensively altered that it would be difficult to determine their original appearance today. The complete carpentry specifications recorded in the mechanics' contract document typical middle-class housing for the period in Boston. They also provide an example of Bryant's specification writing for a house quite different from Thornbury Plantation, though the same careful attention to detail is evident.[4]

Each brick house had three full stories and an attic space with twin dormers and a slate roof. There was a side hall plan with a recessed doorway above a basement story built a few granite courses above grade, a standard characteristic of South End housing. These inexpensive houses did not have the typical Boston bow front for parlor windows, just flat stone lintels and a plain cornice at the roof level. Molded door and window casings with corner blocks were also standard. The main entrances had paneled pine doors with sidelights and transom lights, recessed to provide a shelter from the weather, with simple paneled exterior entryways. The specifications give us much more detail about the interior. In the side hall was a circular staircase with a mahogany rail. The newel posts were iron and the balusters round pine interspersed with iron for added strength.

Each house had closets containing three drawers and six clothes hooks. Kitchens were in the basement, along with the washroom and furnace. A wooden ell at the rear contained privies. Seven-foot board fences closed off the backyard of each house from its neighbors. Although second-floor iron balconies were a common feature on many of these South End houses, we know from historic photographs that they were not present here.

These building contracts document that Bryant designed a large number of such houses in the early 1840s. Some did include the bow front, such as a pair on Garden Court in the North End built in 1844 on speculation for two carpenters, Joseph T. Bailey and Charles E. Jenkins. The surviving four-story house at 6 Garden Court is three bays wide, with a side hall entrance and two bays forming the bow front. A modestly corbelled entablature provides a finish at the cornice level.[5]

Also in 1844 Bryant is believed to have designed a more fashionable three-story bow-fronted house for Jonathan Preston at 21 Beacon Street. Although the house has been demolished, the original drawings survive to document a typical urban residence for a well-to-do Bostonian (figs. 2.1, 2.2).[6] The principal entrance features pilasters supporting a full entablature and pediment framed a recessed paneled door with sidelights and transom. A notation on the front elevation drawings notes that the design was to match the adjoining residence of Gardner Brewer, a properous merchant, land developer, and frequent Bryant client. First-story parlor windows were door height, presumably to open onto iron balconies not shown on the drawings. None of the windows in the drawing show window panes with muntins, suggesting a final detail to be resolved by the purchaser of the house that Preston built to sell. In order to make the drawings presentable for a prospective purchaser, the second- and third-floor windows were embellished with curtains, and a color wash was used to accentuate details. In addition to the main entrance surround, stone lintels for the windows also displayed modest Greek Revival–style headers, and there was a full entablature at the roof cornice. The interior was of course more elaborate than in the South End houses, with both a front and a back staircase and a long parlor that ran the full depth of the residence.

In the same Beacon Street block in 1844 Bryant also designed a house for Theodore Chase, for which the masonry specifications survive. As with the houses in the South End and Thornbury Plantation, these specifications suggest that Bryant may have been years ahead of most of his contemporaries in his efforts to provide detailed documents outlining the work to be done. In some instances, such as the Chase House, the architect was not

Figure 2.1. Front elevation, house at 21 Beacon Street, Boston, for Jonathan Preston, 1844, attributed to Gridley J. F. Bryant, architect. The Boston "bow-front" town house, of which this is an example, did not originate with Bryant. (Courtesy Bostonian Society/Old State House).

hired to supervise the work. The irony of the building contracts for speculative houses is that when an architect was involved in creating the plans
and specifications, they were more likely to result in a building that was
faithful to the designer's intentions. The reason is that if the contractor
departed from the agreed-upon documents, he risked losing the protection afforded in the lien laws. With a project like the Chase House, where
the owner was acting as his own contractor, the architect had little opportunity either to work with the client or to ensure that the contractor properly interpreted the plans and specifications.[7]

Bryant's preparation of detailed masonry specifications is probably one
reason why clients had confidence in his abilities. Although the scarcity of
any surviving written specifications from this period makes it difficult to
compare Bryant's work with that of his contemporaries, a comparison between the drawings for Preston's house and the masonry specifications for
the Chase House with a portfolio of plans and specifications by Edward
Shaw (1784–1859) for another Beacon Hill residence offers some basis

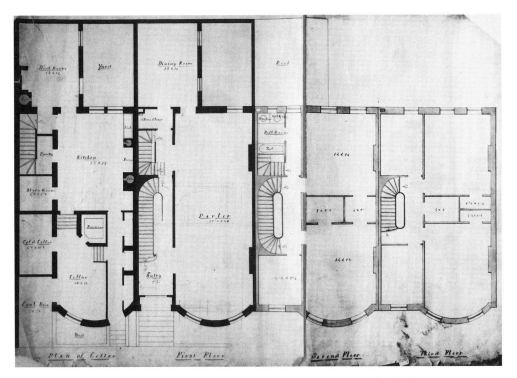

Figure 2.2. Floor plans, house at 21 Beacon Street, 1844. With each floor plan laid
out side by side, this drawing was ideal for a speculative housing project for builders like
Jonathan Preston. (Courtesy Bostonian Society/Old State House)

for understanding Bryant's services as an architect. The house for A. W. Thaxter on Mount Vernon Street designed by Edward Shaw is documented in a portfolio of drawings and specifications dated 1836. Shaw, like most of Bryant's contemporaries, began as a carpenter and became one of the leading architects in Boston. Because much of his work either remains undocumented or has not survived, Shaw is best known as the author of numerous builders' guides. The Thaxter House, a refined bow-front town house in the Greek Revival style, is one of the best surviving examples of upper-middle-class urban housing from that period in Boston. It is similar to the houses for Preston and Chase built a few blocks away eight years later.[8]

A comparison of the drawings for the Thaxter House and the house for Preston is problematical. Whereas the former survives in a portfolio which includes the contract and is presumably complete, the latter consists only of two loose, unnumbered drawings. Shaw's Thaxter drawings include longitudinal elevations, framing plans, details, and even designs for the front and rear yards. Bryant's plans for Jonathan Preston represent a more economical approach in drafting—as one would expect for a house built on speculation. Moreover, Preston himself was a builder and would not have necessarily required construction details, such as framing plans. The basement, first, second, and third floors are laid out side by side on a single sheet as if representing a row of four attached houses. Each floor is distinguished on the plans by different shading of colored ink. Bryant provided Preston a kind of early "pattern book" plan to entice a purchaser.[9] In this case the house was acquired by Edward Brooks, an attorney.

It is in the specifications for Theodore Chase that Bryant's services for a client provide a more striking comparision. For Thaxter, Edward Shaw included printed specifications of approximately 2,000 words for masonry (including slating, plastering, and stucco) and carpentry (including painting and glazing). Bryant's masonry specifications for Chase are for a house of similar size and style, except that it stood on a corner lot and thus had an exposed side elevation. Bryant's document is over twice as long at about 4,700 words with correspondingly greater detail. If the owner, as in the case of Theodore Chase, preferred not to hire the architect to supervise the work, Bryant's specifications would have allowed for much less ambiguity in interpretation by contractors. Even if the architect was to be involved, his duties to negotiate with the contractor on the owner's behalf would have placed fewer demands on his time, given the more explicit construction documents. For men like Shaw, who came out of the building trades,

tradition may have dictated a more personal relationship between architect and contractor. Bryant understood the importance of close working
relationships with skilled contractors, but he also evidently understood
that times were changing. A growing population meant that there would
be many new contractors entering the workforce whose skills and honesty
were untested.

A more direct comparison between the specifications supplied by Bryant
and those of another prominent architect is provided by documents for
two school buildings. In the early 1850s the city printed a series of specifications for school buildings by Bryant and other architects, including one
for a grammar school on Hawkins Street designed by Richard Bond in
1846. Bond's specifications for the windows read as follows:

> All sashes in three stories are to be pine, (nosing form) 1¾ inches thick,
> made and hung in two parts, with weights and line of the best quality
> sash fasteners. The frames are to be made with hard pine pulley stiles
> and beads, and axle pulleys, and all the windows in three stories are to
> finish with inside blinds, 1⅛ inches thick, hung in four folds and in two
> parts in height. They are all to fold back into flat boxings or recesses on
> the walls and hung with hinges, and fitted with fastenings of the best
> quality. The attic and cellar windows are to be made with pine sashes and
> frames. The cellar windows are to be hung with strong hinges to swing
> up, and fitted with suitable fastenings.[10]

Compare the section on windows in Gridley Bryant's specifications for a
grammar school on Tyler Street in 1847:

> All the windows (excepting those in the cellar) are to have double box
> frames, with two inch pine plank sills and yokes, __ inch hard pine,
> pulley styles, five eighths of an inch inside beads, and five sixteenth of an
> inch parting beads. The sashes are to be made of pine, one and three
> fourths inch thick, moulded, coped and lipped. They are all to be double
> hung with the best white window lines, iron pulleys with steel axles, and
> round iron counter weights. All the sashes are to be fastened with strong
> bronzed sash fastenings, to cost $5.50 per dozen. All the windows in the
> first story are to be fitted with one and one fourth inch framed blinds,
> two parts to each window, hung in light box frames, with weights, lines,
> and pulleys, in the same manner as the sashes, excepting that they are to
> run up above the tops of the windows, in close boxes and to have satisfac-
> tory knobs, rings, or handles, on the bottom rails, to draw them down.
> The windows in the second story are to have inside shutter blinds,
> one inch thick, made in eight parts to each window, hung with iron

butt-hinges, and fitted with bronzed hooks and staples, and rosewood knobs, and to fold into boxings. The cellar windows are to be made with plank frames, rabbeted for the sashes, and to have double sashes, hung with iron butt hinges to the tops of the frames, fastened with strong iron buttons, and fitted with catches to hold them open when desired.[11]

It is unlikely that Bryant was paid more for his work, as the city would not have been able to justify an additional expense for more elaborate documents for comparable grammar schools. Like the Thaxter House specifications, Bond's instructions recall an earlier time when he was himself trained as a carpenter. Bryant's more explicit instructions suggest his understanding of changes in the building trades, now that contractors could be less skilled and the products available in a more industrialized society made with less care.

BRYANT'S SUCCESSES in obtaining commissions for houses in the city must also have led to residential projects in the towns that closely surrounded Boston. Communities such as Dorchester, Roxbury, Newton, Watertown,

Figure 2.3. Jeremiah Hill House, Brookline, 1843, Gridley J. F. Bryant, architect. Circa 1888 photograph from C. B. Webster's *Brookline*. Bryant's design was for a Boston bow-front house in a country setting. (Courtesy Trustees of the Brookline Public Library)

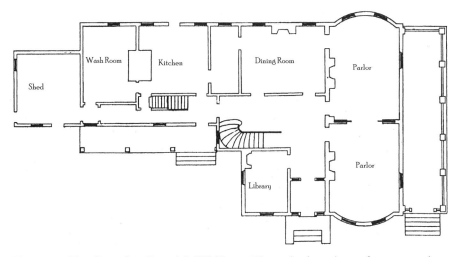

Figure 2.4. First-floor plan, Jeremiah Hill House. The author's conjectural reconstruction of the floor plan is based on a drawing by Coolidge, Shepley, Bulfinch & Abbott, August 2, 1927.

Somerville, Cambridge, and Brookline grew increasingly attractive to Bostonians who desired a home in the country. The architects for the houses built in these early suburban communities in the 1840s are generally more difficult to document. A rare exception is a country house erected in Brookline in 1843, a wood frame Greek Revival counterpart to Bryant's urban residences. Built by Bryant for Jeremiah Hill, the house, currently known as the Kennard House, after a later owner, is intact except for the demolition of the of kitchen wing in 1993 (figs. 2.3, 2.4). The structure represents a traditional approach to residential design at a time when *Landscape Gardening* (1841) and *The Architecture of Country Houses* (1842), the first publications of Andrew Jackson Downing illustrating new architectural styles, were just gaining widespread attention. Though located on a large lot with little to constrain how the house could be sited, it was built with an urban-style side hall plan and bow-front façade. As in the urban houses, the double parlor is located in the bow-front bay adjoining the stair hall. Unlike in a row house, the side elevation is not blocked by a neighbor, allowing for the placement of a piazza running the length of the building. On the other side of the house the architect placed the kitchen wing with a second porch running perpendicular to the main block. The origins of this L-shaped plan call for further investigation, as it became very typical for rural dwellings all across the country throughout much of the nineteenth century. [12]

While Bryant was no doubt grateful for the work, the Kennard House illustrates the persistence of the fashion for Greek Revival architecture in Boston. In his 1842 letter to Richard Upjohn, Bryant reported that there were only two major building projects in Boston at that time, the United States Custom House and the Merchants' Exchange. Both are important local examples of the Greek Revival style. The Custom House, which still stands at the foot of State Street, was originally designed, by Ammi B. Young, in the form of a massive Doric temple constructed of granite. Begun in 1837 when the style was at the height of architectural fashion, it took ten years to complete. The Merchant's Exchange, with its façade of granite, stood as part of a block of buildings on State Street. Built in 1841–42, it was the last major Boston project by Isaiah Rogers.

The changes in architectural styles that came about in reaction to the Greek Revival style occurred first in domestic architecture with the construction of a picturesque villa in the town of Brookline not far from Jeremiah Hill's country house. Theodore Lyman, the former mayor of Boston, owned a country estate in Waltham that had been built by his father in 1793. By the early nineteenth century, Brookline was a more fashionable location for a country house than Waltham. Prominent members of the Perkins, Cabot, Sears, and Lawrence families had already taken advantage of the rural ambiance of Brookline, with its close proximity to Boston. Lyman hired Upjohn to design an Italianate villa that was as modern and progressive as any house featured in Andrew Jackson Downing's new publications. In November 1843 a young architect named Arthur D. Gilman began his long public campaign to advance the cause of progressive architecture by publicly condemning the designs for a new Greek Revival–style church in Boston. In concluding his public criticism, Gilman stated: "In domestic Architecture, the exquisite villa in the Italian style erected at Brookline during the last season for the Hon. Theodore Lyman, and the gem of a suburban cottage on the middle road to Cambridge (from the designs of Mr. Bryant of Court Street), will do more to encourage a real and practical reform than all the books from Vitruvious, down to Robinson." I have not been able to identify the cottage in Cambridge to which Gilman refers, but this praise is a remarkable indication that Bryant was fully prepared to offer more modern residential design, should he find a receptive client.[13]

One early evidence of his ability to design in new architectural styles can be found in the portfolio of the Henry Williams House drawings in Salem (figs. 2.5, 2.6). The design accepted for the 1846 house suggests timidity

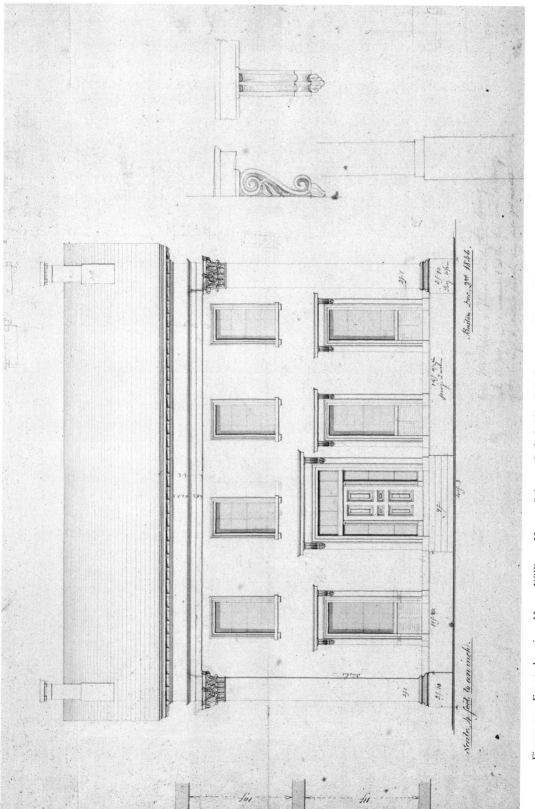

Figure 2.5. Front elevation, Henry Williams House, Salem, 1846, Gridley J. F. Bryant, architect. The house as built shows a conservative approach to new stylistic fashions. (Photograph courtesy Peabody-Essex Museum)

on the part of the client regarding the newer styles. As built, the house features a traditional gable roof perpendicular to the street with an elevation framed by corner pilasters and entablature. The more "modern" details include modest Italianate trim in the form of cornice modillions and brackets supporting a portico over the main entrance. The curious asymmetrical four-bay façade shown in the elevation appears to be a local tradition, but it again suggests a conservative client. More unusual is an alternative scheme advanced by the architect. The portfolio includes a

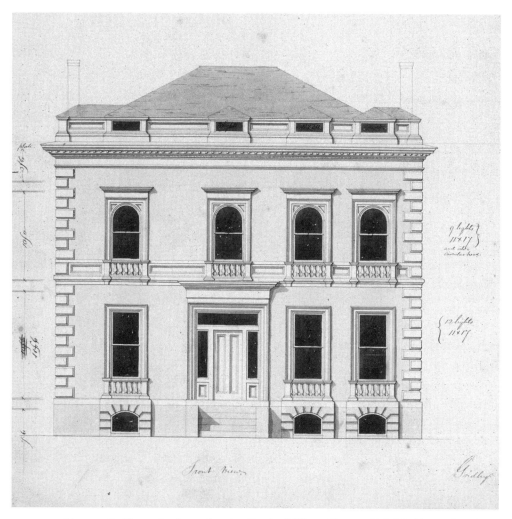

Figure 2.6. Alternative front elevation for the Williams House, 1846. Had Bryant's early interpretation of an Italian palazzo been selected, it might have revolutionized Salem architecture. (Photograph courtesy Peabody-Essex Museum)

Figure 2.7. Edward Deacon House, Washington Street, Boston, Jean Lemoulnier, architect, with Gridley J. F. Bryant supervising architect, 1846–48. Bryant's involvement no doubt provided a level of comfort for the client in the execution of the designs of this untested French architect. (Courtesy Earle G. Shettleworth, Jr.).

color rendering for a house with the same floor plan (and asymmetrical four-bay front), but with a façade inspired by an Italian Renaissance palazzo as popularized in England by the work of Charles Barry and others.

In 1846 Bryant had another opportunity to acquire valuable experience in modern residential design. In that year a Frenchman named Jean Lemoulnier established his practice as an architect in Boston and was hired to design an important mansion on the outskirts of the city. The house for Edward P. Deacon on Washington Street stood near the neck of land that then connected Boston to the mainland (fig. 2.7). The house was remarkable for its location at an edge of the city where there were no other expensive homes and before land was filled on either side of the neck. Even more remarkable was the design for the house, an example of the latest in modern French-inspired domestic architecture. The interior was lavishly ornamented in the French Renaissance style, while the exterior marks the first use of a mansard roof in New England. Gridley Bryant was hired as the supervising architect to oversee the construction of Lemoulnier's seminal design. Even though it would be several years before Bryant himself worked in the style named after the Second Empire of Louis-Napoléon, his involvement as supervising architect is noteworthy. Little is known about Lemoulnier, but he evidently was not trained as an architect. Bryant's involvement very likely minimized any difficulties between the newly arrived French designer and local builders.[14]

WHILE THESE projects kept Bryant in the forefront of domestic architectural design, he found a good deal of work designing large commercial blocks once the depression had ended. In a publication on the historical development of Boston which appeared in 1848, Henry Dearborn provided a lengthy account of the use of granite for recently constructed commercial blocks in the city. For Dearborn, granite buildings represented first-rate construction. It is clear from his account that during the years 1844–46 a large number of structures with granite fronts were built, and it was in that brief period, which saw the completion of the massive Custom House, that Boston truly became the "granite city." The architects for most of these blocks remain unknown, but Bryant certainly designed his share of them. One area notable for a concentration of these new granite blocks was Milk Street.[15]

Chief among these structures was a four-story building erected in 1845 behind the Old South Church on Washington Street as an investment by the proprietors of the Old South Society. A photograph taken about 1880 is perhaps the best surviving view of a building that, owing to the curve of the narrow street, was typically photographed obliquely (fig. 2.8). As was characteristic of the 1840s, the building supported a gable roof parallel to the street with a body that was of brick construction, though the brick portion was not visible from the street. A granite front was divided into three sections of stores by massive square piers. Each section contained three bays recessed behind pilasters which rested on a substantial belt course corresponding to the level of each floor. The four piers that ran the entire height of the façade supported a full entablature with a small pediment over the center three bays. This center section projected slightly forward to suggest a frontispiece. With its boldly articulated pilasters and belt course and deeply recessed windows, the Old South Block epitomized the trabeated character of the Greek Revival style. Like Ammi B. Young's Boston Custom House, then nearing completion, and Richard Bond's 1844 design for Horticultural Hall on School Street, the Old South Block represented the last phase of Greek Revival architectre in Boston. These and other buildings demonstrate that vigorous interpretations of the style were still possible even on the eve of new stylistic changes.

No sooner was the Old South Block barely completed than a dramatically different architectural style was introduced for urban architecture. In late 1845 Hammatt Billings designed the new block for the Boston Museum on Tremont Street using the urban palazzo of the Italian Renaissance as inspiration. The entire façade of brown sandstone with round-arched windows and cast iron balconies stood in dramatic contrast to the heavy granite commercial blocks that lined the streets. In the same year, the Boston Athenaeum held a competition for the design of a new building for its library and art gallery. Both Bryant and Bond entered submissions, although their drawings have not been positively identified. Those by George M. Dexter and the winner, Edward C. Cabot, display an awareness of the

Figure 2.8. Old South Block, Milk Street, Boston, 1846, Gridley J. F. Bryant, architect. The Old South Block, on the left, was perhaps Bryant's last great commercial block in the Greek Revival style. Just beyond on the same side of the street is visible the mansard roof tower of the 1873 Rialto Building by Bryant & Rogers. (Courtesy Boston Athenaeum)

new trend in which inspiration derived from the Italian Renaissance. Dexter clearly based his submission on Sir Charles Barry's Travellers' Club in London, a popular English interpretation of Italian Renaissance architecture. Cabot went directly to the source with a design based on an Italian palazzo. The other Boston architects took note of this new style, which would change the so-called Boston granite style as interpreted by Bryant and his contemporaries.[16]

Bryant's early response to this change in style for granite commercial architecture is evident in a block of stores built in 1846 at the corner of Washington and Winter streets. One section of this building still survives at 429 Washington Street, where one can see the modest Renaissance-style window trim and cornice modillions. The granite facing for the entire block originally turned the corner on Winter Street, hiding its brick construction from the main thoroughfare. Moreover, the rounded corner was another Renaissance-derived feature that softened the harsh geometric lines characteristic of the Greek Revival style. With this block, Bryant took a major step toward the Italian palazzo style which he would fully embrace in the 1850s for his well-known surviving granite warehouses, as well as major pubic buildings.[17]

In the 1840s a new type of architecture was developed in response to the growing railroad industry. As the early wooden train sheds and passenger depots proved impractical as fire hazards for large urban terminals, architects began to design masonry structures in picturesque styles patterned after their European counterparts. Bryant would design several railroad stations in his career, but the Eastern Railroad's depot in Salem, constructed in 1847, was perhaps the most impressive (fig. 2.9). The design for the stone façade is said to have been the idea of one of the owners who had been to Europe, and indeed, the Thuringer Bahnhof in Leipzig could have served as inspiration. Whatever the source, Bryant developed this idea in his own dramatic fashion. The basic form of the Salem station derived from the gate of a medieval city. But instead of horse-drawn wagons, steam engines entered through the gates on this new, modern thoroughfare of commerce.[18]

In 1847 Bryant learned that the new Custom House to be built in New Orleans was to be constructed of Quincy granite. Ever ambitious to expand his options, he began a campaign to secure the appointment as agent for the federal government in Boston. In this capacity he would be responsible for procuring, inspecting, and shipping the granite for the new building. Certainly Bryant, an architect intimately familiar with the stone and with

Figure 2.9. Eastern Railroad Station, Salem, 1847, Gridley J. F. Bryant, architect. The importance of the railroad as an engine of economic prosperity was reflected in the design of this station, which rivaled anything built in Boston at the time. (Courtesy Earle G. Shettleworth, Jr.)

the Quincy quarry, would have been a logical choice. In the National Archives are several testimonials from prominent Bostonians urging the secretary of the treasury to appoint the Boston architect. Typical is one from Congressman Robert C. Winthrop, who stated, "Mr. Bryant is highly esteemed here as a skillful & judicious architect, & as a trustworthy & honest man." Other prominent Bostonians, including Abbott Lawrence and Samuel A. Eliot, also sent letters of recommendation. Clearly, Gridley J. F. Bryant had arrived at a point in his career where he had earned the respect of Boston's "Brahmin" class. Although the appointment to act as agent for the granite used in the New Orleans Custom House eluded him, Bryant was well positioned to embark on a career that would put him very much in the public eye.[19]

3

Architecture and Reform

THE GREAT social reform movements that swept Boston during the early nineteenth century offered architects opportunities to develop original design solutions for specialized buildings. Traditionally, buildings erected for charitable causes operated under very tight budgets, and the resulting architecture was often plain in appearance and conventional in plan. Typical is Bryant's design for the Mariners House, erected by the Boston Port Authority in 1846 (fig. 3.1). Still standing in Boston's North End neighborhood, the Mariners House is four stories high with flat stone lintels, a gable roof, and cupola. On the first floor were shops where seamen's wives and widows could sell handmade goods for extra income. The upper floors contained rooms for sleeping. Only the pediment over the entrance suggests a stylistic treatment. Of course, a building located near the waterfront constructed to provide respectable housing for visiting seamen would not need to offer more than simple, clean accommodations. This is reflected in the traditional character of this architectural design.[1]

Bryant's personal attitude toward the various reform movements in education, the treatment of prisoners and the insane, and slavery is not known. A Whig in his political sympathies, he presumably became a Republican when that party emerged as the alternative to the Democrats. It is worth noting, however, that his architectural office at 4 Court Street was in the same building that contained the office of Charles Sumner, one of Boston's leading "conscience Whigs" and an antislavery spokesperson. Nonetheless, it is not known if Bryant actively identified with any political cause beyond supporting the candidates promoted by the wealthy elite of Boston. Primarily, Bryant wished to offer his clients the most advanced and efficient design for their needs, and he may have found that the most effective way to do so was to work with specialists in a given area of reform.

The reform of public education in Massachusetts was one of the most important successes of the 1840s. Horace Mann led the effort when, in 1837, he helped to create the first state board of education, on which he served for eleven years.[2] Mann and others were responding to the changes brought about in society by the industrial revolution and the rapid growth in population, especially through emigration. They held that the traditional pattern of minimal public education combined with reliance on the family would no longer suffice to produce a citizenry capable of self-government.

Figure 3.1. Mariners House, North Square, Boston, 1846, Gridley J. F. Bryant, architect. This view, from *Boston Notions,* 1847, illustrates the sober and respectable home Bryant designed for seamen which was very compatible with the traditional architecture of this North End neighborhood. (Courtesy Earle G. Shettleworth, Jr.)

The educational reformers sought a uniform curriculum, as well as better training and higher pay for teachers. Naturally, improved schoolhouse design was also an area of concern. The major changes taking place in Boston were touted in the city almanac for 1849: "The vast progress that has been made in the system of instruction, and the character of the schools, has been fully equaled in the improvements of the school houses. To those who remember the small rooms, the inconvenient forms, and the torturing benches of the old schools, the present noble buildings and spacious, convenient and finely-furnished rooms are a perfect luxury."[3] Gridley Bryant's involvement in these "noble buildings" was significant.

Boston demonstrated its commitment to educational reform during the years 1840–48 with the construction of eleven new grammar schools and three primary schools. By contrast, in the previous decade only four new grammar schools had been built. Primary schools did not even exist in separately dedicated structures prior to 1848. Bryant designed at least two of the new grammar schools, both of which were important as models of their kind, as well as one of the new primary schools. He probably collaborated closely with Joseph V. Ingraham, a well-known Boston school reformer. Ingraham's role in the new school designs is not recorded, but his contribution to school reform was acknowledged when one of the new primary schools was named after him within a few months of his death in 1848 at age forty-eight. Bryant's Quincy Grammar School on Tyler Street (fig. 3.2) and the Bowdoin Grammar School on Myrtle Street were both dedicated that year. Fifty years later, a commemorative newspaper article proclaimed the Quincy School the "first modern school in America." This accolade was due both to its organization and to its design.[4]

Under the old system of public education for grammar schools, each building had two "masters." One was designated the writing master (including mathematics) and the other the reading master; one taught in the morning and the other in the afternoon. Each was entirely responsible for all of the students in his particular area of study. This system opened the way for conflict between masters and parents, with no higher authority to arbitrate between them. Moreover, there was no uniform curriculum. In a major reform, resisted by the masters, who guarded their autonomy, the Quincy School was assigned a principal who was solely responsible for the operations of that institution. Under the principal, a corps of teachers was hired, many of whom were women. Up to that time few women had been allowed to teach, there being a generally held belief that they could not handle the boys.

Bryant's design for the Quincy School featured two exterior staircases linked by a central hall. On either side of the hall were classrooms containing individual desks for each student rather than rows of benches. On the fourth floor was an assembly hall where the principal could speak to the entire school. In the attic was space for gymnastics. Whereas a stove traditionally heated the older schools, the Quincy School had a furnace, as well as a ventilation system to circulate the air. The exterior was a plain, traditional design with a gable roof. Pedimented gable ends and trabeated door surrounds provided an element of Greek Revival design. As with the Mariners House, the exterior of the school fit with the traditional architecture

Figure 3.2. Quincy School, Tyler Street, Boston, 1847, Gridley J. F. Bryant, architect. Although called the "first modern school" in Boston, Bryant provided a traditional late Greek Revival–style exterior for this South End neighborhood. This circa 1900 photograph appeared in a report of the Boston School Committee. (Courtesy State Library of Massachusetts)

of the neighborhood, elements of which are still evident on sections of Tyler Street.[5]

Like the Quincy School, most of the other schools built at this time were very conservative in terms of appearance. An exception was Bryant's other 1848 design, the Bowdoin School. Perhaps because it served upper-middle-class residents of Beacon Hill rather than the middle-class residents of the South End (and was built exclusively for girls rather than boys), the Bowdoin School was the first in the city to have a modern exterior design. Inspired by the Italian Renaissance, this building had a hipped roof with modillions, quoins, a second-story oriel window, and round-arched windows on the ground floor. In terms of exterior design, it can be said that the Bowdoin School was a prototype for many of Bryant's public buildings erected over the next ten years. In plan, however, the Bowdoin School reflected the traditional master system.

Plans and specifications for both the Quincy School and the Bowdoin School were first published in the 1854 edition of the highly influential publication by Henry Barnard, *School Architecture; or Contributions to the Improvement of School-houses in the United States.* This publication also featured a third Bryant design for a school erected in 1847–48, the Putnam Free School in Newburyport, Massachusetts (fig. 3.3). Significantly, Barnard featured an exterior view of the Putnam School in his book. As one scholar has documented, Henry Barnard was an admirer of the German education system. The Germans were in the forefront of educational reform, at least in Bavaria and Prussia. The new architecture in both of those regions derived from the Italian Renaissance; it was called *Rundbogenstil* (round-arched style). The depiction of predominantly round-arched windows and doors on buildings such as the Putnam Free School is significant in a publication that does not otherwise devote much attention to building exteriors. Though not explicitly stated by Barnard, the visual connection with German educational reform in the Putnam Free School was probably not coincidental.[6]

A fourth Bryant design for a school, built in 1847–48, is a scaled-down version of the Putnam School. This was the Boynton High School in Eastport, Maine, near the Canadian border. Like the Newburyport school, the one in Eastport indicates that Bryant was well on his way to developing a regional practice and was introducing the latest architectural styles to locations well beyond the Boston metropolitan region. Indeed, Bryant repeated variations of his modified *Rundbogenstil* for high schools in Lynn, Massachusetts (1850), and Dover, New Hampshire (1851).[7] While it is not

Figure 3.3. Putnam Free School, Newburyport, 1847–48, Gridley J. F. Bryant, architect. As featured in an 1854 edition of Henry Barnard's *School Architecture,* this early example of modern *Rundbogenstil* design had a counterpart in Bryant's Bowdoin School on Beacon Hill, built at the same time. (Courtesy Earle G. Shettleworth, Jr.)

known if the Bowdoin and Quincy schools of 1848 were Bryant's first designs for public education, he clearly had caught the crest of a wave in terms of capitalizing on his demonstrated expertise in model designs. In addition to the schools in scattered locations such as Lynn, Dover, Natick, Newburyport, and Eastport, between 1849 and 1852 the architect designed or remodeled nine grammar schools and five primary schools in Boston.

THE PUBLICATION of his school designs in Barnard's book contributed to Bryant's reputation beyond Boston, but greater fame came with his work in the design of prisons. Gridley Bryant's long career of successful commissions for large public buildings really began with the Suffolk County Jail on Charles Street (figs. 3.4–3.7). This project got under way in 1845, when the need for a new jail led to Bryant's first design solution. The existing jail on Leverett Street, designed by Alexander Parris, was completed in 1822. As early as 1836 there was public acknowledgment of its inadequacy. The

Figure 3.4. Suffolk County Jail, South Boston proposal, 1845, Gridley J. F. Bryant, architect, assisted by Alexander Parris. This printed rendering by Hammatt Billings gave emphasis to the keeper's house in an attempt to minimize neighborhood opposition. (Courtesy Historic New England)

granite building lacked proper lighting, ventilation, and heating, security was poor, and no space was allocated for religious instruction. Prisoners had no opportunity to work and were "left to brood in melancholy over the past, or to devise new plans of crime." As part of his response to the published request for proposals, Bryant stated that he had made a detailed estimate of the cost of erecting a new jail by consulting with Parris, who assisted him in compiling the estimates. This enabled Bryant to advance confidently a stylistically radical proposal for the exterior of the new jail (which was refined by the building committee before the plans were made public).[8]

Bryant understood that cost was only one factor in getting a new jail built. As is common today, so in the nineteenth century there was local opposition to constructing a jail in the vicinity of a residential neighborhood. The city fathers had to find a site that was affordable in terms of land acquisition and, given future growth of the city, would not be inconveniently sited in ten or twenty years. The choice of South Boston was certainly affordable, as the city already owned the land. Moreover, there were already an almshouse and other institutional structures in the immediate vicinity. This location, however, part of which survives undeveloped today as Independence Square, stood in a growing neighborhood of middle-class residential housing, and many of these homeowners viewed the construction of a new jail as a threat to their investment. Moreover, across the street

Figure 3.5. Preliminary design, Suffolk County Jail (Charles Street Jail), Boston, 1848, Gridley J. F. Bryant and Louis Dwight, architects. This printed rendering by Hammatt Billings shows the jail as viewed from the southwest. This elegant drawing appealed to civic pride to win over skeptics of penal reform. (Courtesy Historic New England)

was the Perkins Institute for the Blind. The views of several wealthy Bostonians who supported that institution (another reform of the period) would have to be considered. Bryant, who had recently moved from South Boston to the South End, undoubtedly understood the concerns of the neighbors and tried to anticipate them with his proposal.

Up to that time, the standard jail design in New England had called for a severely plain building virtually devoid of architectural character. Bulfinch's Middlesex County Jail, built in 1815–16, was an example, as was Parris's jail on Leverett Street that was to be replaced. Elsewhere in the country, where prisons were designed with architectural character, as was the case in Philadelphia and New York, the solution typically involved adopting a style that was forbidding, like a fortress (Philadelphia) or a tomb (New York). Architecture that would intimidate the occupants and anyone who might be thinking of committing a crime was part of the intention. Bryant adopted neither approach. Instead, for the South Boston site he designed a building that was one of the earliest examples of the influence of the German *Rundbogenstil* in Boston. He enlisted the aid of Hammatt Billings, an architect and popular illustrator, to prepare a color rendering of his design to be lithographed and published in order to allay the concerns of the neighbors. Billings was in fact one of the most talented architects to emerge in the 1840s. As noted in the previous chapter, his 1845 design for the Boston Museum introduced a revival of the Italian palazzo style. It is likely that Billings worked with Bryant far more than has been documented.[9] Indeed, it is possible that the South Boston proposal was a collaboration between Bryant and Parris for the internal arrangements of the jail, and between Bryant and Billings for the exterior.

The exterior was the most progressive aspect of the design. The section for housing the jail cells was rather modestly detailed in terms of architectural ornament, but did feature very large round-arched windows, and stone trim and quoins, all characteristic of the *Rundbogenstil*. Like the tail

Figure 3.6. Suffolk County Jail, Boston, 1849–51. The completed jail is viewed from the southeast in this circa 1870 photograph. (Courtesy Earle G. Shettleworth, Jr.)

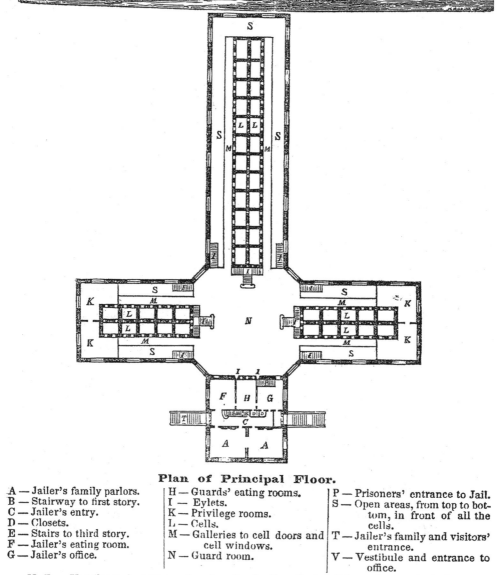

Plan of Principal Floor.

A — Jailer's family parlors.
B — Stairway to first story.
C — Jailer's entry.
D — Closets.
E — Stairs to third story.
F — Jailer's eating room.
G — Jailer's office.

H — Guards' eating rooms.
I — Eylets.
K — Privilege rooms.
L — Cells.
M — Galleries to cell doors and cell windows.
N — Guard room.

P — Prisoners' entrance to Jail.
S — Open areas, from top to bottom, in front of all the cells.
T — Jailer's family and visitors' entrance.
V — Vestibule and entrance to office.

N. B. — Ventilators in centre and end walls of cells.   Each cell has a door and window.

Figure 3.7. Principal floor plan, Suffolk County Jail, Boston, from 1851 *Report of Prison Discipline Society*. This floor plan, along with the Billings rendering, was widely publicized. (Courtesy Earle G. Shettlerworth, Jr.)

wagging the dog, the keeper's house would stand in front of the two wings of the jail, making the latter look more like appendages to a house rather than an institution for criminals. The design of the house was patterned after a traditional three-story Federal period residence with a five-bay façade and hipped roof. Window and door cornices and quoins contributed to a more fashionable appearance. This design provided a radical contrast to the very austere House of Industry and House of Reformation already standing near the proposed site in South Boston.

The interior plan, though not innovative in terms of solutions for penal reform, does provide a benchmark for Bryant's development as one of the leading experts in prison architecture in the country. There were two schools of thought in regard to jail design, popularly known as the "Philadelphia Plan" and the "Auburn Plan." The former derived its name from the famous Eastern State Penitentiary in Philadelphia. The philosophy behind this prison was that only through solitary confinement could prisoners avoid the bad influence of other inmates and learn the skills of self-improvement. The Auburn Plan, named after a prison in New York State, imposed solitary confinement at night but strict discipline and supervision while inmates worked with other prisoners during the day. Security derived in large part from the concept of a jail within a jail, whereby rows of cellblocks were constructed back-to-back with no cell built on an outside wall. This system was progressive in the sense that it assumed that the prison administrators could take an active role in reforming inmates. Although critics pointed out that prisoners invariably found ways to communicate and frustrate the notion of complete control exercised by authorities, state legislators were inclined to support this system because having prisoners work was a source of income to defray operating costs.

Bryant's plan for the South Boston jail was only slightly more progressive than Charles Bulfinch's state prison in Charlestown, built in 1805–6. The rows of cellblocks were built against the back wall, each cell having an exterior window. These windows were long and narrow to prevent escape but were glazed to admit light and provide ventilation. Similarly, the long, round-arched windows on the front of each wing admitted a great deal of natural light to the interior. Cell dimensions varied, depending on the reason for incarceration. Those charged with a serious crime occupied cells that measured six by eleven feet, while debtors and witnesses had thirteen-by-eleven-foot cells. A boiler in the basement provided heat through pipes that extended up into the central corridors, another major improvement in jail architecture. The large keeper's house included space for women and debtors, as well as the keeper's family. Mayor Josiah Quincy Jr., son and namesake of the mayor who built the Faneuil Hall Market buildings, understood the value of high-quality architecture in terms of improving the public image of the city. Evidently, however, the Common Council did not agree with the mayor on the design for the keeper's house. They voted to accept the design for the jail while preferring Richard Bond's plan for the keeper's house. No record has survived of Bond's scheme for the house or the jail, but it presumably made less of an architectural statement.[10]

Opposition from the citizens of South Boston resulted in no jail being built in 1845. Notwithstanding the architectural attractiveness of the presentation, the residents did not want their neighborhood to become the "Botany Bay" of the city, containing all the public institutions for criminals, the poor, and the insane. While efforts to find a new site continued, Bryant's design for the jail underwent a major revision. In 1846 Louis Dwight, president of the local Prison Discipline Society and a passionate advocate of the Auburn Plan, published a "Plan for a New Prison" in the society's twenty-first annual report. In Dwight, Bryant had found a collaborator to provide the intellectual grounding for the architect's great powers of persuasion.

Louis Dwight (1793–1854) was from Stockbridge, Massachusetts. He received his education at Yale and the Andover Theological Seminary and was ordained as a minister in 1822, though his health prevented him from establishing a career in the ministry. After visits to the penitentiary in Baltimore and the infamous jail in Connecticut where prisoners slept in mine shafts, Dwight found his calling in prison reform. In 1825 he founded the Prison Discipline Society in Boston and served as secretary. Through the annual reports of this organization, he became involved in prison reform throughout the country. With a skill in statistics and organizing data, Dwight produced annual reports that served as a clearinghouse for anyone interested in penal reform.

Dwight's own view was that the Auburn system was unquestionably superior to the Pennsylvania Plan, and he used his annual reports to support that bias. With the religiously motivated beliefs of a zealot, Dwight antagonized many local supporters, who dubbed his organization the "Auburnian Society." Prominent reformers such as Samuel Gridley Howe, Horace Mann, Dorthea Dix, and Charles Sumner favored the Philadelphia system of solitary confinement. These individuals, however, were frequently involved in other causes (Howe with the blind, Mann with education, Dix with the insane, Sumner with antislavery), leaving Dwight to dominate the field of penal reform in Boston. With offices in the same Court Street block occupied by Gridley Bryant, Louis Dwight was well positioned to convert the architect of the 1845 South Boston jail scheme.

Dwight's 1846 plan for a new jail naturally reflected the principles of the Auburn Plan. There would be radiating wings based on the prison-within-a-prison system in which rows of cellblocks were built back-to-back with no outside walls. Large windows in the exterior walls would, however, provide abundant natural light. A central octagon from which the wings radiated allowed complete supervision by the guards. The "radial prison plan" had originated in England in the late eighteenth century and had been developed in different variations. (The concept of a central hub with radiating wings was used in the Philadelphia prison, but it was not integral to the concept of solitary confinement.)[11] At the same time, there were centralized facilities, such as kitchens, a chapel, and a laundry. The octagon also served as a centralized gathering point for prison activities. That each cell was to have only a single occupant provided isolation for inmates when they were not under direct supervision.

Dwight's plan failed when the South Boston site was rejected because of neighborhood opposition. Although the Leverett Street Jail site was too small, the mayor and Board of Aldermen voted in August 1848 to hire Gridley Bryant to prepare plans and specifications for a new jail on the site of the existing Leverett Street facility. In September, Bryant's plans and specifications were made available to contractors. While these preparations were under way, a group of citizens petitioned the mayor to change the location from Leverett Street to a new site on the Charles River near the bridge to Cambridge. Although it would require landfill, this location on the north side of Grove Street faced no neighborhood opposition. To the east were the Massachusetts General Hospital and the new Harvard Medical College (the latter designed by Bryant). To the west on Charles Street (which would later be extended in front of the jail) was the site of the planned Massachusetts Eye and Ear Infirmary, designed by Edward C. Cabot. Mayor Quincy, nearing the end of his term, acted quickly to acquire the land. Requests for proposals addressed to pile drivers, masons, stone-cutters, stone contractors, and wharf builders, and to blacksmiths for the wrought iron, were advertised in November and December.[12]

The new site, allowing for the construction of a larger jail, still had its opponents. An article in one newspaper published in December 1848 and signed "A Mechanic" offered a lengthy critique of the proposed design, focusing largely on what the writer perceived as flaws from his perspective as a potential masonry contractor. The article also reflected the views of many citizens who believed that prisons were for punishment, not for reforming criminals.[13] In 1849 the new mayor, John P. Bigelow, agreed with these critics and later argued that the theory behind the Auburn Plan was unproven as it had not stood the test of time. He hired Alderman Jonathan Preston, an experienced architect and builder, to develop a less costly proposal. Preston was asked to prepare estimates for renovating the existing jail buildings. His proposal was submitted in February 1849, but the Board of Aldermen rejected it in favor of building a new jail on the Grove Street lot. In order to win support for the new jail, a compromise was reached to reduce the amount of land purchased by 300,000 square feet. Accordingly, the building was made to fit the site by extending the east wing and shortening the north and south wings. By May the building was at last under contract; it was not completed until November 1851.[14]

The Bryant-Dwight plan was at last accepted, but not without serious opposition. The two men had formed a marriage of convenience in which it was in both of their interests to promote the accepted plan. Dwight strongly believed that his solution represented the most advanced thinking in penal reform and deserved to be replicated throughout the country. Bryant no doubt agreed with Dwight's theories, but he also recognized that the Charles Street Jail (as the Suffolk County Jail was popularly known) could be highly beneficial to his own career as an architect. This explains the publicity campaign they undertook in 1849. A color rendering by Hammatt Billings had been published in 1848. This view showed the building as originally conceived, with the north and south wings longer by one bay each and the east wing shorter. The cupola was originally taller and served the purpose of allowing light into the central octagon. To reduce costs, it became little more than a clock tower. It was the original design that was translated into a woodcut and was published, along with a principal floor plan, in the *Puritan Recorder* on May 31, 1849, and in the *Boston Evening Transcript* on July 10. Bryant also submitted this perspective view and plan to the British architectural journal *The Builder,* which published the design on May 5, 1849, making the Charles Street Jail the first constructed American design to appear in a foreign architectural magazine. As there was no American architectural journal at that time, this was the most important professional outlet for a man of ambition.

The Charles Street Jail is extraordinary for its elaborate masonry exterior. As with the proposal for the South Boston site, Bryant succeeded in persuading the city to support a design that went beyond the basic demands of incarceration. With its dramatic site on the Charles River adjacent to the bridge leading to Cambridge, the building occupied a highly visible location. Adopting the latest architectural fashions, Bryant used the Italian Renaissance palazzo for inspiration, demonstrating a masterly handling of granite. The city already had an example of the powerful effect created by massive granite walls in the Italian palazzo style with the new Beacon Hill Reservoir erected behind the State House. This granite masterpiece, built between 1847 and 1849, was admired by architects throughout its short existence. It is significant that its design, a complete rejection of the Greek Revival style, was begun just as the United States Custom House was completed.[15]

The exceptional masonry of the exterior of the Charles Street Jail is evident in the tall, round-arched windows framed in granite quoins. The quoins are the same quarry-faced stone used for the walls, which in turn are set off by the use of ashlar stone for the keystones, belt courses, and quoins at the outside corners of the buildings. The round-arched motif continues in the multiple chimneys, a purely decorative detail that survived in the final design while other, more fussy details, such as the cupola and corbelled cornices shown in the published rendering, were sacrificed. When it was completed in 1851, the city of Boston had a prison that reflected the most progressive thinking in penal reform, as well as a major architectural landmark that bolstered its popular self-image as a modern city. By adopting a progressive architectural style, Boston made an unambiguous statement about its commitment to penal reform.

Bryant and Dwight wasted no time in promoting their theories of prison design. Operating through Dwight's Prison Discipline Society, the two men answered queries from around the country. Indeed, it seems as if the entire United States suddenly woke up to the need for a new approach in the design of prisons. In 1850 the two men won the commission to enlarge the Massachusetts State Prison in Charlestown. This involved constructing a stone octagon "guard house" and enlarging an existing structure that consisted of the original granite jail, designed by Bulfinch in 1805, and the subsequent addition from 1829 by Alexander Parris. The importance of this project for the two men is that it demonstrated how an existing structure could be modified to save costs and still result in an example of model prison design. Built before the Charles Street Jail was even completed, this project answered the concerns of many cost-conscious communities that could not afford an entirely new structure.

The state of Rhode Island accepted the Bryant-Dwight concept of enlarging the state prison in Providence and hired the designers in April 1850 to prepare plans and specifications. The enlarged complex was completed in 1852. Also built in this period before Dwight's death in 1854 were the Norfolk County Jail in Dedham (1851–52), the Hampshire County Jail in Northampton (1851–52), and the Essex County Jail in Lawrence (1853). The Dedham and Lawrence jails were smaller versions of the Charles Street Jail, albeit with Gothic and Tudor ornament rather than Italian Renaissance. Perhaps a more medieval architectural style appealed to provincial communities. The jail in Northampton is more conventional in plan and provides evidence that Bryant and Dwight were not averse to other solutions.

Although aggressive promotion gained Bryant national publicity, it proved difficult to succeed in getting designs built in distant locations. Bryant knew from his own experience that expensive public buildings did not come easily. It took the presence of the architect on the scene, constantly managing and promoting the design in the face of parsimonious public bodies, often abetted by jealous local architects. A case in point was the large jail for the city of Baltimore, a commission, modeled on the Charles Street Jail, that Bryant won in 1856. True to form, he managed to get a woodcut of the design featured locally in *Ballou's Pictorial* magazine. A year later, however, the mayor of Baltimore and his allies on the city council had second thoughts about an architecturally elaborate design for a prison. Construction was halted until a local firm could provide a more modest plan to complete the building.[16]

LOUIS DWIGHT's theories of penal reform also found ready application in the treatment of the poor and delinquent, and the two men had extraordinary success in adapting their Charles Street Jail design for other kinds of inmates. Indeed, to call their success extraordinary is not an overstatement when one realizes that, before the Charles Street Jail was finished, several commissions came into their office. Clearly there was a need among social reformers for new ideas in architecture. Bryant and Dwight formed their association at just the right time to answer that need.

In 1847 there was a cholera outbreak in Boston that was particularly hard on the poor. This epidemic signaled the beginning of a long campaign to construct a free city hospital, which Bryant was selected to design fourteen years later. The city's first almshouse was in the center of town near the Boston Common. Both the House of Reformation and the House of Industry (workhouse) were built in South Boston in the mid-1820s. The immigration stemming from the famine in Ireland contributed to putting a great strain on these institutions, and this problem came to a head with the 1847 cholera outbreak when temporary buildings had to be erected for quarantine purposes on Deer Island. While the epidemic played itself out, the response among the city's reformers was to construct a substantial building on Deer Island to replace temporary structures. As stated in a city report, "It cannot however be denied that American poor are very averse to being placed in contact with foreigners, especially when the numbers of the latter so greatly preponderate."[17] The consensus was that the mostly Irish poor flooding into Boston should have to come through a public institution for inspection and, if necessary, treatment before being let loose into society. In effect, by 1849, Boston was to have its own Ellis Island.

In June of that year, as construction of the Charles Street Jail was just beginning, the city offered a $300 premium for the best design for what was called an almshouse. In fact, the new building was to serve as a quarantine station and hospital for immigrants. No information has come to light regarding how many architects responded, but Bryant and Dwight's proposal was selected. Their solution was a variation on the Charles Street Jail, adapted as an almshouse (fig. 3.8). Since the governing principle behind the design of both was control and reform of the inmates, the Charles Street Jail design was easy to adapt for this purpose. As with the jail, a color rendering of the Deer Island Almshouse was lithographed for publicity. This time the delineator was Joseph R. Richards, a young architect in Bryant's office who was his chief draftsman. A woodcut rendering and the first-floor plan with a lengthy description was submitted to *The Builder* in London and published in June 1850. This time a full page was devoted to the rendering, an honor more often reserved in that journal for large country homes belonging to the wealthy.[18] As the British journal noted, this was not the typical American almshouse. Like the Charles Street Jail, the building was architecturally distinctive, mostly owing to its picturesque configuration, consisting of a central octagon with a cupola and four wings with corner towers featuring conical roofs. Although two of the towers contained staircases, their primary use was as water closets. The actual detailing of the brick building was rather plain, as one would expect for a building for that purpose. Nonetheless, because of its distinctive configuration, the building made a strong architectural statement, especially standing on an island in Boston Harbor. It is safe to assume that *The Builder* was correct in saying that it was unlike any other almshouse in the country.

The interior was organized for processing new arrivals, segregating

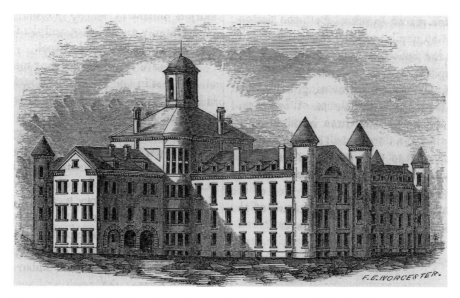

Figure 3.8. Deer Island Almshouse, Boston Harbor, 1849–51, Gridley J. F. Bryant, architect. For a brief period this building served as the Boston Ellis Island. From *Sketches and Business Directory of Boston and its Vicinity,* 1861. (Author's collection)

them by sex, age, and condition. They were even segregated in the dining rooms, which were divided into four eating areas. One was for the old and infirm men, one for working and healthy men, one for lying-in women (a term for pregnant women, though it must also have included old and infirm females), and one for working and healthy women. The emphasis on a carefully processed control of inmates is included in the description provided by *The Builder:* "The paupers, as they arrive, are received at a central point, under the eye of the superintendent, in his office, as they approach; thoroughly cleaned, if necessary, in the basement central apartments for cleansing, and distributed, when prepared for distribution, to those parts of the building assigned to the classes to which they belong."[19] Although this seems oppressively bureaucratic to modern thinking, it is worth remembering the wretched conditions many of the arrivals had left behind in their native lands. At any rate, such conditions did not often lead to sympathy for the newcomers, who, in supposed contrast to American poor, were often referred to as "ready-made" paupers.

Like the Charles Street Jail, the Deer Island Almshouse was not completed until late 1851. In 1850 Bryant and Dwight secured the commission for the Cambridge Almshouse, a stone structure employing the same plan. Sometime at the end of that year, the Bryant and Dwight plan was selected

for the Maine State Reform School in Cape Elizabeth, just outside Portland. Begun in the spring of 1851, this building still stands on an elevated
site near the airport. It is the most architecturally dramatic of this series of
designs, having the size of small jail but with polygonal corner towers and
Gothic stone lintels over the windows and doors. The central octagon has
the obligatory cupola to light the great interior space, but it also provides
the crowning decorative feature. Once again, the team of Bryant and
Dwight managed to persuade a public committee to fund the construction
of a building that not only would assist in the control and education of
wayward inmates but also would house the least desirable elements of society in a building of exceptional architectural distinction. The purpose of
the Cape Elizabeth institution was not just to incarcerate its inmates but to
reform them. Constructing the building on a farm ensured that inmates
would benefit from productive labor. At the same time, as with all these
institutions, strict control was important. The Bryant and Dwight design
provided for security and close supervision but also included schoolrooms,
workrooms, and a chapel. Architectural beauty was important not only for
the edification of the inmates but also for the benefit of the wealthy citizens whose taxes funded its construction. Contemporary accounts noted
that the building could be seen to advantage from the Western Promenade,
Portland's most exclusive residential neighborhood.[20]

As mentioned earlier, another important reform effort that began in
the 1840s was the movement to construct a free city hospital.[21] As with the
almshouse on Deer Island, the impetus accelerated with the cholera epidemic of 1849. People in the early nineteenth century generally avoided
hospitals except for a major illness or when they were in need of an operation. While principles of sanitation were only imperfectly understood, it
was recognized that a building housing many sick people was not the best
environment for promoting recovery. Consequently, most people preferred to receive care in their homes. There were notable exceptions, such
as in the case of the poor, whose own living conditions were not conducive
to rest and recuperation; "respectable domestics" living in the attics of
their employers' homes; or people visiting from out of town who became
sick or had an accident. It was these groups that were intended to benefit
the most from a public hospital offering care that was either free or at
minimal cost.

A very clear and explicit distinction was made between paupers and the
"deserving poor." As advocates for the hospital stated in one report, "We
would not have this hospital for the reception of the degraded victims of

vice and intemperance, or a home for the hopeless pauper." The suspicion of many citizens that a city hospital would draw people who belonged in an almshouse led the proponents to drop the word "free" from their efforts to promote a public hospital. Because many citizens were afraid that a hospital would be the source of disease that could spread into adjoining neighborhoods or would attract precisely those "degraded victims of vice and intemperance," the location and design of the building was critical in obtaining public support. It took more than ten years to overcome the opposition to building the hospital in Boston. Bryant's well-honed skills at working to obtain public support played an important part in the success of the project. He had previous experience in designing a medical institution with Harvard's Medical College in 1847. Bryant also designed the Lying-In Hospital on Springfield Street in the South End, erected in 1855, a substantial brick structure with a mansard roof. This building played a role in the struggle for a city hospital as well. The creation of a hospital for pregnant women was an important reform effort. Apparently it was also a premature experiment, as the hospital closed soon after it was completed, but the building became a candidate for conversion into a new city hospital. For many supporters, the South End was the most desirable location for a hospital as it was in the middle of the fastest-growing neighborhood in the city, and unlike South Boston or East Boston, it was not separated from the rest of the city by water.

Seeking authorization from the state legislature to create such an institution in late 1857, hospital proponents purchased the old lying-in hospital for use by the new institution. Opponents, including many people who had invested in the development of the South End, managed to place a proviso in the bill that any hospital established in the city could not be built within three hundred feet of an existing church or school. The lying-in hospital building was located next to a school. The proponents refused to give up and, indeed, may have welcomed being forced to design and build a new structure that would incorporate the latest ideas in hospital design. In December 1860 the city accepted a bequest from Elisha Goodnow of $26,000, which required that a hospital be built either in South Boston or in the South End. Early in 1861 an architectural competition offered a $300 premium for the best design. The only architects in the competition who have been identified were the winner, Gridley Bryant; the second-place entrant, George Ropes, who was awarded $100; and three other firms that received $50 in compensation: John H. Rand, Woodcock and Meacham, and Carl Fehmer. Another architect, Elbridge Boyden, also apparently entered; his drawing was published in a book on hospital design later that year. One entry by William G. Preston, then studying architecture in Paris, missed the deadline.

All of the firms would presumably have become familiar with a report on the latest theories of hospital design by Dr. Henry Clark, the city physician. Dr. Clark's report, "Outlines for a Plan for a Free City Hospital," included an elevation drawing, floor plan, and landscape plan by Joseph R. Richards, an architect who had worked for Bryant. The theory proposed, called the "pavilion plan," was based on the Lariboisier hospital in Paris. These schemes typically called for a central administration building and groups of separate two- or three-story buildings divided into wards. These so-called pavilions were arranged to maximize the benefits of natural sunlight and good ventilation. Open colonnades linked all of the pavilions and the administration buildings. This arrangement answered the concerns of many who preferred a more homelike environment and segregation of patients according to sex and illness (and perhaps income). Fully aware of the objections voiced by local property owners, Dr. Clark included a landscape plan in his proposal. His report stated, "The grounds may be laid out tastefully with shrubbery, flowers, trees, and fountains, so as to make the whole as attractive to purchasers of lots for private residences in the vicinity, as if it were only a pleasure park."[22]

Opposition was led by William W. Clapp Jr., a South End resident and owner of the *Evening Gazette* newspaper. Clapp argued that locating a hospital in the neighborhood would amount to a "downright breach of good faith to land owners and residents" who had made improvements. With allusions to the Charles Street Jail and the Deer Island Alms House, Clapp thundered, "Setting aside that Boston, by the extravagance of its charities, is already offering a premium on pauperism, and encouraging idleness, deception and sloth by its too commodious receptacles for criminals, and its bountiful supply of the fat of the land to all who apply, it is now proposed to add a place for the reception of those whose indulgences rob them of health."[23] The strong views of local citizens such as Clapp played a major role in how Bryant's design evolved.

A perspective view and landscape plan documents Bryant's wining entry (fig. 3.9).[24] The layout consisted of a central administration building and six two-story pavilions, all linked by curving colonnades. The architectural style was Italianate. The dome atop the administration building with its ribbed roof surmounted by a lantern suggested inspiration from nothing less than St. Peter's Basilica in Rome. Each of the pavilion buildings had hipped roofs, quoins, and round-arched first-story windows. This complex was to be set amidst landscaped grounds with curved paths that provided a park-like buffer on every side. The land purchased for the site, bounded by Harrison, Springfield, Albany, and Concord streets, then marked the farthest limits of urban development. As if to make it clear that this institution would not intrude on the neighborhood, it was to be oriented west toward Springfield Street.

It is not known who in Bryant's office may have assisted in the vision of sunny Italy for a hospital design. Possibly William S. Park, who had traveled in Europe prior to working in Bryant's office, played a role. In any case, this scheme evidently met with the approbation of the physicians but not the neighbors. In a process that was not atypical of public projects at that time, the designed underwent a radical change sometime between its publication on June 13, 1861, and that fall, when ground was broken. On November 8 the Board of Consulting Physicians, which had advised the city on the hospital design, issued a remonstrance protesting the changes that

Figure 3.9. Competition drawing, Boston City Hospital, Gridley J. F. Bryant, architect. The successful competition drawing published in an 1861 *City Report* reflected the latest reform theories in hospital design and also responded to opposition from South End neighbors. (Courtesy Earle G. Shettleworth, Jr.)

Figure 3.10. Boston City Hospital, view from Worcester Square, circa 1870. Bryant was instructed to revise his design to make it more compatible with local architecture. (Courtesy Earle G. Shettleworth, Jr.)

had been made by the architect. In particular, the doctors objected to the fact that there were fewer pavilions, and that each structure had been enlarged from three stories to four. Basically, these changes increased the density, which was contrary to the theories of hospital design they had been expounding. The hospital committee and building committee for the city replied that they had been advised by the city council that the authorization for construction had been for a site on Harrison Avenue (not Springfield Street), which required facing the buildings north. As the lot was rectangular, this reorientation toward the narrow end of the lot meant that fewer, taller buildings were necessary to maintain proper light and exposure. (Fig. 3.10.)

This narrow legalistic defense did not account for the change in style from Italian Renaissance to French Second Empire. The new administration building owed its inspiration to Les Invalides in Paris, while the pavilion structures acquired mansard roofs. The new orientation placed the complex on an axis toward Worcester Square, the residential neighborhood across Harrison Avenue. In this way, the entire complex was made architecturally a part of the predominant style of the South End neighborhood. It was also argued that reducing the number of buildings would produce cost savings, although this hardly seems credible, given the enlargement to the administration building that was necessary to make it correspond to the taller pavilion buildings with their mansard roofs. It was

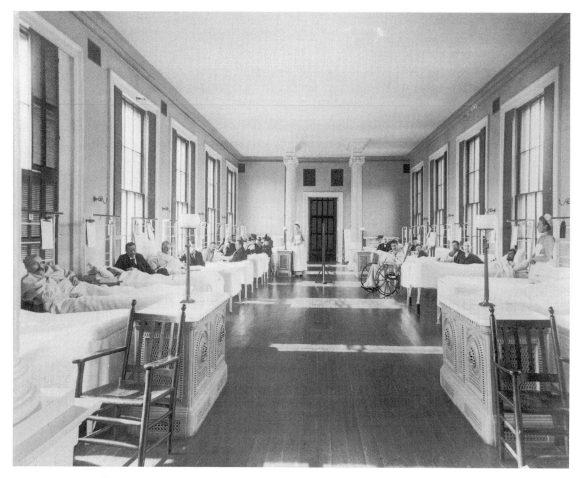

Figure 3.11. Men's Ward, Boston City Hospital. This circa 1890 photograph shows the natural light and tall ceilings typical of the wards, with ventilation ducts hidden in classical columns at the end of the room. (Courtesy Boston Medical Center)

these roofs that particularly concerned the physicians, as they could antici-pate their being adapted from attic spaces into less desirable wards.

Bryant's published defense of the changes explicitly states the impor-tance of making the design more, to use a modern term, "contextual." Bryant wrote that he had been instructed to revise the plans by adding mansard roofs. "They also required to be so located upon the site as to cause the longer side or principal portico façade of the centre building to face Harrison Avenue, . . . it being understood that the intention was to produce additional architectural effect in the central building, and in each of the pavilions as seen from Harrison Avenue."[25]

Although some physicians may have been unhappy with changes in the design, the hospital achieved what was intended. A photograph of one of the wards taken in the 1890s reveals spacious, well-lighted conditions that clearly met the standards established in the theories of the pavilion plan. It is true that the landscape grounds soon gave way to the construction of new hospital wards and ancillary structures, but by then low-density schemes for medical care were no longer viewed as practical by the medi-cal community (fig. 3.11).

With the Civil War having just broken out, it is remarkable that this com-plex was begun at all. Once again, Bryant's abilities to revise his designs to meet the concerns of many opponents helped to carry the day and realize this important public benefit. While these projects garnered Bryant much publicity, they were only part of his contribution to the transformation of Boston from the congested eighteenth-century city of Charles Bulfinch to a modern Victorian era metropolis. But Gridley Bryant's success in secur-ing commissions for institutional buildings was more than equaled by his success in the private sector.

4

Transforming Boston

BRYANT'S SUCCESS in winning commissions for public buildings garnered the architect considerable publicity, as well as important contacts with wealthy citizens. In the early 1850s Bryant's office was turning out drawings for the almshouses in Boston and Cambridge and large jails in Boston, Cambridge, Dedham, Lawrence, and Northampton. At the same time, the architect was busy working to secure the major prize of designing an addition to the Massachusetts State House. Bryant did not hesitate to supplant other architects when he thought he had a better solution. In the days before the establishment of professional standards through organizations such as the American Institute of Architects, his aggressive competition may have caused resentment among his peers, but it was not considered unethical.

In 1851 the Committee on Public Buildings of the state legislature endorsed a plan by Bryant for constructing two additional stories on the 1831 north wing at the rear of the State House designed by Isaiah Rogers. The principal concern in this expansion was to provide a fireproof area for the State Library. Bryant's proposal was not accepted, and in 1852 the committee procured three alternate plans for a new north wing by the architectural firm of Towle and Foster. The legislature adopted one of these schemes, at an estimated cost of $65,000. For unknown reasons, Bryant was then hired to supervise the project.[1] By the time construction began in 1853, Bryant had persuaded the governor and Governor's Council to adopt his own newly revised scheme for the north wing. This substitute far exceeded the Towle and Foster proposal and ended up costing $243,203. Adding insult to injury, Towle and Foster had to petition the legislature to be paid for the preparation of their plans. Bryant's attitude toward his fellow architects in this matter has not been recorded. Presumably, all was fair in the marketplace of ideas. In this case, it is highly likely that the recent burning of the Library of Congress in Washington, D.C., was a factor. The architect of the United States Capitol, Thomas U. Walter, had designed a new "fireproof" library in 1851 that included the first cast iron ceiling in the country. Undoubtedly Bryant was aware of Walter's innovation, as his design for the new wing of the State House, which was to include the library, featured both exterior and interior finishes of cast iron.[2]

For much of the nineteenth century, cast iron was thought to be one of the most fireproof materials available.[3] The extensive use of cast iron in the new wing, however, made the addition much more expensive. The columns supporting brick segmental arches for the floors as well as most of the interior and exterior finishes were cast iron. Even the doors and the inside window architraves were iron. The roof was made of wrought iron covered with sheet copper. In terms of the exterior design, it was stylistically compatible with the original State House by Charles Bulfinch. Bryant, who clearly distinguished the new work from the old by providing a setback in the east and west walls, employed the same neoclassical vocabulary used by Bulfinch, albeit with the addition of larger-scale embellishments characteristic of the period, such as heavy architrave trim around the windows and doors. In 1856, two years after the addition was completed, the London architectural journal *The Builder* published a perspective view, plan, and description of the design, showing the twin "turrets" Bryant had proposed but which were never built (fig. 4.1). These small towers were intended to balance visually the large Bulfinch dome, which, owing to the extension formed by the new north wing, would no longer be in the center of the structure. It is possible that Bryant's inspiration for the two towers derived from Christopher Wren's St. Paul's Cathedral in London. Certainly the architect would not have hesitated in drawing upon such a major English landmark.[4]

BY 1860, Gridley Bryant had become one of the most successful architects in Boston. According to Henry Bailey, Bryant's income rose steadily from $1,000 in 1840, to $5,000 in 1843, to $13,500 in 1845, to $25,000 in 1865.[5] Since we do not have income figures for other architects, it is useful to compare personal worth as recorded in tax records for Bryant and his contemporaries. Bryant's taxable personal estate increased from $8,000 in 1849 to $10,000 in 1850, doubling to $20,000 in 1851. In 1860 it stood at $40,000, certainly exceeding that of most other architects who lived in

Boston at the time. For example, that same year William Sparrell, a designer of long standing but of no remarkable ability, had personal wealth valued at $3,000. William Washburn, well known for his expertise in hotel design and as a president of the Board of Aldermen, had a taxable valuation of $4,000. Jonathan Preston, himself a former alderman, had a valuation of $5,500, while Nathaniel Bradlee's was estimated at $10,000. Of course, these figures do not reflect income. Hammatt Billings, for example, had taxable personal wealth valued at only $5,000 despite the fact that he was enormously successful as a popular illustrator as well as an architect. We know from James O'Gorman's biography of Billings that he enjoyed living well but had problems managing his money, which is probably reflected in the low figure recorded for his personal wealth.[6] Some of these architects—Bradlee and Preston, for example—had extensive real estate interests, which Bryant did not. To appreciate Bryant's economic status, it is also useful to draw comparisons with Beacon Hill residents of various professions. Many had personal wealth valued in six figures. Bryant's tax bracket was more comparable to that of men such as Dr. Oliver Wendell

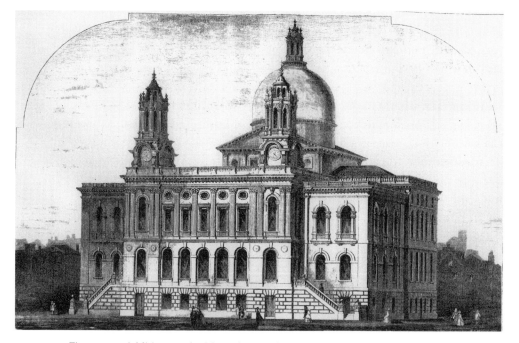

Figure 4.1. Additions to the Massachusetts State House, Boston, 1853–54, Gridley J. F. Bryant, architect. This drawing from the April 5, 1856, issue of *The Builder* was one of several designs Bryant had published in this British architectural journal. (Courtesy Boston Public Library, Fine Arts Department)

Holmes ($35,000); attorney Francis C. Loring ($40,000); Caleb Curtis, the president of an insurance company ($50,000); and John D. Bates, a merchant ($55,000). Of course, Bryant's comfortable situation had little bearing on his lack of social standing.

How he managed take on so much work had much to do with his success in employing the talents of other architects. It has commonly been assumed that he must have had a large office of draftsmen, as was typical for successful architects by the late nineteenth century. Absent office records, we can only try to piece together who worked for, and with, Bryant over the years. The available circumstantial evidence does not suggest that he maintained a large office, but he may have hired men for specific jobs as needed. Indeed, given the limited number of drawings typically generated for a given project, it is unlikely that it would have been economical for any architect to keep a large staff. Several architects are known to have worked for Bryant during the 1850s who later went into independent practice. From these names the number of his employees at various times can be estimated, though there may well have been others as yet unidentified.

From 1840 until 1867 Bryant's office was at 4 Court Street, a three-story block at the corner of Washington Street. With its close proximity to the county courthouse, the vast majority of tenants in that building were lawyers (called "counselors" in the city directories). In 1851, for example, a year in which Bryant was exceptionally busy working on several major public buildings, the city directory does not list any draftsmen at that address and only one architect, Luther Briggs Jr., who trained under Bryant in 1842–44 and presumably then shared work with him. In contrast, no fewer than twenty-two attorneys maintained offices at 4 Court Street, including Charles Sumner, the antislavery senator, and John A. Andrews, who would become the state's governor during the Civil War. It was not a large building, and these other tenants would presumably have left little room for an architectural office with many employees. The only other occupant of 4 Court Street at the time was Ezra Lincoln, a civil engineer who, like Briggs, may have had a business relationship with Bryant.

The city directories, of course, are a very imperfect source for identifying employees. For one thing, students known to have worked for Bryant were never listed until they achieved a paying position as draftsman or architect. Moreover, the manner in which architects shared projects could vary considerably. We have some evidence of the kinds of arrangements Bryant typically made in a letter he wrote to Alexander Parris in 1846. In addition to revealing that the relationship between the two men had changed considerably since Bryant had apprenticed in the Parris office ten years earlier, the letter shows that agreements could be flexible:

> If you commence business in the office, do you wish to consider that any job you may secure is for yourself individually, or for our mutual benefit, provided that I in return make you a proposition that whatever surplus business I may have more than I can attend to myself with Parker & other students, shall be for our mutual benefit & be divided as we hereafter agree.
>
> Will it be agreeable for you to assist me (as you have done for the last week) under any circumstances, provided we do not agree as to any other matters before named & do you wish me to make you an offer for so doing, or will you say what you expect.[7]

The full text of this letter gives us a good deal of information. Significantly, it establishes that Bryant maintained Parris's great architectural library during these waning years of his former mentor's career. There is also reference to students working in Bryant's office, although only one, Parker (presumably Charles E.), is named. No record is available indicating what he charged his students. It would provide a fascinating insight into the workings of an architect's office in the early nineteenth century to know what students had to pay various architects. One instance for which we do have a record is that of George M. Dexter, who in 1851 was charging apprentices $200 per annum, not an insignificant investment.[8]

The letter to Parris concludes: "I go to Gloucester to day & shall be happy to converse with you, or receive a reply in writing on Thursday, as there are some matters yet unsettled between Mr. Billings & myself that have a bearing upon any arrangement to be made with any one else." This reference to Hammatt Billings suggests the transitory nature of arrangements made with various designers. Later correspondence with another architect, John Hubbard Sturgis, documents the conflicts that could develop over fees where there was some question as to which architect had "brought in" the job, and therefore deserved part of the commission, although he may not have had any hand in the actual design. In this instance Bryant was prepared to give up $900 in fees, provided Sturgis could obtain assurances from the client that the commission for the Old Colony Railroad depot had been secured by Sturgis alone and not during "your time under our contract."[9]

In the absence of architectural plans and specifications, the evidence for Bryant's working arrangements with other architects remains fragmentary and does not clearly indicate how he ran his office. Generally, surviving architectural drawings carry only Bryant's name until later in his career. During his association with Arthur Gilman, from 1860 to 1867, drawings record the full names of both architects as equals. Then, from 1867 until around 1877, when there was an actual partnership with Louis P. Rogers, the drawings are signed with the firm name, "Bryant & Rogers, Architects." It is known that Bryant also worked on individual projects with a number of established architects, such as Hammatt Billings, George Snell, and Charles E. Parker. Presumably those drawings listed the names of both architects as equals.

We do know the names of a few architects who trained under Bryant in the 1840s and later became well established in their own right. Alexander Esty and Charles E. Parker first worked for Richard Bond. Luther Briggs trained with his father-in-law, Alexander Parris. Their length of employment with Bryant is not known, as the names of these men never appeared in the city directory at 4 Court Street. The inadequacy of directory listings as a source of documentation is illustrated in the case of Joseph R. Richards. Bryant once testified that Richards had worked for him for nine years, rising to the position of chief draftsman. As with Briggs, Parker, and Esty, however, Richards was never listed in the city directories at 4 Court Street. Since Richards was a paid draftsman rather than a student, his absence from the directories is particularly puzzling.[10]

Joseph Richards worked for Bryant until 1853. Several other draftsmen have been identified through the directories as having worked at 4 Court Street during the 1850s: Charles A. Cummings, Willard T. Sears, Rheimunt Sayer, William S. Park, Samuel W. Richards (brother of Joseph), and Louis P. Rogers. Some of these men—Cummings and Sears, for example—may have been associated with Bryant for only a short period. By the end of the decade, Samuel Richards, Sayer, Park, and Rogers appear to have been working in Bryant's office. There may have been others whose names are not known, but the evidence does not suggest large numbers of employees.[11]

Certainly to work for Bryant during the 1850s afforded extraordinary opportunities for involvement in a great variety of projects. During the first half of the decade, Bryant's office received commission for a large number of public buildings. By the middle of the decade the architect had become deeply involved in several large construction projects in the private sector. His period of seemingly unchallenged dominance began in the early 1850s and lasted about two decades, until the great Boston fire of 1872. Louis

Dwight, his zealous collaborator in the design of institutional structures, died in 1854, but the loss of this connection with the Prison Discipline Society probably only resulted in a decline in Bryant's attempts to obtain commissions outside New England. In any case, Boston was entering a period of major development in its commercial districts, and it is to Bryant's involvement in that work that we must now turn.

BY THE 1830s the wharf area of the city had begun its transformation from the brick buildings of Charles Bulfinch and others to granite warehouses. The Commercial Wharf, designed by Isaiah Rogers in 1832, originally extended from Richmond Street to the harbor (the building was cut into two sections by the construction of Atlantic Avenue in 1868). Rogers's great warehouse was built of rock-faced ashlar granite blocks relieved by smooth stone for the trim. The use of this smooth stone gives the building a touch of Greek Revival–style neoclassicism that does much to relieve what would otherwise have been a stark, almost brutal appearance.

In 1851–52 and just down the street from the Commercial Wharf, Milton Stone erected a granite block that set a new standard in architectural fashion for mercantile warehouses. Stone employed an English-trained New York architect, Calvert Vaux, who adopted the Italian palazzo style for the Boston waterfront.[12] Bryant's response was his design for the Mercantile Wharf Block. With facades on 33–81 Commercial Street and 33–81 Mercantile Street, the block was the first of his major urban development projects and continued the trend toward making Boston's warehouses more architecturally stylish (figs. 4.2, 4.3). The Mercantile Wharf Corporations acquired a lot on the east side of Commercial Street between that road and the Philadelphia Packet Pier. Here former mayor Josiah Quincy led the effort to construct a block of warehouses six stories high and over 450 feet long. Sixteen lots were laid out, the pilings driven, and foundations prepared before many of the lots were sold. With construction having begun and several lots acquired by wealthy capitalists, the remaining seven unsold parcels were auctioned in April 1856. An illustration and description of the completed building appeared in *Ballou's Pictorial Drawing-Room Companion* early in 1857.[13]

The design for this block adopted the Italian palazzo style. Bryant relieved the façade of rock-faced granite with pilasters in the form of quoins dividing each warehouse and continuous belt courses marking each floor. The low-pitched (and barely visible) hipped roof has a granite cornice supported on brackets. In the treatment of the stone, the cornice and belt

Figure 4.2. Mercantile Wharf Block, Boston, 1856, Gridley J. F. Bryant, architect. As evident in this circa 1875 photograph, Bryant's granite warehouses were built with the rear elevation having direct access to wharfs. This is no longer the case today owing to landfill. (Courtesy Earle G. Shettleworth, Jr.)

courses were given a smooth finish, while the pilasters created the effect of quoins with generous tooled margins. Margins also highlight the stone where it frames windows and doors. For the ground-level entrances, the doors and flanking windows have segmental arches with keystones repeating the quoin motif.

In 1857 Bryant became involved in his second major warehouse project, the State Street Block (fig. 4.4). Foundation work began in the spring of that year for the Long and Central Wharf Corporation. This development was located in front of the United States Custom House on filled land between Long Wharf and Central Wharf. As with the Mercantile Wharf Block, sixteen lots were laid out for public auction. All the pilings had been driven and foundations completed by the time the land was auctioned in June 1857. Prospective buyers were informed that they would have to pay a share of the foundation work for their lot, and that all warehouses were to be built "agreeable to designs, drawings and working plans prepared by Gridley J. F. Bryant, Architect." Moreover, all masonry and timber framing

Figure 4.3. Detail, Mercantile Wharf Block, Silas Pierce & Co., 59–61 Commercial Street, Boston. This circa 1875 photograph illustrates a typical entrance to this granite block of warehouses. (Courtesy Earle G. Shettleworth, Jr.)

Figure 4.4. View of State Street Block, Boston, 1857, Gridley J. F. Bryant, architect. This illustration may have been published to promote sales of the warehouses. It both captures the massive size of the building and provides a contrast with Ammi B. Young's Greek Revival–style United States Custom House. The Custom House was a major landmark and very expensive to build, and Bryant was not averse to reminding Bostonians that it was dwarfed by his State Street Block. (Courtesy Historic New England)

had already been contracted for; the purchasers would be expected to acquire what was needed to conform to Bryant's designs.[14]

The building is Bryant's masterpiece of granite commercial architecture. In his prospectus Bryant sought to assure investors that there would be no architectural frills. Yet his description makes it clear that the exterior would be designed in a monumental style that befitted a building that would block what had been an unobstructed view from the water of the great Custom House: "The effect to be produced is obtained by arched openings, horizontal fascias, and belts between each of the stories, upright pier-block divisions between each warehouse with those of the street story finished with bold rustic blocks, and by a corbel table cornice which crowns the entire length of each facade." On the west façade, facing the Custom House, the center bays are "crowned with a massive circular pediment, in the tympanum of which it is proposed to introduce some appropriate device or inscription commemorative of the erection and uses of the block." The sculpture includes a globe, symbolizing international commerce. Notwithstanding the purported lack of architectural frills, Bryant understood how the stone could be carved and arranged to great architectural effect. The prospectus continues with a description of the treatment of the masonry: "The principal part of all the stones of the facades are designed with rough split faces encircled with tooled marginal lines on the edges of the exterior face of each stone. The faces of the fascias and belts of each story are designed as dressed stone, as are also all the window heads, keystones, arches, capitals, rustics, and main cornice." One of the conditions of the purchase was to forbid the construction of "Lutheran windows" (dormers), although skylights were acceptable; perhaps it was thought that dormers would spoil the architectural effect of the roofline.[15]

The State Street Block (as it came to be known) included a mechanical system for operating internal lifts. In the attic of building number nine was a steam engine and boiler to power the hoists in all of the units. The connection shafts for operating the lifts ran through the building at attic level. The boiler room was designed to be fireproof, with a floor and ceiling constructed of wrought iron beams within brick arches, and brick walls. Sadly, much of the architectural effect of this great building was lost when over half of it was demolished for an elevated highway; a variety of poorly designed additions cut into the roof of the surviving sections.

The planning and design of two large granite warehouses with multiple owners provided Bryant the experience he needed to tackle a much larger urban development project. This was the transformation of Franklin Street (then known as Franklin Place) into one of the most architecturally spectacular, albeit short-lived, commercial districts in the history of Boston (fig. 4.5). Were one to visit Boston's wholesale district in the early 1850s, it would have been evident that a great many of the streets still retained their residential architecture. It is easy to assume that Beacon Hill was always the principal neighborhood for the wealthy to live, given its elevated location above the streets leading down to the harbor. Yet many wealthy Bostonians lived in houses on streets such as Franklin, Summer, and Winter well into the nineteenth century, and many of these houses still stood against the tide of commercial expansion as late as 1850. One of the premier survivors was the row of Federal-style townhouses known as Tontine Crescent, designed and partially financed by Charles Bulfinch in 1793–94. The original development called for two crescent-shaped rows of houses with a small oval-shaped park in the center. Although only the south row and the park were actually built, the shape of Franklin Street became defined by this development. Within the next few years, substantial houses were built opposite Tontine Crescent. Franklin Place ended at Federal Street, where the Federal Street Theater and Holy Cross Church, both also by Bulfinch, were located.

The redevelopment of this area, begun in 1857 and completed during the Civil War, included the acquisition and demolition of Tontine Crescent and the houses on the opposite side of the street. It also included the extension of Devonshire Street to Franklin Street and the demolition of buildings in order to create Winthrop Square. Also, Milk Street was cut through to Franklin from the north. Holy Cross Church, designed in 1800, which stood at the east end of Tontine Crescent, was one of the last Federal period structures to be demolished. The development involved several different property owners and required the cooperation of the city. Bryant's role was clearly pivotal. At the end of 1858, when the construction on both sides of Franklin Street had been completed, the *Saturday Evening Gazette* accorded Bryant special praise: "Not only as an architect has he laid us under obligation, but he has shown no little tact in bringing together purchasers, and, by devoting time, has laid before them plans for uniformity of action which have resulted in great pecuniary benefit to them." Even his friends across the Atlantic in London noted the architect's success. In commenting on the Franklin Street development, *The Builder* observed: "Mr. G. J. F. Bryant, architect, has planned no less than about forty-five first-class stores here in a single year! Fortunate Mr. Bryant!"[16]

Bryant's role as chief designer of the development is known. Less well

Figure 4.5. View of Franklin Street toward Devonshire Street, Boston. Most but not all of the buildings in this view were designed by Bryant. Note the second block on the right with its single warehouse by an unknown architect that breaks the symmetry of Bryant's design for the row (to the right of the flagpole). (Courtesy Earle G. Shettleworth, Jr.)

documented is his authority over building owners who chose other architects. The Nathaniel J. Bradlee Collection in the Boston Athenaeum contains a set of drawings for 57–59 Franklin Street that may illustrate a typical arrangement with other designers. This was the Arch Street corner of a block Bryant designed in 1858. This end of the block was owned by J. Bowdoin Bradlee, presumably a relative of the architect Nathaniel Bradlee. The drawings document that Nathaniel Bradlee was hired to design the interior, but that for the exterior, with the exception of minor changes to doors on the side and rear, he copied Bryant's elevations. The one actual drawing by Bryant in this portfolio is an elevation for the cast iron storefront. In another instance, however (the store at 65–67 Franklin Street), the owner decided to follow the usual tradition of designing a building that rose up an additional story, thus spoiling the architectural uniformity of the block. That single exception stands out only because of Bryant's overall success in persuading most property owners to accept his vision of urban development.[17]

Unlike in the Mercantile Wharf Building and the State Street Block, the predominant architectural style of the Franklin Street development derived from Paris during Louis-Napoléon's Second Empire. All of the buildings were built of granite, and those on the south side, where the street reflected the curve of the old Tontine Crescent, supported mansard roofs. The dominant motif of the mansard roof continued into Winthrop Square as well. These roofs would later be blamed for the rapid spread of the infamous fire in 1872, but they also contributed greatly to the architectural beauty of the area. In addition to its architectural uniformity, the development was successful because the new buildings respected the crescent shape of Franklin Street, creating a sweeping curve down Devonshire Street. At that corner stood the Cathedral Building, built on the site of the old Catholic church and embellished with elaborate stonework designed by Bryant in collaboration with Hammatt Billings.[18] It is important to remember that these buildings did not house stores and offices in which one would have expected architectural embellishments of this quality. Rather, this was the city's wholesale district, where products were stored and sold in bulk.[19]

Turning the corner in front of the Cathedral Building, one faced the newly created Winthrop Square and the magnificent palatial warehouse for wholesale dry goods erected by James F. Beebe and William F. Weld in 1860–62 (fig. 4.6). With its richly embellished façades, in another neighborhood this extraordinary block might have been mistaken for a hotel.

Figure 4.6. Weld-Beebe Block, Winthrop Square, Boston, 1860–62, Gridley J. F. Bryant, architect. Winthrop Square was created as part of the redevelopment of Franklin Street and provided a piazza for Bryant's grandest commercial palace. (Courtesy Earle G. Shettleworth, Jr.)

This was Bryant's premier commercial block and the crowning achievement of the entire Franklin Street development. When this area was rebuilt after the 1872 fire, no effort was made to replicate the architectural standards established by Bryant. Instead, different architects designed the new commercial blocks in a variety of materials and styles typical of the piecemeal method of urban development in American cities.

Franklin Street and Winthrop Square represent only a portion of the many commercial blocks designed by Gridley Bryant in the years leading up to the Civil War. One small two-story structure that must have been fairly typical is documented in a portfolio of drawings in the Fine Arts

Department of the Boston Public Library. Built for Moses Grant in 1857, the design is for a "flatiron" structure at the corner of Friend and Union streets. There are nine sheets of drawings, thirteen pages of handwritten specifications, and a printed contract form with blanks to be filled. Unlike the Bradlee drawing for the Franklin Street block, these plans do not include detailed drawings for the interior of the store, which would be modified to suit whoever leased the property.

BRYANT'S ROLE in the Franklin Street development came about at a time when a large number of talented architects were active in the city. Much of the work of these men has been lost, first in the great fire of 1872, then in subsequent development of the central business district. In the 1850s several prominent designers who were older than Bryant either were nearing the end of their careers (Richard Bond, George Dexter, Edward Shaw) or had moved away from Boston (Isaiah Rogers, Ammi B. Young). A few of the older architects were still quite active, such as Jonathan Preston, who took on a young partner in William Ralph Emerson, and William Washburn, who developed a particular niche by specializing in hotel design throughout the region. Hammatt Billings also had a regional practice, but he was better known for his work designing monuments and as a popular illustrator.

Apart from large development projects such as the State Street Block and Franklin Street, much of Bryant's commercial work was comparable to that of a number of young architects. Already mentioned is his former student, Charles E. Parker. Also important was Nathaniel Bradlee, the successor to George M. Dexter's firm. Like Bryant, Bradlee managed to publicize many of his projects in the newspapers. Edward C. Cabot obtained many commissions through his wealthy family's connections. George Snell arrived from England around 1850 to design the Music Hall, a major building in its day. Less well known is John R. Hall, but the old St. James Hotel, still standing on Franklin Square, is an indication of his importance. Arthur D. Gilman, with whom Bryant later collaborated (see chapter 6), was another important competitor. Toward the end of the decade, other notable architects included George Meacham, S. S. Woodcock, and Thomas W. Silloway. Meacham and Woodcock were briefly in partnership and won a competition to design the Public Garden.

Many of these architects derived much of their income from specializing in particular types of buildings (like Washburn), or in developing their own property. Jonathan Preston had long been involved in real estate development. Indeed, for much of his career he listed himself as a mason in the city directories, and evidently did not begin to think of himself as an architect until around 1850. The design capabilities his firm offered improved significantly in 1853 with the addition of William Ralph Emerson, first as a draftsman and then as a partner. Another architect who actively designed and developed property was Charles K. Kirby. His one exceptional design was the first Boston Public Library building, a commission he won in a public competition in 1855. This impressive Italian Renaissance–style structure stood on Boylston Street opposite the Common. As there is nothing else comparable in Kirby's known work, it is tempting to speculate that the design was "ghosted" by another architect.

Among those who developed a specialization, church building proved lucrative. Alexander Esty is remembered for several stone church buildings in the Boston metropolitan area. Thomas Silloway, trained as a Universalist minister, designed or remodeled hundreds of churches in small communities throughout New England. John Stevens was another architect who left lavishly designed churches in many towns. Another area in which all of these men were active was the large market for residential architecture. As the development of roads and railroads contributed to the industrial prosperity of the small cities and towns of New England, many large homes were built in the latest architectural fashions. Architects who lived in suburban towns outside the city often found a great deal of work in their place of residence. Luther Briggs in Dorchester, George Meacham in Newton, Joseph Richards in Cambridge, S. S. Woodcock in Somerville, and John R. Hall and Nathaniel Bradlee in Roxbury were all prominent in the towns where they lived and probably designed many more buildings there than have yet been documented.[20]

It was a prosperous time for architects in general, and with so many fine designers at work in the city, Bryant's rise to prominence in so many areas of architecture was no small accomplishment. The many commercial blocks Bryant designed for wealthy merchants often led to residential projects for the same men. One of the finest documented examples is north of Boston in the city of Salem. Bryant's great railroad station in that city, discussed in a previous chapter, no doubt enhanced his reputation locally. The survival of original drawings for a large brick town house in Salem provides evidence of Bryant's skill in residential design that, as I have noted, often remains undocumented in the work of most architects during the early nineteenth century.

In 1851 John Tucker Daland hired Bryant to design his new Salem

FRONT ELEVATION

Figure 4.7. Front elevation, John Tucker Daland House, Salem, 1851, Gridley J. F. Bryant, architect. This Italianate palazzo represents the architect's skills in designing a large-scale urban dwelling before he came under the spell of French architecture. (Photograph courtesy Peabody-Essex Museum)

residence. Now part of the Peabody Essex Museum (and for many years the library for that institution), the house exhibits Bryant's mastery of a style that he adopted not only for residences but also for commercial blocks and all manner of public buildings (fig. 4.7). Inspired by the Italian palazzo style, the Daland House is the largest surviving example of residential design by Bryant. In the context of Salem, the house is in the tradition of the three-story brick Federal-style residences for which that city is famous. The difference between this house and the earlier Salem mansions is not only the new architectural vocabulary apparent in the brownstone trim but the larger scale as well. All of the rooms, even the third-story bedrooms, are spacious with tall ceilings. There are two pairs of chambers with connecting dressing rooms on the second floor and four large chambers, three small bedrooms, and two dressing rooms on the third floor. In addition, the house has several deep closets. The connecting drawing rooms and large entrance hall bespeak a family that entertained on a lavish scale.

The original portfolio of seventeen working drawings in the Peabody Essex Museum documents this project. As was typical for the early nineteenth century, minimal graphics were required, even for so large and ornate a mansion. This is evident in the front elevation drawing, where dimensions are carefully marked, and details such as windows and balusters are delineated on other sheets. In this case the original specifications have not survived, but we can presume they would have provided much of the detailed instructions not shown on the various other drawings. Only the detail sheet showing window construction is colored to enhance graphically the architect's intentions. The owner and builders signed the portfolio of seventeen drawings in the presence of the architect, who added his signature as a witness. A smaller, eighteenth drawing, dated March 1852, documents major revisions to the main entrance as delineated on the elevation sheet. Although Bryant was not generally known for his residential work, the John Tucker Daland House clearly establishes his skills at designing homes for the wealthy merchant class of Massachusetts.[21] The Daland House also demonstrates that Bryant found time to travel outside Boston in search of work. Indeed, his efforts took him to the farthest reaches of Maine and, vicariously through the federal government, to the Pacific coast.

5

From Down East to San Francisco Bay

By his own account, Gridley Bryant was a man of extraordinary energy. Not content to work in the Boston area, he made extensive use of the new railroad lines built throughout New England to establish a regional practice. As with his work in the Boston area, securing commissions for prominent public projects was important as a means of enhancing his reputation in a given locality. Yet in his day as in our own, public projects tend to take a great deal of time and effort if they are to be carried to a successful conclusion. With elected officials as clients, there is inevitably opposition on behalf of citizens who resist spending money on architecture beyond the bare necessities.

Many of the projects Bryant designed in Maine are particularly well documented, and his work in that state constitutes a significant part of his practice. It was not uncommon for Boston architects to secure major commissions "Down East." Charles Bulfinch supplied the design for Maine's new state house in 1829, and Richard Upjohn designed some of his most important early projects in Maine. Bryant stands out among his fellow Bostonians, however, for the number of major projects he took on, especially in the 1850s. His work in Maine, as far as is known, began in Eastport with the Boynton School in 1848 and the United States Custom House in 1849. Though remote from much of the state, Eastport, on the far northeast coast, was easily accessible by steamer. His fame in connection with the Charles Street Jail probably led directly to the commission for the Maine State Reformatory in Cape Elizabeth, now part of the city of South Portland. That building (an illustration of which was featured in at least two local newspapers), as well as Bryant's skills at self-promotion, began to give the architect a statewide reputation.[1]

Figure 5.1. Maine State Reformatory, Cape Elizabeth (now South Portland), Maine, 1851–53, Gridley J. F. Bryant, architect. Constructed as a reformatory for boys, Bryant's distinctive architectural landmark was clearly visible from the Western Promenade, Portland's wealthiest neighborhood. (Courtesy Maine Historic Preservation Commission)

As noted in a previous chapter, the design for the reform school in Cape Elizabeth combines features of the Deer Island Almshouse and the firm's jails. Constructed of brick, the building, with its Tudor Revival window and door arches, has a pronounced picturesque character (fig. 5.1). Indeed, a Portland newspaper at the time commented that the building (still prominently visible outside Portland) could be "viewed with fine effect from the western promenade in the western part of our city."[2] Not a few citizens must have expressed surprise, if not outrage, at the state's construction of such a grand structure to house wayward boys who, it was commonly believed, lacked only proper discipline. Bryant understood that a certain percentage of people would never be won over to public expenditures for architectural aesthetics. For many citizens, however, it was important that these buildings reflect well on their community as evidence of their progressive spirit.

Simultaneously with the state reformatory, Bryant secured the commission to design the Fryeburg Academy in western Maine (fig. 5.2). This small school is similar in its exterior architectural details to the reform school. Both employed stone Tudor arches over the windows and doors as the dominant architectural motif. Yet the Fryeburg school is a much smaller structure and exhibits a freely interpreted use of masonry for stylistic features. The basic design is a square box with three bays on each elevation, a hipped roof, and a cupola for the bell. As with his other institutional buildings, Bryant introduced very large double-tier windows separated by paneled spandrels to permit ample light and ventilation. In addition to the window and door arches, decorative effect was provided in the roof of the main structure and the enclosed entrance vestibule. Both included brick corbelling of a refined and rather delicate character. At the corners, stone

Figure 5.2. Fryeburg Academy, Fryeburg, Maine, 1852–53, Gridley J. F. Bryant, architect. Located in the western part of the state, this school is perhaps Bryant's most fanciful in its ornamental treatment for an institutional structure. (Courtesy Maine Historic Preservation Commission)

quoins terminating in a stone entablature combined with the corbelling to frame each elevation. As an early photograph of the school reveals, the building stood in a field on the outskirts of Fryeburg, creating an impressive architectural landmark for this small town of mostly wooden houses and shops.[3]

The first of Bryant's several county projects in Maine dates from 1854, with the fireproof additions to the York County Courthouse in Alfred. The old wooden Greek Revival–style courthouse received flanking wings of brick construction and, as was invariably the case with all of Bryant's public buildings, a prominent belfry. The addition of the fireproof wings probably saved valuable records when the wooden center section burned in 1933.

Whenever Bryant was hired to design a major public building in a community, his presence may well have led to numerous private commissions that remain undocumented. One instance of this presumed geographical connection is known through the survival of original drawings. The Joseph Titcomb House still stands in an excellent state of preservation in Kennebunk, a few miles east of Alfred (fig. 5.3).[4] As mentioned, Bryant's training under Alexander Parris was in the Greek Revival style. Although he had embraced new stylistic fashions and the taste for picturesque architecture popularized by figures such as Andrew Jackson Downing, the foundations of his training rested firmly in traditional neoclassical architecture. Bryant's own design proclivities are difficult to discern, in part because of the variety of architects he worked with, and in part because of the rapid changes in architectural styles during this period of American history. Yet there is a common thread in much of the architect's work. The house for Joseph Titcomb is in many respects representative of the "essential Bryant," if one can make such a statement about an architect with such a long and varied career. That the exterior design shares striking similarities to the Eastport Custom House of 1849 supports this speculation.

The style of the Titcomb House might be described as American "country Palladian." The house has a gable roof with wide overhanging eaves supported on block modillions, a central pavilion, and an entrance portico featuring the architect's favorite motif of segmental arches supported on chamfered posts. Drawing on the Italian Renaissance, the exterior is faux ashlar masonry in wood with window surrounds copied from archaeologically correct Italian sources. Even the twin chimneys are in the spirit of the blocky masonry of the house. It is a remarkable essay for a small town in rural Maine, as the house is a forthright expression of the long tradition of Palladian design in Western architecture. A rather plain variation of this

Figure 5.3. Joseph Titcomb House, Summer Street, Kennebunk, Maine, 1854, Gridley J. F. Bryant, architect. This view, taken from an 1856 map of York County published by J. L. Smith, conveys Bryant's intention that this wooden house would appear to be of masonry construction. (Courtesy Maine Historic Preservation Commission)

design, built in the same year for Aaron Hobart Jr. in East Bridgewater, Massachusetts, can be attributed to Bryant.[5]

This same affinity for classical traditions can be seen in his other major private school design in Maine, the Maine State Seminary (now Bates College) in Lewiston. Designed in 1856, this project was intended to be much larger than Fryeburg Academy, as it encompassed a campus plan of at least three buildings. There appears to have been a preliminary design for the school in the Greek Revival style, though it is likely that Bryant persuaded the trustees to adopt more stylistically fashionable plans. He would have been able to offer as a model his newly completed design for Ballou Hall at Tufts College in Medford, Massachusetts. Bryant's accepted plan for the Maine school, illustrated in a school catalogue in 1860, shows a classroom building, Hathorn Hall, flanked perpendicularly by dormitories (fig. 5.4). This view also shows multiple circular walks and carriage paths laid out in a manner similar to that of his initial landscape plan for Boston City

Hospital. Only one of the two dormitories was built, and no formal land-scape plan appears to have been executed.[6]

There is additional evidence that the design for the campus developed to reflect a grander vision than many of the school's supporters had origi-nally anticipated. In November 1856, O. B. Cheney, who would become the school's president, issued an appeal to financial backers to make good on their pledges. He confessed: "I must say, then, that the friends of the institution at the beginning, did not anticipate the erection of buildings

Figure 5.4. Bates College, Lewiston, Maine, 1856–57, Gridley J. F. Bryant, architect. The initial campus plan consisted of Hathorn Hall, with its Corinthian portico and high basement, flanked by Parker Hall set in a field north of the great Lewiston mills. (Courtesy Maine Historic Preservation Commission)

on so broad a scale, and not so great an expense as upon the plan now determined upon, and which is under careful direction of a distinguished
architect, Mr. Bryant, of Boston. Not that such buildings were not desired,
but our friends could hardly believe that the necessary funds could be secured."[7] This statement, combined with the dramatic revisions made to
the initial plans for the school, is circumstantial evidence of Bryant's role
in urging the building committee to develop a more ambitious design for
their new school.

Bryant's design for Hathorn Hall is for a three-story brick building with
a grand portico at one end supported on Corinthian columns. (The design
for Ballou Hall at Tufts employed the Ionic order.) In the center of the
roof is a tall bell tower. The cornices, with block modillions, break into full
pediments over the entrance pavilion and in the flanking gable ends. Its
site on a raised terrace reinforces the classical monumentality of the building. Bryant's original plans for the dormitory show a three-story structure
with a nearly flat roof disguised by a neoclassical balustrade. The dormitory as built, named Parker Hall, eliminated the balustrade in favor of a
hipped roof with multiple dormers, giving the building an extra story, as
well as chimneys that do not show on the elevation drawing. Subsequent
changes in the twentieth century extensively altered Parker Hall.

The school's trustees promoted Bryant's campus design through an illustration published in the school newspaper in 1860. Lewiston was a rapidly developing industrial city in the 1850s, and this ambitious scheme fits
with its development as one of Maine's major urban centers, rivaling the
older cities of Portland and Bangor. The Civil War, and the loss of so many
prospective students to the army, must have retarded the growth of the
school. Indeed, the second floor of Hathorn Hall remained entirely unfinished for thirteen years. When the building finally opened in 1857, it contained six recitation rooms and two literary rooms on the third floor, while
the ground floor held the president's office, the library, a chapel, and scientific rooms.

In late 1855 Bryant followed up his additions to the York County Courthouse with a series of courthouse and jail designs for a number of Maine
counties. Directly opposite Lewiston on the Androscoggin River is the city
of Auburn, Maine, where Bryant designed a combined courthouse and jail
for Androscoggin County. The exterior of the courthouse was based on a
prototype established with the Lying-In Hospital in Boston, built the previous year. These are rectangular brick structures with an entrance portico
at one narrow end. Windows are set within broad pilasters linked by courses

of brick corbelling. The pavilion roof (not a true mansard) forms a steeply pitched hip with overhanging eaves. The upper section of the roof is flat to accommodate a bell or clock tower, a feature Bryant invariably persuaded his clients to include. The entrance portico, a tripartite Palladian arrangement, was another highly characteristic feature of Bryant's designs.[8]

As Robert MacKay has documented, the jail section of this complex is based on a jail in Hartford, Connecticut, that Louis Dwight had identified as a model for small institutions of that type. This is not surprising, considering the limited options available for small county governments, which typically did not have large prison populations. MacKay has documented that Bryant refined the Hartford jail plan and published a model of his own with his next project, the Kennebec County Jail in Augusta.[9] Designed in 1857, this jail is remarkable for several reasons. The exterior view and plan were published in a New York Prison Association report in 1869, possibly influencing small jail designs throughout the country. The structure was also probably chosen for publication because it was Bryant's most stylish small jail. Constructed of granite instead of brick, it is an exceptionally elegant building (fig. 5.5) with a front dormer and flanking towered bays that embellish the hipped roof in a way that is more suggestive of a French mansard roof. Bryant had actually developed a scheme to construct an addition to the existing courthouse next door, but the county commissioners opted for a new building at a cost of over $52,000. In a famous story that was used to criticize the building as too lavish, it was said that when Senator Stephen A. Douglas of Illinois visited Augusta, he mistook the jail for the state house.[10]

While the Kennebec County Jail was under construction, Bryant received the commission to design a jail for Washington County in Machias. This brick building, for which original plans and specifications survive, is the smallest of the group of jails. It cost less than $24,000.[11] Although the typical entrance portico was sacrificed to save costs, Bryant did succeed in persuading the county commissioners to include an ornamental bell tower. He won them over by arguing that the bell could be rung in times of emergency, although no bell was ever installed. Round-arched windows and distinctive brick corbelling under the eaves of the hipped roof provided a modicum of ornamental flourish (fig. 5.6).[12] Given the rarity of a jail break in a rural community such as Machias, it is extraordinary that the county commissioners saw the need to endorse features that suggested a concern for high security. The building provided a compact version of the firm's "Auburn Plan." On the two principal floors, six cells are clustered in the

Figure 5.5. Kennebec County Jail, Augusta, Maine, 1857–59, Gridley J. F. Bryant, architect. This is the most elegant of a series of small jails and courthouses designed by Bryant.
(Courtesy Maine Historic Preservation Commission)

core of the building, away from the outside walls (fig. 5.7). Catwalks surround the cellblocks. The jailer's house forms a separate wing on the front
of the building; from within his residence he could monitor the cellblocks
through "eyelets" in the walls (fig. 5.8). On either side of the guardroom,
two-sided oriel windows allowed views from within the exterior side walls
(the rear wall had no windows).

In the original plans Bryant suggested that there be prominently embla-
zoned on the front façade the name of the institution: "Washington County

Jail & House of Correction." Although the name was never applied to the building, the philosophy these words imparted—a "house of *correction*"—found expression in the plans. As Bryant noted in his proposal to the county commissioners, "It will be found to combine all the important principles of prison construction, acknowledged to be of the utmost importance in the erection of these structures, to wit: classification, supervision, security, light, heat, ventilation, humanity, employment, instruction, religious worship, correction." [13] What is remarkable about the Washington County Jail is that the commissioners in this remote corner of Maine evidently completely accepted the reformist principles advanced by Bryant's designs.

Bryant's next Maine county building, the Aroostook County Courthouse in Houlton, was designed in 1858 and built the following year. Located in

Figure 5.6. Side elevation, Washington County Jail, Machias, Maine, 1858, Gridley J. F. Bryant, architect. This drawing illustrates the importance of windows to provide light and ventilation for the inmates. (Courtesy Washington County Commissioners)

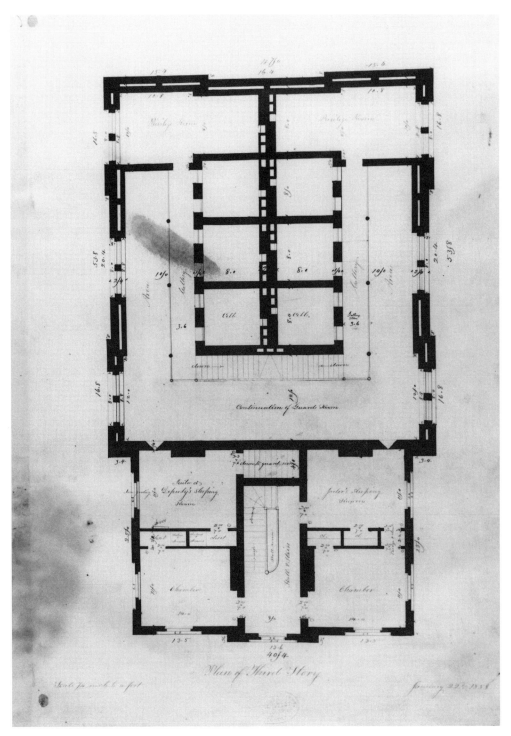

Figure 5.7. Third-floor plan, Washington County Jail. The central block of six cells on each floor provided little avenue for escape. (Courtesy Washington County Commissioners)

Figure 5.8. View of cellblocks from peephole in jailer's residence, Washington County Jail. This photograph illustrates the abundance of natural light, as well as the concern for strict supervision of prisoners. (Photograph by Lyman Holmes)

the far northern part of the state where there was not yet even a railroad line, Houlton was not a place where one would expect to find the work of a leading Boston architect. It is known that Bryant visited Machias (which was accessible by water), but it seems unlikely that he traveled to Aroostook County. By then, however, his reputation in Maine, combined with his long, detailed written instructions, would have made it feasible to meet the needs of clients in that remote part of the state without traveling there. The building was very similar in design to the Androscoggin County Courthouse, and it is likely that the county commissioners had visited Auburn. They may even have met Bryant in Auburn or Augusta and conducted subsequent communications by mail. In order to save over $2,000 in construction costs, the commissioners altered Bryant's plans, mostly through the substitution of less expensive materials, for example, wood gutters instead of copper, glass of single instead of double thickness, and wooden steps and railings instead of stone and iron. About half the savings came through the elimination of a full cellar. These savings reduced the cost to less than the low bid, which was $14,400.[14]

Bryant almost succeeded in ending this decade of work in Maine with a new state prison in Thomaston, but he had less success with the state legislature than with county commissioners. In 1858 Governor Lot M. Morrill appointed James G. Blaine to head a commission to look into the construction of a new state prison. Commissioner Blaine wrote Bryant in October of that year asking for a design for a new prison with a capacity of 250 and provisions for enlargement "without impairing its general features." Blaine, a former governor, had participated in the dedication of the Kennebec County Jail in Augusta, and Bryant's reputation for expertise in prison design was such that Blaine felt he could apply to him directly rather than requesting proposals from a variety of firms. The architect's report included a single sheet of drawings offering a "bird's eye view" (Bryant's phrase) of the entire complex and its floor plans. A description of the building was also specifically requested. The design reflected the classic Dwight-Bryant scheme developed ten years earlier, except that the architectural style was updated to French Second Empire. Bryant was by now comfortable enough with the subject to expand his "mechanical description" to include theories of penal reform advocated by his late partner.[15] As a backup, or perhaps in quick response to a discouraging reaction from the legislature, in November 1859 Bryant prepared a portfolio of two less ambitious designs. One scheme was for enlargements to the existing prison, while the other was for a new structure with but one prison wing extending from the hexagonal guardroom–administration building. (These drawings—two sets of colored perspective views and floor plans—still survive in the Maine State Library.) Bryant thus prepared three different schemes for model prison reform, making every effort to alleviate the deplorable conditions prevailing in the existing structure.

In the end, the legislature chose not to accept any of Bryant's plans. The state prison continued to be remodeled with little attention to theories of penal reform. The architect's success in Maine, however, continued at the local level. In 1862 the town of Alfred hired Bryant to prepare plans for two buildings, a school and a town hall. Both projects, for which original drawings survive, are remarkable in their simplicity and lack of pretension (fig. 5.9). Though designed by a Boston architect who was then involved in creating many of the most stylistically fashionable buildings in New England, the town hall and school could both be mistaken for the work of a local builder. Modestly embellished in the Italianate style, the designs suggest the long New England tradition of Greek Revival–style public buildings. For Bryant, as with any successful architect, knowing his clients was the key to success.

Alfred, notwithstanding its location as the county seat, had long since lost any pretensions to major economic development. This was not the case for the towns of Auburn and Skowhegan, communities with significant industrial activity. Both municipalities hired Bryant, in 1865 and 1868, respectively, to design brick town halls with very stylish mansard roofs. In both cases, the arrangement was to use the ground floor for stores to obtain rental income to defray construction costs. A beautiful color elevation drawing survives for the Auburn building (fig. 5.10), documenting once again Bryant's recognition of the importance of graphics to promote his reputation and the value of the project. For the Auburn town hall, we know that Bryant's involvement was restricted to the exterior design and the plans for the upper floors. The cost-conscious town fathers, who were planning a new building only because the old one had burned, modified Bryant's design. Local firms then designed the three stores, and the contractor for the building was authorized to reduce the costs of the exterior by substituting plain granite lintels for carved sandstone window

Figure 5.9. School House, Alfred, Maine, 1862, Gridley J. F. Bryant, architect. Built at the same time as the Boston City Hall, this small rural school does not suggest the hand of one of the leading architects in New England. (Courtesy Maine Historic Preservation Commission)

Figure 5.10. Presentation drawing, Auburn Town Hall, Auburn, Maine, 1865, Gridley J. F. Bryant, architect. This unsigned color rendering of the front elevation shows the combined town hall with stores. The design was modified by the contractor to save money in construction. (Courtesy Maine Historic Preservation Commission)

surrounds. The designs for the dormers were also simplified. In order to compensate for making the building plainer, the slope of the mansard roof was given a curve in the contractor's revisions.[16]

In the 1870s, another jail in Bangor (Penobscot County) and a court-house in Rockland (Knox County) would bring Bryant and his then part-ner, Louis Rogers, back to Maine. Original drawings survive for both buildings, which involved no new approaches to design but are architec-turally elegant statements in the tradition of Bryant's earlier work. The Bangor jail followed the design of the Machias jail, except that the cell wing is granite and the keeper's house brick with granite trim and the ar-chitect's traditional Palladian portico.

THE ECONOMIC return on projects in these distant locations did not neces-sarily justify an architect's commitment in travel time. Architectural draw-ings alone did not then earn architects large fees; often several sheets of plans and elevations for a proposed design would bring in only $25 to $100. For example, in 1844 Bryant designed a house on Beacon Hill that was estimated to cost $9,800. For plans and specifications he was paid $75. These probably consisted of floor plans and elevations, plus separate speci-fications for masonry and carpentry. The preparation of more extensive construction plans could require full- or quarter-scale detailed drawings on a heavy cartridge paper, amounting to two to three dozen sheets. Speci-fications would also be prepared, which typically involved one set for car-pentry and one set for masonry.[17]

While the architect's thoroughly prepared drawings and specifications perhaps made it less critical that he be hired for supervision, providing con-struction oversight was preferable. This was also where the fees were to be earned. Bryant designed interior alterations to Holden Hall at Harvard (a small building) in 1850, for which he was paid $650, as his work included supervision of the construction. To take the example of a larger structure built at the same time, the Deer Island Almshouse cost $177,088.36, of which Bryant was paid $2,282.45 for plans, surveys, and architectural ser-vices.[18]

We know that Bryant traveled a great deal, and even then he was not necessarily paid to supervise construction, though at Bates College he was hired to provide that service. That put him across the river from Auburn when the Kennebec County commissioners came to visit his Androscoggin County Jail on June 4, 1857. His presence in Auburn no doubt helped se-cure the Kennebec County Jail commission, but it is not known if he was hired to provide supervision for that project. For projects in which Bryant mailed his plans and specifications but did not provide construction supervision, he may in some instances have known the contractor and relied on his competence. The relations between architects and contractors during this period is one about which little is known. The Androscoggin Courthouse and Jail and the Washington County Jail were both built by Albert Currier of Newburyport, Massachusetts. Bryant had worked earlier with this contractor on the Essex County Jail in Lawrence, and the two men probably had a good working relationship. For the Washington County Jail, Currier actually built his own brickyard in the vicinity, ensuring a steady supply of bricks to complete the project on time. In the case of the Aroostook County Courthouse, seven contractors submitted bids. Curiously, the low bidder, Harrison D. Clement, at $14,400, was located in Lawrence, Massachusetts, making him also the farthest away. The highest, at $19.185.72, was from the nearest location, not far from Bangor. Either Clement had some experience working on Bryant's projects or else he foolishly underbid. In any case, since the Aroostook County Courthouse is located 375 miles from Boston, the contractor would have had to travel by road on the old military highway north of Bangor, as there was no railroad to Houlton.[19]

Perhaps the best illustration of Bryant's practice of providing drawings for buildings at distant locations while deriving substantial income from construction supervision closer to home is his work for the United States government. As early as 1849 Bryant began aggressively to pursue contracts with the federal government for both design services and construction supervision. The Treasury Department was responsible for most of the public buildings erected in the early nineteenth century. (Military facilities and lighthouses fell under the control of the Army Corps of Engineers.) During a brief period prior to the establishment of the Bureau of Construction and the appointment of Ammi B. Young as supervising architect in 1852, major public buildings, such as customhouses, were often designed by a variety of local or regional architects. The treasury secretary and local officials, such as custom collectors, selected these men. In the case of major buildings, where several local architects might have supporters, competitive plans could be considered. For locations where there were no prominent local architects, the selection process may have been less competitive.[20]

Bryant's first effort had been an ultimately failed attempt to be appointed as the Boston agent for securing the granite necessary for construction of the massive New Orleans Custom House in 1848. Surviving records are incomplete, but it is evident that he marshaled the support of many politically influential citizens to receive the New Orleans appointment. Apparently, he was initially successful, only to have the offer rescinded for unknown political reasons. Perhaps in compensation, he was hired as the architect for the Eastport Custom House in Maine in 1849.[21] A friend in that area, James P. Wheeler, whom Bryant had met while attending the Gardiner Lyceum, had acted on Bryant's behalf to secure the commission to design the local high school in 1848. This coincided with a report to the United States House of Representatives that led to authorization to build a new customhouse in Eastport.[22] The building burned in 1887, and the only surviving images are a photograph of a fire-gutted shell and a sketch published after the fire. These are enough, however, to show that Bryant's design provided that physically remote port with the flavor of the "new" Italian Renaissance style. As previously noted, there is a strong similarity to the design for the Titcomb House in Kennebunk. Though not in the palazzo style that Treasury Department architect Ammi B. Young built all over the country in the 1850s, the Eastport Custom House broke with the neoclassical tradition made famous by the government work of Robert Mills.

More characteristic of early-nineteenth-century federal government architecture was Bryant's design for the San Francisco Custom House (fig. 5.11). As in Eastport, there was no local architect sufficiently competent to press his own claim for the commission. Bryant had at least one champion in Congressman Samuel A. Eliot of Massachusetts, who wrote a strong letter of endorsement to Treasury Secretary Thomas Corwin in December 1851: Mr. Bryant has done a great deal of work for me, & I have been familiar with what he has done for other people, for about fifteen years, & have never had the least occasion to complain either of the manner in which he had done the work, or of the price he has charged for it; nor have I known any one else to complain. He is faithful, remarkably industrious, energetic & every way competent & I have always found him ready either to adopt good suggestions from other people, or to make better ones himself.[23]

Eliot had first come to know Bryant when the young architect was working on the alterations to the city hall while Eliot was mayor of Boston. He later had an opportunity to call upon Bryant to supervise work at Harvard College, including emergency repairs to Gore Hall in 1852 after the construction of the building's Gothic towers was determined to have been defective and they had to be rebuilt. Eliot, in his capacity as treasurer of

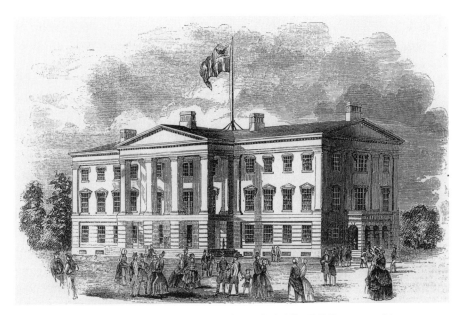

Figure 5.11. San Francisco Custom House, 1851–56, Gridley J. F. Bryant, architect. Featured in *Gleason's Pictorial Drawing-Room Companion* on May 29, 1852, this was one of many instances when Bryant illustrated his work in popular pictorial journals. (Author's collection)

Harvard, blamed Richard Bond, the original architect. Bryant's services were secured to rebuild and reduce the height of the towers. The endorsement of men like Eliot must have carried weight, especially since the president at the time, Millard Fillmore, was a member of Eliot's Whig Party.[24]

Bryant's selection for the San Francisco project was not without informal competition, however. Thomas U. Walter, the Philadelphia architect, had been hired to prepare plans early in 1851. Although Walter's design was rejected, he was asked to revise it at the same time that Bryant submitted his own plans. The records are not complete, but apparently Bryant had been asked to arrange for the procurement of the cast iron to be used in the building, and the Boston architect managed to obtain permission to develop plans for the entire building, possibly unbeknownst to Walter. In November, Treasury Department officials wrote to Bryant indicating that they were considering drawings from more than one other designer and were waiting for his submission before making a decision. By the end of the year, Bryant had been selected to develop the plans. The Army Corps of Engineers was assigned to supervise the construction.[25]

It is almost certain that Bryant never traveled to San Francisco. Instead, he prepared detailed drawings, lithographed copies of which survive in the National Archives. The basic design, with its low-pitched gabled roof, pilasters, and projecting cornice supported on piers, calls to mind the Greek Revival structures of the nation's capital. Bryant, however, embellished his building with rusticated basement-level and window trim consisting of cornices supported on brackets, providing a more stylish overlay for this remote outpost of the federal government. A more important feature of the design was its fire-resistant qualities, which enabled the building to withstand the great earthquake and fire of 1906. It was Bryant who persuaded the government to employ the standard fire-resistant technique of constructing floors built on brick arches supported by iron columns. Remarkably, the granite used for the basement story was Quincy stone shipped all the way from Boston. The ironwork, glazing, plumbing, and carpentry also came from Boston. Local brick was used for the superstructure, which was covered with mastic to imitate stone. True to form, as an avid self-promoter Bryant managed to get a woodcut view and description of the building published in *Gleason's Pictorial Drawing-Room Companion* for May 29, 1852.

Notwithstanding the appointment of Ammi B. Young as supervising architect of the Treasury Department in 1852, Bryant was paid $250 to travel to Philadelphia in 1853 to measure the United States Mint there and develop plans for a similar structure in San Francisco. This was not built until 1869, following the designs of then Treasury Department architect Alfred Mullett. Bryant's contribution to Pacific Coast architecture also included advising the treasury secretary on the design of lighthouses. It is probably no coincidence that Bryant's brief success in obtaining government appointments coincided with the fact that the Whig Party controlled the White House from 1849 to 1853.[26]

The architect's next major government job was the Post Office and Court House in Philadelphia, designed in 1862. At this time another former Boston architect, Isaiah Rogers, was at the Treasury Department. Rogers had left Boston about the time Bryant's career was getting under way, and there is no record that the two men were close. In any case, Bryant, at one of the busiest points of his career, was hired both to develop plans for the building and to provide construction supervision. A local architect, John Frazer, was hired to assist in the latter task. The structure, which stood for barely thirty years, was a handsome example of the mansard style, quite typical of what was being built in Boston at that time. With a solid reputation growing among Treasury Department officials, Bryant would win even more lucrative jobs supervising construction in New England over the next decade.[27]

6

Bryant and Gilman

ON THE EVE of the Civil War, Boston had finally recovered from the financial crisis of 1857 and was continuing the great period of residential expansion which had begun in the early years of the decade. Gridley Bryant had been very successful, both locally and regionally, and the fact that the country was about to enter a period of grave crisis did not significantly curtail his practice. The number of talented competing architects only continued to grow. Men such as Nathaniel P. Bradlee, George Snell, John R. Hall, Edward C. Cabot, George Meacham, and Alexander Esty were joined by new faces, including Henry Hartwell (later of Hartwell and Richardson), Charles A. Cummings (later of Cummings and Sears), William R. Ware (later of Ware and Van Brunt), William G. Preston, and William R. Emerson. In the post–Civil War period, these firms would begin to supersede Bryant in competition for local commissions. If he was to meet the challenge offered by these talented architects, he needed to find another designer to work with on a regular basis.

The growth of the city and the surrounding suburbs brought prosperity to the building trades. In particular, there was the continued expansion of the South End neighborhood toward Roxbury and Dorchester, and, in 1857, the decision to fill the Back Bay for a residential neighborhood of upper-class homes. While the South End was desirable for the middle and upper middle classes, the very wealthy did not have a new neighborhood of their own until the Back Bay began to be filled. The man responsible for the design of the Back Bay, as well as setting the architectural tone of the new neighborhood, was Arthur Delvan Gilman, one of the most enigmatic and forceful architects of his day (fig. 6.1). It was Bryant's great good fortune that he was able to join forces with Gilman at this critical period in

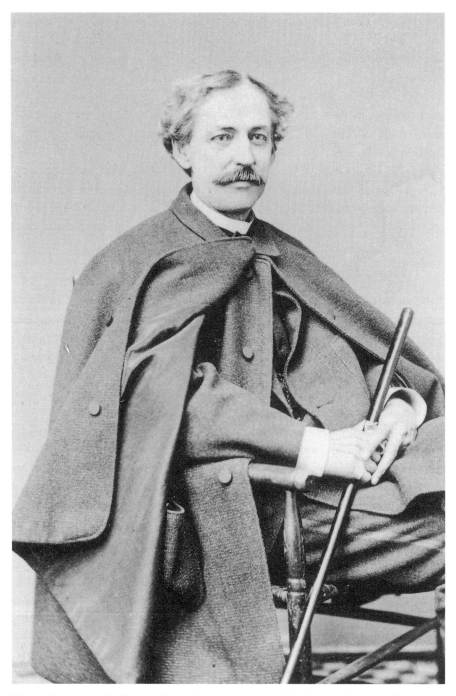

Figure 6.1. Arthur D. Gilman, circa 1870 carte de visite. Handsome, elegant, and a popular conversationalist, Arthur Gilman provided social connections Bryant lacked. (Courtesy Earle G. Shettleworth, Jr.)

the development of the city. Once again, Bryant recognized a route to advance his career by working with someone who could complement his own skills, thereby continuing to maintain his supremacy as the city's leading architect.

Arthur Gilman was born in Newburyport in 1821 and began to work as an architect in the early 1840s; yet his early fame (or notoriety) came through his opinionated architectural critiques that were widely publicized in the press at that time. Gilman's practical training as an architect is not known. He burst into the public consciousness in 1843–44 with a series of letters, articles, and lectures in which he scathingly attacked Boston architecture in general and the Greek Revival style in particular. For reasons that shall become clear, it is likely that Gilman learned the rudiments of building design in the office of Gridley Bryant while poring over the architectural library of Alexander Parris.[1]

Gilman's first known architectural commission came in late 1845. He had spent the two previous years antagonizing many potential clients with his critiques of contemporary architecture. His first published article in January 1843, reviews of Alexander Jackson Downing's *Treatise on the Theory and Practice of Landscape Gardening* and *Cottage Residences,* inspired the public to stop building houses in the form of mock Greek temples and adopt Downing's theories of picturesque landscape design. Significantly, Gilman spoke fondly about vernacular architecture of the colonial period in comparison with what was currently being designed by architects. In language that calls to mind the early-twentieth-century romanticizers of the Colonial Revival style, he wrote, "If the artist would draw an American landscape, he rejoices not in the tall mansion, with its Grecian facade, and its kitchen after the manner of a tail in the rear; but rather in the steep-roofed work of antiquity, with its projecting upper floor, in which the obvious purpose of defense, against the snowstorms and savages of former days, give it grace of fitness, if it has no other." Gilman found unbearably pretentious the image of a Greek Revival–style house and landscape with rows of well-ordered trees and symmetrical walks. In November of the same year, he engaged in a newspaper debate, offering strident criticism of Richard Bond's design for the new Mt. Vernon Street Church on Beacon Hill. The severe granite façade in the form of a Greek temple mounted on a brick building epitomized all that Gilman loathed in contemporary architecture. The Reverend E. N. Kirk, minister of the church, responded with a vigorous defense, and so began the type of public dialogue Gilman evidently relished.[2]

His most famous assault on Boston architecture is his April 1844 review of Edward Shaw's *Rural Architecture.* Shaw, by then nearing the end of his most productive years as an architect, had been trained as a carpenter in the Greek Revival style, and though he introduced designs in the Gothic Revival style, he remained essentially an adherent of neoclassical architecture. For Gilman, a review of Shaw's builder's guide served as an excuse for a comprehensive critique of contemporary architecture, particularly the Greek Revival style, of which there was no more prominent symbol than the massive granite Custom House in Boston, begun in 1837 and not yet complete in 1844. Ammi B. Young's design may no longer have been as fashionable in 1844 as in 1837, but it would be a mistake to imagine that the new architectural styles were sweeping Boston. In the same year the Latin and English High School and the Horticultural Society Hall, both by Richard Bond, joined his Mt. Vernon Church as pure examples of the Greek Revival style. Isaiah Rogers's Merchants' Exchange on State Street, completed in 1842, was yet another major example. Notwithstanding the success of Downing's publications, the Greek Revival style still had many proponents during the 1840s.

Gilman's published critique, followed by a series of lectures at the Lowell Institute in October and November 1844, had a great impact locally. The Boston Custom House was an extraordinarily expensive public building project, and many Bostonians took exception to hearing this major architectural edifice in the very heart of the city's waterfront characterized as "so incongruous and absurd a pile, that we scarcely know where to begin or where to end our enumeration of its deformities."[3] Enumerate he did, in great detail, why the most important building then under construction in Boston represented all that was deplorable in art and architecture and was a monumental waste of money to boot. Gilman's critique was felt so deeply that, within a few months, William W. Wheilden, acting on behalf of Young and the building commissioners, published a twenty-three-page rebuttal. Answering in kind, Wheilden rejected Gilman's criticisms as "narrow, contracted and impolitic."[4]

It was not just the Custom House that was subject to Gilman's stringent attacks. The Merchants' Exchange, as well as several designs by Richard Bond—the Latin and English High School, the Bowdoin Square Church, the remodeled Tremont Temple, and the Harvard Library building—also came under fire. That the Bowdoin Square Church and the Harvard Library were Gothic Revival, a style Gilman approved of in theory, did not spare them. Gilman's understanding of the Gothic Revival derived from Augustus Welby Pugin and the pedantic interpretation of historical styles that characterized all of his writings. It is not surprising, given the nasty nature of Gilman's attacks on architects (who were not named), that Wheilden could conclude: "There is no semblance of justice—no regard for character—no thought for the feelings of others—no estimate of the claims of the city—no consideration for its welfare—neither taste, discrimination nor judgment in such wide sweeping, wholesale denunciation as that we have been considering, and we unhesitatingly denounce it as unbecoming the writer, and unworthy the high character the pages have hitherto sustained, into which it found admission."[5]

Notwithstanding his lack of concern for antagonizing powerful representatives of the city, Arthur Gilman did find work. Perhaps it is no coincidence that the two earliest projects that have been identified are churches outside Boston: St. Paul's Episcopal Church in Dedham (1845) and the Central Congregational Church in Bath, Maine (1846).[6] The two wooden Gothic Revival–style churches, nearly identical to each other, were both based on an English church, St. Luke's in Chelsea. The use of board and batten siding for these churches was a technique developed by the American architect Gilman most admired, Richard Upjohn. Upjohn had left Boston for New York in 1839 but continued to receive important commissions in New England. In Gilman's view, no church in America could surpass Upjohn's Trinity Church in New York City. As for more modest country churches, in 1845 Upjohn had designed two important wooden structures in Brunswick, Maine, a town quite close to Bath. St. Paul's Episcopal Church and the First Parish Church were contemporary with Gilman's Dedham church, which is not surprising, given that the two men had developed a personal relationship.[7]

For domestic architecture Gilman was not necessarily enthusiastic about the variety of picturesque styles advocated in Downing's publications except insofar as they served as an antidote to the Greek Revival style. The Italian palazzo mode for cities and the Italian villa for the suburbs offered, in his view, the best solutions. In particular, Theodore Lyman's country house in Brookline, built in 1842, established a model for emulation. Gilman never passed up an opportunity to praise Bryant's design, and it is significant that in one article in 1843, an unidentified residence in Cambridge designed by Bryant received praise in the same sentence.[8]

Bryant and Gilman's early friendship is difficult to document. In addition to the aforementioned 1843 letter, there is a copy of Pugin's *Contrasts: or, A Parallel between the Noble Edifices of the Middle Ages, and Corresponding Buildings of the Present Day; Shewing the Present Decay of Taste* which Gilman inscribed to Bryant in June 1845.[9] As mentioned, it is not known where Gilman received his training in building construction (as opposed to architectural theory), but it may well have been in Bryant's office. In all of Gilman's animadversions on the Greek Revival style, it is noteworthy that architects whose work he criticized (Ammi B. Young, Isaiah Rogers, and Richard Bond) were all competitors of Bryant. Even more significant is the fact that there is one architect of many major Greek Revival–style buildings whose work is spared any criticism: Alexander Parris. It was Parris who trained Bryant and also hired Upjohn when that architect was struggling for commissions in Boston.

Gridley Bryant was trained in the Greek Revival style, but he is said to have been an admirer of men who could write well and had a scholarly background.[10] The intemperate, pedantic Gilman was an unlikely match for a man like Bryant, whose great strength was his ability to work with a variety of individuals. Yet Gilman was certainly in the forefront of architectural theory and would have had much to offer Bryant in that regard. Moreover, Gilman was fundamentally conservative in his outlook. He condemned in no uncertain terms the architecture not only of the Greek Revival but also of the Federal style of Charles Bulfinch. Instead, Gilman admired the eighteenth-century architecture of the colonial period. In his view, the Federal and Greek Revival styles were an aberration from the fundamental principles of Art. While it is unlikely that Bryant completely subscribed to this view, there came a time when the two men found that circumstances enabled them to work together in harmony for a few very productive years.

GILMAN'S OWN artistic development prior to 1859 can be divided into two periods. From the first period, leading up to his trip to Europe in 1853, only a few commissions are known, mostly churches. Like Upjohn, Gilman favored the Gothic Revival but would also work in the Romanesque style. Two major residential commissions for country houses date from shortly before he left for Europe: Fernhill, the William P. Winchester Estate in Watertown (now part of Cambridge), and the H. H. Hunnewell Estate in Needham (now part of Wellesley) (figs. 6.2, 6.3). The Winchester house, Fernhill, is no longer standing. It occupied a commanding site on a bend in the Charles River. Its brick exterior, with its full entablature, pedimented central pavilion, and roof balustrade, was more in character with Georgian neoclassicism in the manner of James Gibbs and Colin Campbell than with the picturesque Italianate style of Richard Upjohn. This feeling of an

Figure 6.2. Fernhill, the Winchester Estate, Cambridge, 1849–50, Arthur Gilman, architect. This view taken during an unidentified military ceremony shows the house after it had been acquired by Mt. Auburn Cemetery in 1885. (Courtesy Trustees of the Brookline Public Library)

eighteenth-century English estate is also evident in the exquisite little neo-classical boathouse that stood at the bend of the river. The almost rustic simplicity of this boathouse, with its Tuscan order and over-scaled mutule, suggests something of the spirit of the Covent Garden chapel in London by Inigo Jones, built in 1630–31. The house dates from 1848–49; its owner, William Winchester had little time to enjoy the novelty of commuting to Boston on the Charles River, as he died in August 1850.[11]

The Hunnewell House, still standing on a large intact estate adjacent to Wellesley College, has a more delicate and refined elegance that is very much in keeping with its beautiful landscaped setting. Both houses have five-bay façades, low-pitched hipped roofs masked by balustrades, central pavilions, and entrance porticos supported by Ionic columns. Yet the Hunnewell House features a bowed pavilion and relies less heavily on large-scale trim for ornamental effect. Like the Winchester Estate, this house displays Gilman's affinities for eighteenth-century neoclassicism. Built in 1851–52, it was first enlarged in 1866 with a substantial neoclassical conservatory. Family records list Bryant as the architect of that addition, as well as of a lovely Second Empire–style cottage at the main entrance to the estate. It seems likely, however, that Gilman, who was then based in New York but still working with Bryant, was involved in the design of both structures.[12]

A third important early project by Gilman is the town hall in Exeter, New Hampshire (fig. 6.4). Gilman designed this building in 1855, when he was in a brief partnership with Benjamin Dwight. Like the two aforementioned houses, Exeter Town Hall demonstrates Gilman's appreciation

Figure 6.3. Hunnewell Estate, Wellesley, 1851–52, Arthur Gilman, architect. At right is attached conservatory added by Bryant in 1865. (Courtesy Earle G. Shettleworth, Jr.)

Figure 6.4. Town Hall, Essex, New Hampshire, 1855, Gilman & Dwight, architects. The design combined the modern *Rundbogenstil* with a cupola inspired by American architecture of the eighteenth century. (Courtesy Essex Historical Society)

of eighteenth-century Georgian traditions. He strongly believed that windows, as important functional elements of a design, should be explicitly acknowledged in terms of ornamental trim. Here, the two floors of round-arched windows provide abundant natural light and suggest a vigorous appreciation of the *Rundbogenstil*. At the same time, the neoclassical entrance portico and cupola boldly affirm the town's colonial heritage.[13]

Upon his return from Europe in 1854, Gilman established an office that exhibited his artistic tastes. A brief description survives in the account of a visiting architect from New Orleans, Thomas K. Wharton:

Met an appointment with Mr. Bryant at 11—he spent an hour with me introducing me to several friends—amongst whom we called upon Mr. Gilman, Architect, who has just returned from Europe and brought some fine works of art which appear to advantage in his well lighted and handsome rooms on Tremont Street—his office is quite a gem in its way, beautifully situated, spacious and furnished with every architectural convenience, and the walls exhibit abundant proof of the talent of its occupant—an article, too, in today's "Journal of Music" entitled

"Pilgrimage to Salisbury" shows him to possess fine literary taste, and intense appreciation and love of English scenery—he designed and executed the elegant "Winchester" mansion at the foot of Mt. Auburn which
we admired so much during our visit to Mt. A.[14]

In Europe, Gilman visited France and Britain, where he met and social-
ized with prominent architects (Sir Charles Barry and Sir Charles Cockerel) and literary figures (William Makepeace Thackeray) and visited many
great cathedrals. His tour of France also included cathedrals, but in the
one published account of this trip, Paris is not mentioned.[15] Yet it was Paris
that clearly had the most profound impact on his thinking about architecture. Visits to ancient cathedrals and, comparatively speaking, ancient architects (Barry and Cockerel were nearing the end of their lives) may have
served only to reinforce many firmly held opinions. Gilman acquired the
view that modern Paris and its rebuilding under Emperor Louis-Napoléon
represented the apex of Western civilization, and this belief would have a
profound impact on Boston.

In 1857, Gilman became involved in the planning efforts to fill in the
Back Bay for residential development. Various sources after the fact ac-
knowledge that it was Gilman's plan for platting the Back Bay neighborhood that was accepted. Up until then, the standard approach to urban
planning in Boston had been to follow the English precedents of using
small semi-private parks or squares to break the linear pattern of street
layouts. Louisburg Square on Beacon Hill and Worcester Square in the
South End are typical examples of this approach. David Sears, who offered
an alternative plan for the Back Bay, would have continued that tradition.
Gilman's concept, by contrast, was based on the approach taken by Baron
Haussmann, who was then supervising the reconstruction of much of Paris
under Louis-Napoléon. The accepted scheme for the Back Bay centers on
a broad central avenue (Commonwealth) bisected by a tree-lined mall.
This avenue is on axis to the Public Garden, as are the flanking parallel
streets, Beacon, Marlborough, Newbury, and Boylston. The shorter perpendicular side streets run from Boylston Street to Beacon Street on the
Charles River.[16]

Gilman also introduced the French concept of luxury apartment houses
to Boston. The established tradition had been, again following the English
example, blocks of row houses. Row houses continued to be favored by
most wealthy Bostonians, but with the Hotel Pelham erected in 1857 at the

corner of Boylston and Tremont streets, Gilman designed a building that featured a complete residence on each floor. The exterior of the building was designed in a very simple mansard style reminiscent of a Parisian apartment house.[17]

When filling of the Back Bay at last began in 1859, the first buildings were erected on Arlington Street facing the Public Garden, and on sections of Beacon, Marlborough, Commonwealth, and Newbury streets up to Berkeley Street. The association between the two architects began with the earliest construction in this neighborhood. In the absence of original plans and specifications, newspaper accounts provide the best source for determining who designed these buildings. Some were by Bryant and Gilman, others by Bryant or Gilman alone, and this seems to fit the pattern of loose association on a variety of projects.

This work also coincides with Gilman's having moved into Bryant's office at 4 Court Street. Although they had been friends for years, the reason they chose now to work together probably had to do with Bryant's well-known capacity for work. Gilman would have recognized that he had an opportunity to establish an architectural pattern for the new Back Bay neighborhood, making it conform to his Parisian vision. But he could do this only by taking on a large number of projects during the first years of development. For that he needed Bryant. Also in Gridley Bryant's office at that time were William S. Park, Samuel W. Richards, Rheimunt Sayer, and Louis P. Rogers. Within a few years, Edward H. Kendall, James G. Hill, and Carl Fehmer would replace Richards and Sayer. Whether these three men, all of whom later became prominent architects in their own right, joined in order to work for Bryant or Gilman is not known. It can be presumed that they made significant contributions to the work that came out of 4 Court Street. As there was no formal partnership, these men may have found themselves collaborating on joint projects, or on commissions for Bryant and Gilman alone.[18]

The first project the two men collaborated on was the Arlington Street Church, generally recognized as Gilman's masterpiece (fig. 6.5).[19] At the time there were two prominent architectural styles for church architecture, Gothic Revival and Romanesque (often referred to as Italianate or Lombardic for the Lombardy region of northern Italy). In Boston, the Gothic was the most popular style, especially for Episcopal and Catholic churches. Congregationalist, Baptist, and nondenominational churches often favored the Romanesque. The Unitarians of the Arlington Street Church consulted several architects for a design, including a former member of their congregation, the architect Edward C. Cabot. Remarkably, they selected Gilman's interpretation of an eighteenth-century Georgian church.

A close reading of Gilman's writings reveals his admiration for local examples of eighteenth-century church architecture. When, in 1857, Christ Church in Cambridge was contemplating additions, Gilman argued that

Figure 6.5. Arlington Street Church, Boston, 1859–62, Bryant and Gilman, architects. The first church built in the new Back Bay neighborhood, this was also the beginning of Bryant and Gilman's collaboration. (Courtesy Earle G. Shettleworth, Jr.)

the 1760 Peter Harrison design was a magnificent example of a specimen from the period of what were referred to as "Queen Anne's churches" and should not have its proportions altered by an enlargement. Significantly, his solution was to move the old church back on the lot and construct a duplicate in stone, albeit on a larger scale. In other words, the proportions of the design were inviolate, but the scale and materials adopted for a new structure were not.[20]

Gilman had had an opportunity to model a new church on Christ Church with St. Andrew's Episcopal Church in Chelsea in 1858–59, but he did not in fact attempt to copy the older design. The Arlington Street Church is Gilman's homage to Gibbs and St. Martin-in-the-Fields in London, but it is also a building of its period in the scale of the ornament and the use of New Jersey brownstone on the exterior. For the first church to be built in the new Back Bay neighborhood, Gilman arrived at a solution that was at once conservative and radical. A long newspaper account after its dedication justified the use of a style that marked "a return to those solid and classical principles which were characteristic of churches of a former age but had not been used, with one exception, since the Revolution. The interior plan, with its boxed pews, was if anything even more derivative of eighteenth-century New England churches (fig. 6.6).[21] Not surprisingly, the various congregations that soon followed by moving into this neighborhood built in the more widely accepted Gothic Revival style.

At the same time that the Arlington Street Church was under construction, a number of houses were being built on the prime lots facing the Public Garden. Gilman set the tone in terms of scale and architectural style with his mansard-roofed dwellings. In the blocks between Arlington and Berkeley streets, Gilman offered a variety of approaches to urban design. At the corner of Arlington and Commonwealth, the house designed for John Bates is a freestanding single-family residence with an exterior of monochromatic sandstone which calls to mind the town houses of Paris. On the corner of Arlington and Beacon is a row of three houses designed with Bryant for John Simmons. This group forms an interesting comparison with a similar block of three houses built on Arlington Street in 1860, designed by Richard Morris Hunt of New York.[22] Also designed with Bryant was a row of eight houses on the south side of Commonwealth Avenue built of brick with sandstone trim. Across Commonwealth Avenue at the corner of Berkeley Street is Gilman's most elegant and refined interpretation of Second Empire style, a freestanding double house for Samuel Hooper and his son designed with Bryant (fig. 6.7). Hooper acquired

Figure 6.6. Interior view, Arlington Street Church. No project better illustrates Gilman's love of eighteenth-century Georgian architecture. (Courtesy the Bostonian Society/Old State House)

several house lots in order to accommodate the residence, which looked like a single-family home and was comfortably positioned with a comparatively large amount of open yard on the west side. Like the row of eight houses across the street, the Hooper residence is constructed of pressed brick that sets off the soft tones of the sandstone trim. Each window is framed with sandstone that, in the case of the Hooper House, has delicate floral carvings in a Renaissance motif. The roof of the Hooper House has two colors of slate in a chevron pattern that emphasizes the European

Figure 6.7. Samuel Hooper Houses, 25–27 Commonwealth Avenue, Boston, 1860–61. Byrant and Gilman were provided a rare opportunity to design a house in the Back Bay with a side yard owned by the client. (Courtesy Boston Athenaeum).

picturesque origins of the design. This house is the best example of Gilman's understanding of contemporary French residential architecture.

The choice of an architectural style inspired by the Paris of Louis-Napoléon was clearly Gilman's vision of the single most appropriate style for American domestic architecture. At the same time that the Arlington Street Church and these houses were under construction, as well as the great Weld-Beebe warehouse on Winthrop Square and the Boston City Hospital, Bryant and Gilman secured the commission to design a new city hall. With other architects following suit in the choice of this style, Boston was being transformed, architecturally at any rate, from the "Athens of America" to the "Paris of America," and the two men who were chiefly responsible were Gridley Bryant and Arthur Gilman.

BOSTON CITY HALL (fig. 6.8), the first Second Empire–style municipal building in the country, was directly based on the new additions to the Louvre in Paris by L. T. J. Visconti and Hector Lefuel. The project originated in 1860, when seven architects were invited to submit plans to remodel the existing city hall on School Street. This building had been constructed as the county courthouse in 1810–12 according to the designs of Charles Bulfinch. Bryant, along with Jonathan Preston, had remodeled the building in 1840 for use as a city hall, which perhaps gave him an advantage in the selection process. The other architects solicited, in addition to Bryant, were Edward C. Cabot, Nathaniel Bradlee, S. S. Woodcock, Joseph R. Richards, W. R. Emerson, and Hammatt Billings. Cabot and Bradlee, the most experienced along with Bryant, chose not to submit designs. Woodcock and Emerson had only recently begun to practice as architects on their own, while Richards had trained under Bryant. Only Billings would have been as respected as a long-established designer, but his record of building supervision in the absence of his brother Joseph (or other architects) was spotty. It was, therefore, not surprising that Bryant was selected.[23]

Bryant's scheme, published in a report of the Committee on Public Buildings, was radically different from any other design developed by his firm. He had been made aware of the latest interpretations of French Renaissance architecture with the Deacon Mansion in 1847, the first building in Boston to employ a mansard roof. Since that time, Bryant's work with the mansard, or Second Empire, style had previously been somewhat tentative. Buildings such as the Post Office Block on Summer Street, the Cheshire County Courthouse in New Hampshire, and the Kennebec

County Jail in Maine employed a pavilion roof with ornamental dormers which suggested the character of the Second Empire style but were not really mansards. His city hall proposal, however, was quite different. Here was a full-blown example of the type of design then current in Paris, considered by many to be the world's capital in terms of artistic tastes. Although Gilman is not mentioned in the city report, one must conclude that he played a major role in choosing a style that marked such a radical break with the city's long tradition of looking toward Britain for guidance in architectural matters.

In 1862 the city authorities decided to demolish the old structure and design a new building. For this work Arthur Gilman was selected along with Bryant. (The staff at Bryant and Gilman's office at 4 Court Street included Edward H. Kendall, who had just returned from studying architecture in Paris and would have been able to assist in the design details.)

Figure 6.8. City Hall, Boston, 1862–65, Bryant and Gilman, architects. Rendering by Carl Fehmer at the time of dedication in 1865. Unlike many later public buildings in the Second Empire style, this city hall is a faithful homage to contemporary French architecture. (Author's collection)

Although the Civil War had already begun, proponents argued that the depressed economic conditions made it advantageous for the city to secure labor and materials for a second major capital improvement project. This was a year after Bryant had begun the Boston City Hospital, a design transformed from Italian Renaissance to French Second Empire. Perhaps more significantly, 1862 was also the year that the Weld-Beebe Block on Winthrop Square was completed, the monumental culmination to Bryant's great Franklin Street redevelopment efforts and his masterpiece of Second Empire commercial architecture.

Though now taken for granted as a typical Victorian municipal building, Boston City Hall, when it was completed in 1865, had no precedent in terms of its lavishly ornamented, French-inspired exterior. The light-colored Concord, New Hampshire, granite of the exterior stonework had more in common with the Chelmsford granite used in the old city hall than with the ubiquitous Quincy granite. The design for the new building dispensed with the pavilions on the flanking wings dictated by the configuration of the old city hall. The result was a squarer building with a correspondingly grander central pavilion. A dominant design motif is the superimposed orders in which tall round-arched windows are closely framed by rusticated piers on the ground story and twin pilasters above. Add the heavy belt courses in the form of entablatures and the three-tiered porticos on the central pavilion and the result is a building whose front elevation has virtually no plain wall surface. According to the architects, the style of the building "will doubtless ere long be fully recognized by sound architectural critics as the true vernacular style of our age and country." Given how quickly the style spread to towns all over the country in the 1870s, this prediction was borne out, albeit for a short period.[24]

The interior was largely gutted in 1971, which is a sad loss in the history of American public architecture. The original plan was very compactly organized, and interior finishes reflected a cost-consciousness one would expect during wartime. Had this same building been constructed in the prosperous "Gilded Age" of the late 1860s and early 1870s, grander spaces might have been developed. As it was, the central staircase of butternut was more typical of the materials and scale of a large private mansion than of a government office building. Even the public spaces, one for the aldermen and one for the mayor and Common Council, were more reminiscent of an early-nineteenth-century church than a late-nineteenth-century auditorium. The architects made use of the abundance of large windows by placing the staircase in the center of the building and all the rooms on outside walls. The two public meeting rooms were located in the central pavilion within the principal façade.

The relatively simple interior finishes reflect the strong opposition the designers encountered in constructing the building. Many years later Bryant recounted the difficulties: "Oh, we were called boodlers and jobbers and every opprobrious name in payment for our struggle in erecting that monument to the city in School street. One of the last biting criticisms was, 'We have waited twenty-six years for a City Hall, and now we've got some walls with a staircase inside.' " Bryant's answer was a practical defense of his and Gilman's plan: "Many people didn't then recognize the utility of ample corridors and having all the rooms have the light and air of an outside exposure."[25]

THE ASSOCIATION between Bryant and Gilman produced two other major public buildings, Lynn City Hall and the New Hampshire State House. The city of Lynn had been one of the centers of shoe manufacturing for many years and, unlike Boston, had a substantial industrial base to finance a new city hall. A lot was purchased and plans procured in 1863, but by that time the costs of labor and materials were rising rapidly. After the destruction of the existing city hall in a fire in 1864, the need for a new building was no longer debatable. The names of other architects who submitted plans are not known, but in 1865 Bryant and Gilman were selected, probably in large part owing to their reputation for having designed Boston City Hall. The cornerstone was laid in November 1865, and the building was dedicated two years later in November 1867. The total cost was over $289,000, of which Bryant and Gilman were paid $8,000. This amounted to almost 2.8 percent in commissions, a figure that compared favorably to their fee for Boston City Hall, a $505,000 building for which the architects were paid a little over $11,000, or not much more than 2 percent.[26]

For the Lynn City Hall (unlike Boston City Hall) the architects had the advantage of an open site on the city common and Park Square that better showed off the design. Although described at the time as "Italian Renaissant," the building bore all the characteristics of Gilman's passionate adaptation of French Renaissance style as interpreted in the Paris of Louis-Napoléon (fig. 6.9). Whereas the mansard-roofed fourth floor of Boston City Hall is barely a full story, the third-story mansard of Lynn City Hall typified what came to be a hallmark of the style. It was a crowning feature of the building, exhibiting fully ornamented dormers embellished with iron cresting. The most prominent feature was the four-stage tower, a highly visible

Figure 6.9. City Hall, Lynn, Massachusetts, 1865–66, Bryant and Gilman, architects. Lithographic print of a lost architect's rendering. A prosperous industrial city, Lynn built a city hall that rivaled that of Boston. (Courtesy Michael J. Lewis, who donated the print to Historic New England)

element, given the building's advantageous site. Gilman later adapted the design for this tower as one of the subsidiary towers on his proposed New York State Capitol. In some respects, Lynn City Hall also shared a similarity with Gilman's residential work. It was constructed of smooth, pressed red brick with sandstone trim, against which the ornamental treatment of the cornices, windows, and doors stood in bold relief. Sadly, the building burned in the 1930s.[27]

Gilman's participation in the design for remodeling the New Hampshire State House is less well documented. The available contemporary records in New Hampshire for the 1864–66 project mention only Gridley Bryant as architect. Gilman's involvement is noted only in a vanity publication for which he no doubt supplied information after moving to New York.[28] The design for the New Hampshire State House, compared to Bryant's other statehouse designs, also suggests Gilman's participation. In terms of Bryant's legacy, the New Hampshire State House is important as the only state house he worked on that survives largely intact.[29]

Bryant's first effort at working on a statehouse was in Massachusetts. He lived to see his 1853–54 wing demolished for a larger extension in 1889 by a former draftsman of his, Charles Brigham. He had, however, developed several far more drastic proposals prior to that which would have left little of the Bulfinch State House. In September 1866 a commission appointed by the Massachusetts legislature hired Bryant and Alexander Esty to develop three schemes to provide for more space. It is not known why Esty was selected to work with Bryant, but there may have been objections from other architects who had experienced so little success in obtaining major public commissions. In any case, Esty had trained with Bryant, and the two men presumably got along professionally. They produced three designs, two for enlarging the existing building and one for an entirely new structure. The proposals would have introduced a great domed building on Beacon Hill not unlike the capitols of several midwestern states erected in the 1870s and 1880s. Fortunately, these proposals were rejected in favor of preserving the Bulfinch design, at least on the exterior. Bryant's other unsuccessful efforts to obtain major statehouse commissions included a proposal to rebuild the burned Vermont State House in 1857, two proposals to enlarge the Bulfinch statehouse in Maine in 1867 and 1876, and a competition entry for the Connecticut State House in 1871 (the latter two with Louis P. Rogers).

Bryant was successful In New Hampshire possibly because the project advanced at a rapid pace that was quite extraordinary for a major public project in the late nineteenth century. The New Hampshire legislature had procured three plans to enlarge the 1816–19 statehouse and hired Bryant to evaluate them in terms of their effectiveness in meeting the needs of the state. Bryant's report of April 30, 1864, included his own set of plans and estimates for two alternatives that he, naturally, felt were superior. The legislature debated Bryant's proposals in June and July 1864 and approved the plans on July 15. Work began in September of that year. The remarkable speed with which this project was undertaken was in part due to the

Figure 6.10. Additions and alterations to State House, Concord, New Hampshire, 1864–66, Bryant and Gilman, architects. A limited budget resulted in an exceptionally elegant design that the architects probably considered insufficiently opulent. (Courtesy Earle G. Shettleworth, Jr.)

curious arrangement under which the city of Concord entered into a competition with Manchester for the right to keep the state capitol. Having gained the honor, the winning municipality was obligated to pay substantial sums for the construction work.

Notwithstanding New Hampshire's traditional parsimony, the legislature accepted the more expensive scheme for the new state house (fig. 6.10). On the exterior a third story was added in the form of a rather modest mansard roof which does not command the prominence normally associated with the Second Empire style. The dominant features of the exterior are the two-story granite portico and domed lantern. Rather than a monumental portico with columns a full two stories tall (as in Bryant's proposal for Vermont), the New Hampshire building has a two-tiered portico, the Tuscan order on the ground floor supporting a Corinthian order, on which the pediment rests. This use of superimposed orders was unique for an American statehouse and suggests the influence of French architecture. The lantern, as noted in the local newspaper, was based on "the celebrated dome of Hotel des Invalides at Paris, an architectural work of the highest order of merit." The walls and fenestration were also altered with the addition of ashlar granite, quoins, and new round-arched windows on the second-story level. In his report, Bryant repeated what had become the standard Bryant and Gilman line with regard to architectural style: "It will at once be recognized, by all those conversant with such matters as the prevailing style of modern Europe, a style which the taste of the leading architects of Paris in particular, have largely illustrated, under the patronage of the present Emperor, in most of the great modern works of the French capital."[30]

The interior alterations included enlarging and remodeling the Senate and House of Representatives chambers with neoclassical pilasters and cornices; when the building was remodeled again in 1909, these were replicated for those enlargements. The most significant change to the alterations Bryant and Gilman had made to the exterior was the removal of the mansard roof for a more substantial third story. Although a complete architectural history of the New Hampshire State House remains to be written, it is evident that a great many of the Bryant and Gilman alterations remain, giving the state a rare surviving example of a statehouse from this mid-century period, before the more extravagant styles of the post–Civil War years.

THE LACK of solid documentation for Gilman's involvement with this project is probably due to his relocation to New York City in 1865. Bryant and

Gilman maintained their loose association for the project that first took him to New York: a massive hotel at the south end of Central Park for Hiram Cranston. In scale, the design for this Second Empire–style structure called to mind the Hôtel de Ville in Paris, which burned during the Commune in 1871. The appearance of the New York project is known only through a rendering by Louis P. Rogers published in *The Builder* on August 3, 1867. The move to New York, Gilman wrote his friend New York senator Andrews Dickson White, was "the summit of my wishes." To White he also made clear his belief that the style of Louis-Napoléon's Paris was superior to all others, particularly the newly fashionable Venetian Gothic. For that style, made famous in this country by architects such as Peter P. Wight and Jacob Wray Mould, he had only contempt: "The idiotic and feeble minded youth who comprise the American Architectural Mutual Admiration Society have retired from the competition [for the design of the hotel] in disgust, and betoken themselves for solace to the Pre-Raphaelite stripes and fizgigs and peaks-poppies on the end of long sticks, and black letter legends cut on forty different colored stones, in short the exaggerated ecclesiastics-gingerbread-horse-with-a-gilt-tail style, in which Mr. Wight and Mr. Wray Mould are such proficients."[31]

The hotel project was never built, perhaps because its promoter, Hiram Cranston, had been a notorious Copperhead Democrat during the war. Gilman nonetheless chose to remain in New York, where he was for a time one of the architects of the New York State Capitol building. Gilman's initial success was due in part to his great popularity in social circles as "one of the most gentle and racy of humorists."[32] Edward H. Kendall accompanied him from 4 Court Street, and the two men briefly formed an association similar to the one Gilman had had with Bryant. He built a home on Staten Island, where he designed St. John's Episcopal Church in the Clifton neighborhood in 1869. As it happens, this was the same neighborhood where H. H. Richardson lived, although there is no record that the two ever met. Indeed, it is unlikely that they would have gotten along, given the fact that both men were used to being the center of attention in any social setting.

Gilman's arrangement with Kendall did not last, and his practice declined. One of his major New York projects with Kendall was the Equitable Life Insurance Company, which was won in a competition with H. H. Richardson, George Post, and Richard Morris Hunt in 1867. When an addition was made to that building in 1875, Kendall alone was the architect. Gilman's well-known willingness to express his opinions frankly, without concern for whomever he offended, very likely contributed to his resignation from the New York State Capitol project. The world of New York politics was quite different from that of Boston, something Bryant surely realized when he chose to remain in his native city.

Contemporary accounts indicate that Gilman died in 1882 "after a long and wasting illness." He passed away in the home of his mother-in-law in Syracuse, where he is buried. The sixty-year-old architect was survived by his wife and one son.[33] The Bryant and Gilman association had been a period of intense creativity in which the two men dominated Boston architecture for seven years. Given Gilman's narrow views regarding architecture, it is unlikely that it could have lasted much longer even if they had both remained in Boston, where changes in the profession and in architectural fashions required a greater adaptability than Gilman's career suggests he possessed.

7

Bryant and Rogers

THE POST–CIVIL WAR period brought economic prosperity and change in the architectural profession. In 1865 fifty-seven firms were listed in the Boston city directory. By 1872 that number had almost doubled. Bryant had remained eager to work with a variety of designers on various projects even during the years when he and Gilman shared an office. In 1865–66 he collaborated on several projects with John Hubbard Sturgis, an English-born architect who had arrived in this country with plenty of pedigree but few contacts among Boston's businessmen. It was Sturgis who made measured drawings of the John Hancock Mansion on Beacon Hill before it was demolished. This recording an eighteenth-century building is considered by many historians as an important milestone in the Colonial Revival movement. Bryant and Gilman, who had the commission to design new double houses on the site, were also involved in an effort to reconstruct the Hancock House in the Back Bay as a governor's mansion. Sturgis's drawings, made in 1863, may have been intended primarily to facilitate that effort. After Bryant and Sturgis had worked on a few projects, Charles Brigham, a draftsman in Bryant's office, left to form a partnership with Sturgis. Sturgis and Brigham would soon become a leading artistic force among those who favored the Venetian Gothic style as advocated by the English art critic John Ruskin. Given the long-standing Anglophile proclivities of many Bostonians, what is now often called the High Victorian Gothic style found a receptive audience among the wealthy in Boston.[1]

The changes in fashions in the postwar years soon challenged the supremacy of Second Empire–style architecture derived from the French Renaissance. (It is probably no coincidence that a decline in the popularity of French architecture coincided with the collapse of Louis-Napoléon's

Second Empire in France.) With Arthur Gilman no longer available to supply comfortable assurances of "correct" architectural theory, Bryant would have had to keep pace with the times if he wanted to maintain his professional standing. The changes following the Civil War included a renewed interest in the establishment of professional standards for architects. In 1865 William R. Ware organized the first school of architecture in the United States at the Massachusetts Institute of Technology. The American Institute of Architects (AIA), which had for many years been inactive, met in New York and elected Richard Upjohn its president. Gilman, when he relocated to New York, reportedly gave a vigorous talk at the AIA convention held in that city in 1867.[2]

The same year saw the formation of the Boston Society of Architects. In May, nine architects met in Nathaniel J. Bradlee's office to lay the groundwork for the organization. In addition to Bradlee, they were Edward C. Cabot, William Ralph Emerson, Henry T. Hartwell, W. P. P. Longfellow, A. C. Martin, S. J. F. Thayer, and Henry Van Brunt. Also invited but unable to attend were Charles A. Cummings and William R. Ware. Only Bradlee and Cabot had been in practice for more than ten years, so the tenor of the group was dominated by a new generation. At the second and third organizational meetings, twenty-seven architects were in attendance.[3]

All of Boston's architects were invited, but there is no indication that Gridley Bryant had any interest in either the Boston Society of Architects or the American Institute of Architects (which later became its parent organization). Although no record of his opinion on these professional organizations has come to light, one can make certain suppositions. He had acquired much of his own training in the traditional manner by working in an architect's office. Bryant had trained other architects in the same way, a method he no doubt considered well suited to the needs of the profession. The new generation of architects, however, included many who had traveled in Europe, or had even been educated there. The emphasis on formal academic architectural theory expressed in many of the early meetings of the Boston Society of Architects would no doubt have left Bryant feeling at a disadvantage. Accounts of the early meetings of the Boston Society of Architects include reports of architects critiquing one another's work, and one may suppose that this held little interest for an intensely practical man like Bryant.[4]

Even Arthur Gilman, who probably taught Bryant much that he knew about architectural history, quit the AIA in 1872. His reasons are not known, but his departure may well have been due to disagreements with the younger generation over new architectural theories that began to take hold in the early 1870s.[5] Bryant was not averse to change, but it is unlikely that he had much time for theoretical discussions, and he may have felt uncomfortable with rapid changes in architectural fashions. As mentioned, one of the prevailing styles of the 1870s, which Gilman explicitly rejected and Bryant never used, was the High Victorian Gothic, also known as Venetian Gothic. This style began to change the face of Boston and environs in a number of high-profile projects. Its impact is perhaps not fully appreciated owing to the number of buildings in this style that have since been demolished in the Boston area. Important examples dating from the post–Civil War years include Memorial Hall at Harvard (1865–71, Ware and Van Brunt), the Masonic Temple (1867, Merrill G. Wheelock, demolished), the Hotel Boylston (1870, Cummings and Sears, demolished), the Odd Fellows Hall (1871–72, Hammatt and Joseph Billings, demolished), the Museum of Fine Arts (1870–76, Sturgis and Brigham, demolished), the Boston and Providence Railroad Station (1872–74, Peabody and Stearns, demolished), the New Old South Church (1874, Cummings and Sears), and the Young Men's Christian Union (1875, Nathaniel G. Bradlee, heavily altered).

The changing nature of architecture in Boston probably played a role in Bryant's forming his first and only formal partnership. Louis P. Rogers (fig. 7.1) had worked as a draftsman in Bryant's office since 1855, and probably had entered as a student prior to that. Born in Phippsburg, Maine, on February 12, 1838, Rogers grew up in Malden, a town north of Boston. He apparently received all of his training under Bryant and was grateful enough to name his first child Louis Bryant Rogers.[6] By 1865, the city directory marks his rise from draftsman to architect in Bryant's office. Surviving drawings and contemporary newspaper accounts, however, give no indication that Rogers was equal in status to Bryant and Gilman in their shared projects. The evidence is circumstantial, but it appears that when Gilman and Bryant's New York hotel project failed and the two men parted company, Rogers also left to work on his own. (At the same time, Bryant took in a new Harvard-trained student, Robert Swain Peabody, who left after a year for a European tour.) Louis Rogers may well have expected an improvement in his situation which Bryant resisted. At any rate, this is a reasonable supposition, as Rogers was listed in the 1867 directory as an independent architect at another location. What we do know is that in September of that year, Bryant agreed to form his only formal partnership, with Rogers.[7]

Not only was the Boston architectural community growing, but also there was an increasing trend toward forming partnerships as a way to compete more effectively. In 1867 there were six partnerships in Boston, including the rising new firms of Emerson and Fehmer, Sturgis and Brigham, and Ware and Van Brunt. By 1872 the number of partnerships had almost tripled, including Cummings and Sears and Peabody and

Figure 7.1. Louis P. Rogers, circa 1880? Louis Rogers may have lacked Gilman's social refinements, but his published rendering of a large hotel project planned for New York City suggests a skill at architectural rendering of which little record has survived. (Courtesy Donald Morrow)

Stearns. These changes also coincided with Bryant's appointment, in 1869, as the local supervising architect for the new United States Post Office and Sub-Treasury Building in Boston. As this appointment also included small jobs supervising repairs to government buildings around southern New England, these duties required much of Bryant's attention well into the 1870s. In his campaign to obtain the appointment, Bryant received strong endorsements from many prominent Boston businessmen and politicians, such as Oakes Ames, Henry Wilson, and Nathaniel B. Shurtleff. Alfred Mullett, supervising architect of the Treasury Department, unreservedly endorsed Bryant: "Mr. Bryant is one of the oldest, most competent and industrious men in his profession. He is not only a fine architect but a gentleman of rare business qualifications and possesses in my opinion all the requisites for this important position." That Bryant managed to get along with the demanding Mullett is evidence of his ability to work with many types of individuals. His new role was also a lucrative one. With his appointment to supervise construction of the new Boston Post Office, Bryant was to receive a 5 percent commission.[8]

Not only did Bryant agree to a partnership with Rogers, but also the firm moved out of 4 Court Street to a more fashionable address, 17 Pemberton Square. Following Nathaniel Bradlee's lead, other firms quickly made Pemberton Square the principal address for Boston architects, who converted the area's 1830s town houses for office space. Initially the firm of Bryant and Rogers continued to secure many public projects in the city. During the years 1868–70 they designed seven neighborhood fire stations and nine schools. Among the fire stations, one of the most charming is the small structure for Hook and Ladder Company No. 5 on West Fourth Street in South Boston (fig. 7.2). The wood-paneled doors hung in an opening ornamented by a stone aedicula of pilasters supporting a pediment. The second floor of this central bay forms a frontispiece with paired round-arched windows and projecting cornice. Rather than displaying the usual picturesque millwork that later became associated with the Second Empire style in America, this building emphasized the neoclassical origins of that style.

Since the beginning of the nineteenth century, Boston school architecture had always been conservative in appearance, as if Bostonians wanted to make an architectural statement that reinforced the city's Puritan traditions. Though progressive in terms of layout and internal arrangements, most of the schools Bryant designed were tall brick buildings that were often not highly visible in their urban setting and were minimally ornamented. For the most part, this tendency continued into the 1870s and is reflected in a group of schools designed by Bryant and Rogers.

There were exceptions, though a study of Boston school architecture would be necessary to understand why there were such marked differences in thedesign for some schools. Perhaps it was owing to the political influence of the representatives of different neighborhoods. For example, two six-room schools, the Freeman School (1868) on Charter Street in the North End and the Drake School (1869) on C and Third streets in South Boston, were relatively plain, even somewhat grim, for a period of typically lavish architecture. By contrast, another six-room South Boston school, the

Figure 7.2. Hook and Ladder Company No. 5, West Fourth Street, South Boston, 1869. Bryant and Rogers designed a series of small fire stations, of which this is a rare survivor. (*History of South Boston,* 1901, author's collection)

Figure 7.3. Shurtleff School, Dorchester Street, South Boston, 1869, Bryant and Rogers, architects. This design probably reflects Rogers's free interpretation of popular styles. (Courtesy of the State Library of Massachusetts)

Clinch School, on F and Seventh streets included stylish brick quoins and a mansard roof with prominent dormers. The difference may also have been due to the immediate surroundings. The Clinch School's neighborhood appears to have been more middle class, in comparison to the working-class settings of the other two.[9]

The designs for larger schools, typically including fourteen classrooms and a large assembly hall, evidently afforded more latitude for architecturally stylish exteriors. Two examples were the Lyman School (1869–71) in East Boston and the Shurtleff School (1869) in South Boston. In the case of the Lyman School, which still stands but has been converted into housing, the exterior has nicely detailed brick corbelling and a gable-end entrance pavilion designed in a free interpretation of traditional classical motifs. Similarly, the large Shurtleff School (fig. 7.3) on Dorchester Street, in the same district as the Clinch School, displayed a rather unconventional interpretation of the Second Empire style. For example, the lower portion of the mansard roof was paneled in the form of a continuous string course broken only by the tall dormer windows. Given Bryant's conservative approach to design, these unorthodox interpretations of the style probably reflect the influence of Louis Rogers. In another middle-class neighborhood, the South End, Bryant and Rogers designed the twelve-room Appleton Street School in 1870 (not to be confused with the surviving Rice Manual Training School by Emerson and Fehmer on the same street). The Appleton Street School was little more than a plain rectangular box supporting a generic mansard roof and bell tower.

WHILE BRYANT's firm still dominated the city in securing commissions for public buildings, the private sector had become more competitive. In January 1870 the *Boston Transcript* published a list of significant buildings erected during 1869, many with their architects identified. This unusual account provides historians with a rare record of the architectural profession in Boston for one year.[10] In examining this list, one need only cut out the public buildings to realize that Bryant was just one of many successful architects in the city. Nathaniel J. Bradlee, Ware and Van Brunt, and Emerson and Fehmer are firms that receive frequent mention for their work in that year.

Bryant and Rogers continued to pursue commissions outside Boston. Since office records are lacking for most of these firms, the best-documented projects continue to be public buildings or major commercial structures. Maine remained fertile ground for them, with the Penobscot County Jail in Bangor in 1869, the Boston and Maine railroad station in Waterville in 1872, and the Knox County Courthouse in Rockland in 1874. The surviving documentation for these three projects includes original architectural drawings.[11] In New Hampshire, the architects designed a large Second Empire-style mansion for Frederick Smyth in Manchester, built 1867–73, as well as Milford Town Hall in 1869. Connecticut also proved fruitful. The Orange Judd Hall of Natural Science at Wesleyan University dates from 1870, a commission that may have derived from the success of two remarkable office buildings in Hartford.

Designed in 1869, the Connecticut Mutual Life Insurance Company (fig. 7.4) and the Charter Oak Life Insurance Company buildings were extraordinary commissions for a Boston firm to secure in a major New England city where New York architects were particularly active. Both structures were featured in lengthy accounts in a short-lived New York journal, *The Technologist*. The buildings were constructed with granite facing and included elevators. The taller of the two was the Connecticut Mutual Building. Including the rusticated basement, or ground floor, it stood five stories high, plus an attic level with prominent corner towers and dormers. Although it was erected with traditional masonry load-bearing walls, its tall windows must have afforded well-lighted interior spaces. A photograph of Main Street taken around 1890 illustrates what an extraordinary landmark the building was. The intricate French Renaissance carvings, not only on the towers and dormers but also on the chimneys, suggest a commercial palace. The entrance, a two-tiered structure in which the second floor supported a portico decorated with statuary, also contributed to this palatial image. As described in *The Technologist*, the statuary represented "Justice and Charity protecting the widow and orphan, with

Figure 7.4. Connecticut Mutual Life Insurance Company, Main Street, Hartford, 1869–70, Bryant and Rogers, architects. The Hartford office of the firm was in charge of Francis Kimball, who may have played a major role in the design. (Courtesy Earle G. Shettleworth, Jr.)

Plenty pouring from the cornucopia into the lap of the widow her full and just rights."[12]

The Charter Oak Building was also five stories tall, although the exterior was somewhat more restrained and expressed the influence of "Neo-Grec" fashions in the use of neoclassical ornament without archaeologically correct orders. The ornamental treatment of the pavilion roof was highly elaborate in its own right. Dormers, a balustrade with urns, iron cresting, and chimneys all expressed an architectural voluptuousness more characteristic of New York than New England. The firm's principal draftsman on this project was Francis Kimball, who had evidently been hired by Rogers when that architect was briefly on his own prior to his partnership with Bryant. Kimball's later work as a successful New York architect of ornate office buildings suggests that he played a major role in the design of both Hartford buildings. At any rate, his undoubted talent earned him a position running the new Bryant and Rogers office in Hartford.[13]

In what may have been a first for a Boston firm, Bryant and Rogers had established a branch office in Hartford by 1869. The success, however brief, of this branch office probably had a great deal to do with the energy and talent of Francis Kimball. This presence gave Bryant and Rogers a competitive edge over other Boston firms seeking commissions in Connecticut, although their impact on that state is difficult to assess, as only the building at Wesleyan survives. In any event, the prominence of the two Hartford insurance company buildings no doubt explains why the architects were invited to furnish proposals for a new Connecticut State Capitol in 1871, the only Boston firm to receive an invitation. The other architects solicited, each of whom was paid $1,000, were James G. Batterson and George Keller of Hartford, Napoleon Le Brun of New York, George B. Post of New York, and Thomas Fuller of Albany. In the end, Richard M. Upjohn of New York, who had not been in the original group, was selected.

In 1873, before Upjohn had finally clinched the commission, Bryant testified in support of Batterson, whose supporters were trying to overturn the choice of Upjohn. Batterson, the owner of the New England Granite Company and stone supplier for the Connecticut Mutual Life Insurance Company Building, was not himself an architect. His plans had been developed by Keller, who by 1873 was in practice on his own. Bryant's role as an expert witness was questioned in the newspapers at the time, since he had done business with Batterson's firm, and of course had competed for the project himself. As Henry Russell Hitchcock and William Seale have observed, however, the conduct of all the competitors in the Connecticut

State Capitol project was "ruthless," so Bryant should not be singled out for criticism.[14]

CLOSER TO HOME, Bryant and Rogers designed the town hall (later city hall) in Gloucester, Massachusetts. In 1866 the town of Gloucester had hired Boston architect Benjamin F. Dwight to design a new town hall. That building burned in May 1869, and money was appropriated to construct a replacement. This grand Victorian edifice, which survives very little altered, is a major work by Bryant and Rogers and reveals much about the business of architecture in the so-called Gilded Age in New England.

Gloucester has always been known chiefly for its fishing industry. The popular image of New England fishing ports where men "go down to the sea in ships" tends toward the quaint and picturesque. Gloucester, however, like any substantial town in the nineteenth century, preferred an image of growth and industry, and this is reflected in its municipal building. In 1860 the population of Gloucester was 10,904. Ten years later, notwithstanding the losses from the Civil War, the population had grown to over 15,000. It was in this atmosphere of prosperity that, when the town hall burned in 1869, a consensus developed in favor of building a larger, grander structure. Although there was no formal competition, other architects were consulted. S. S. Woodcock developed plans for a Gothic-style building with "ornamental turrets and a French roof." According to a local newspaper, Bryant and Rogers's design of brick with sandstone trim "provided a marked contrast to the severe simplicity of its predecessor." To the extent that such a comment reflected badly upon Benjamin Dwight, it was perhaps not fair. Surviving documentation in the city archives establishes that Dwight's design was altered to save costs.[15] The architectural fees awarded in the two projects indicate that this was a high-visibility commission of the kind that Bryant and Rogers pursued so aggressively. Benjamin Dwight's design, a brick building with a mansard roof and clock tower, cost over $78,870, for which the architect received $1,515. The Bryant and Rogers design, a larger structure with multiple towers, cost $97,371, for which the firm received $1,350. Another $200 was paid to a man named Fitz Babson for unspecified plans and expenses, as well as $27.75 for landscape plans to R. M. Copeland. The town of Gloucester appears to have gotten more for less. As the plans do not survive for either project, it cannot be determined how much drafting time was required. The Bryant and Rogers specifications, which are in the town archives, include printed

masonry and carpentry contracts. The specifications themselves are twenty-
six pages long, bound and handwritten on ruled paper by Gridley Bryant.
The reverse of each page contains supplemental instructions in another
hand, possibly that of Louis Rogers. In any case, they offer proof that at
this late date, Bryant was still taking the time to write out detailed specifications. His willingness to spend that kind of time on a plan, as well as the
fact that the masonry contractor was Albert Currier, fresh from his work
for the firm on the Milford, New Hampshire, town hall, contributed to the
success of the project.

Begun in October 1869, the building was completed in the spring of
1871, just a few weeks before the citizens of Gloucester voted to incorporate as a city. The design may be as close as the architects ever came to the
High Victorian Gothic style, at least in the use of dark colors and a very
picturesque roof treatment with four pyramidal towers, one at each outside
corner (fig. 7.5). At both major entrances to the building, Bryant's typical
neoclassical porticos were supported by Corinthian columns. The dominant element of the design is the grand tower ornamented in the Renaissance style and capped with a French pavilion roof. This structure, with a
clock and belfry, is similar in character to the neoclassical towers Bryant
proposed for various statehouse projects, as well as the design that was actually built for Lynn City Hall. Indeed, the original design for the Gloucester tower, calling for a belfry surmounting the clock face, was even more
similar to Lynn's. That more traditional arrangement, however, was re-
versed in Gloucester at the request of the building committee. Everything
about this design bespeaks the ambitions of both the architects and the
city fathers, who viewed their community not as a quaint fishing village but
as a growing, modern municipality.

While it may be difficult to characterize a single style for Gloucester City
Hall, its design did emanate from a desire for "striking boldness of artistic
effect," as expounded by the architects. The firm's proposal for the Connecticut State House in 1871 describes a much larger building, but the
theory behind this approach to public architecture could apply just as well
to Gloucester City Hall: "The general design of the exterior is made up of
what may be termed angle pavilions, and the walls or 'curtains' which connect them, and thus together form the lines of advancing and retracting
masses, so necessary to accentuate the light and shade of the exterior com-
position. Without these marked diversities of surface, the effect of so large
a building—particularly when viewed at a distance—would be likely to

become in the highest degree tame, flat and spiritless—causing the edifice to be stamped with an air of monotony, which no amount of richness of variety of detail could possibly be expected to counteract."[16]

WHILE BRYANT and Rogers were in Gloucester designing the city hall, the firm was retained to prepare plans for a granite house on Cape Ann for Jonas H. French. French, the founder of the Cape Ann Granite Company, may have known Bryant previously through his business as a supplier of granite. The plans for the house, dated 1871, feature a one-story structure, built of local stone, with a mansard roof (fig. 7.6). French built up the site

Figure 7.5. City Hall, Gloucester, Massachusetts, 1869–71, Bryant and Rogers, architects. The Town of Gloucester made its transition to a city with the completion of this building. (Courtesy Earle G. Shettleworth, Jr.)

Figure 7.6. Side elevation, Jonas French Cottage, Cape Anne, Gloucester, Massachusetts, 1871, Bryant and Rogers, architects. Constructed of granite for the owner of a local quarry, the house contained elaborate polychromatic ceiling and wall paintings by an unknown artist. (Courtesy The Cardinal House Trust)

to enhance his view; hence the name, "Rock Lawn," given to the cottage. The house, however, does not have the exaggerated vertical proportions normally associated with the Second Empire style, or indeed with the picturesque summer cottages of the 1860s and 1870s. Only the suggestion of a tower formed by the peaked roof of a second-story bay window provides a concession to a picturesque silhouette. The relatively restrained manner with which this house occupies its coastal site is in marked contrast to Gloucester City Hall.[17]

The floor plan takes advantage of the site in the manner that became de rigueur for grand summer "cottages" at the end of the century (fig. 7.7). A large open entrance hall containing a central staircase which opens onto the three principal rooms in the main section of the house, the drawing room, library, and dining room. The kitchen wing is in a separate structure linked by a connector containing a pass-through hall and china closet. By placing the kitchen in a wing linked by a narrow corridor and set back from the ocean-front façade, the design afforded maximum exposure to the principal rooms. The drawing room still retains its original painted ceiling, an extraordinary polychromatic design by an unknown artist. This exceptional artifact lends credence to the story that Mrs. French wished to outdo her neighbor, Mrs. Benjamin Butler, whose granite mansard-style house had been designed by Benjamin Dwight a few years earlier.[18]

Louis Rogers may have taken charge of much of the firm's design work while Bryant was supervising government projects. It was probably Rogers who developed the Second Empire–style design for major additions to the Connecticut State Prison at Weathersfield in 1870. That project was never constructed, but in the same year Rogers traveled to Jackson, Michigan, to prepare sketches for additions to the state prison there, which is believed to have been built. As mentioned, Bryant and Rogers also designed the Penobscot County Jail in Bangor, Maine, in 1869. Rogers went on to prepare, under his own name, a competition entry for the Massachusetts State Prison in Concord in 1874. What this project meant in terms of the Bryant-Rogers partnership is not clear, but it presaged wanderlust on the part of Rogers which ended the partnership a few years later.[19]

ON NOVEMBER 9 and 10, 1872, Boston's great commercial district burned in a massive conflagration. The fire began in the basement of a block at the corner of Summer and Kingston streets. Designed by John R. Hall, this block was typical of the area's ornate four-story granite buildings with a

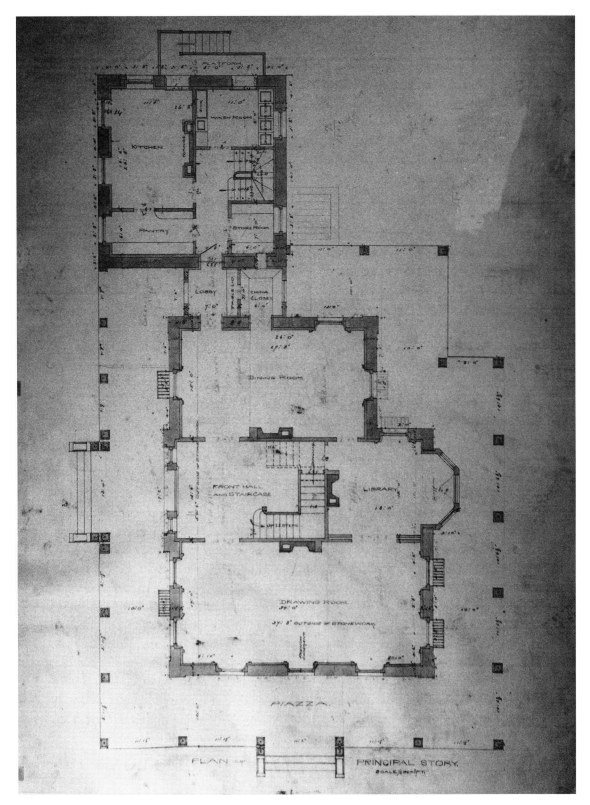

Figure 7.7. First-floor plan, Jonas French Cottage. At a time when ocean front cottages were often built with little consideration for their siting and orientation, the Bryant and Rogers plan was noteworthy. (Courtesy of The Cardinal House Trust)

fifth story in a mansard roof. An account published shortly after the fire describes the flammable conditions that prevailed in these masonry buildings: "There are bales and boxes of dry goods in the basement and on the ground floor, reaching back from Summer street front one hundred feet or more. There are prints and muslins piled on counters ready for display,—a roof full of tinder. In the stores above are cases, packages, and bundles of hosiery, gloves and laces,—more flammable material,—and still higher, in the upper stories, piles of tape and muslin, thread and trimmings, shreds and ravelings, where sewing-girls have been at work manufacturing skirts and corsets. Tinder below and tinder above,—quick fuel for the flames from basement to attic."[20]

The wind swept the fire from building to building, each structure filled with flammable goods. The mansard roof was blamed for much of the devastation, although, as Bryant himself testified after the fire, the problem was more one of materials. Building owners, wishing to save on costs for their commercial palaces, often used wood shingles and wood dormers instead of slate and masonry or metal for the less visible top-floor elements. Typically, blocks of buildings encompassed under a single mansard roof also lacked internal brick firewalls between each store.

With hundreds of buildings lost and around a thousand acres devastated, the Boston fire is less well known nationally only because the great Chicago Fire had broken out the previous year. Gridley Bryant saw much of his life's work destroyed in two days. The hardest blow must have been his Franklin Street development. For barely a decade it was one of the finest concentrations of urban commercial architecture in the country. It would all be rebuilt, but in the traditional manner, in which scores of architects would compete, each producing designs having little in common with neighboring structures. Bryant and Rogers contributed their share of new designs, but with the exception of the long-demolished Rialto Building, little of their new work was comparable to the structures built in the 1850s and 1860s, or indeed to the new work by architects such as Nathaniel J. Bradlee and Peabody and Stearns. The loyal client John Simmons hired the firm to build a new block on Franklin Street, but it is a plain structure with a granite front and no mansard roof. Initially, few merchants had the resources to rebuild in the same scale as before. The new firm of Emerson and Fehmer developed a series of granite blocks with Neo-Grec carvings, an innovative design approach that compensated for limited budgets. It was this firm, and not Bryant's, that was hired by the merchants

Weld and Beebe to replace their great structure on Winthrop Square in 1873.

Bryant himself found his work on the United States Post Office and Sub-Treasury extended, as that unfinished building was damaged in the fire. Indeed, the new structure doubled in size from what had originally been planned. The completed building was typical of the series of magnificent Second Empire–style buildings designed by Treasury architect Alfred Mullett for major American cities.

Shortly after the fire, the city undertook to revise the building laws to prevent such a conflagration from happening again. Bryant, called to testify on the issue of the mansard roof as a possible cause of the fire, defended the design but assured officials that the mansard roof on the new post office building—indeed, the entire structure except for its wooden doors and windows—would be of noncombustible materials. In reconstructing the Rialto Building at Milk and Devonshire streets, Bryant called for the exceptionally elaborate mansard roof and tower to be made of iron backed by plaster of paris. The roof structure itself was also to be of iron.[21]

The most important post-fire structure by Bryant and Rogers still standing is the new building for the *Boston Transcript* newspaper on Washington Street (fig. 7.8). Occupying a corner at Milk Street, the building is constructed with façades of Concord granite and a mansard roof—or rather, it has a fifth floor with three sides of a mansard. On the side where adjoining buildings were constructed on Washington Street there is a brick fire wall mandated by the new building code. This graphically illustrates how the mansard roof had become a purely decorative device to finish off the top floor of a building. With its row of dormers, it is, in fact, barely a mansard. Though built in the waning years of popularity for the style, the Transcript Building is a superb representation of Bryant's legacy of commercial architecture in Boston.

IN ABOUT 1877 Louis Rogers left Bryant and Boston, apparently motivated by the usual desire to advance his career in a new location. The record of his movements is not complete, but by 1879 he was in Washington, D.C., working as chief draftsman in the office of the supervising architect of the Treasury Department, at that time James G. Hill, who had briefly trained with Rogers in Bryant's office. Rogers resigned from that position in September 1880 and, according to one account, later moved on to Kansas City. He was there only a short time before settling in Rochester, New

York, in 1882. Rogers formed a partnership there with John R. Thomas until 1886, then practiced alone, except for one year in partnership with A. Burnside Sturgis and Leon Stern. During his partnership with Thomas, the firm was reasonably successful, but poor health eventually brought him back to Massachusetts and his parents' house in Malden. He attempted to

Figure 7.8. Transcript Building, Washington Street, Boston, 1873, Bryant and Rogers, architects. Built after the great fire which many blamed on the mansard roof, this was the firm's reaffirmation of the Second Empire style. (*King's Hand Book of Boston*, author's collection)

go into the wholesale fish business with a friend in Maine, and for a few years also practiced architecture in Malden. His career, however, had effectively ended in Rochester in 1891.[22]

Gridley Bryant was again without a formal partnership, but for a few years he could draw upon the young draftsmen he trained, sharing various projects and learning about new trends in architecture.

8

An Architect of the Nineteenth Century

THE END of the Bryant-Rogers partnership coincided with continuing radical changes in architectural fashions in the United States. As noted, for a brief period the High Victorian Gothic style had supplanted the Second Empire style in the design of many of the most prominent architectural landmarks. Nonetheless, the High Victorian Gothic also lost favor by the late 1870s. In its place came the Queen Anne style, another English import, and the American Colonial Revival movement. With the completion of Trinity Church in Boston, a revival of the Romanesque style as interpreted by its architect, H. H. Richardson, also began to have a major impact. Richardson himself moved to Brookline, outside Boston, in 1874 after he won the commission to design Trinity Church on Copley Square, but he had already introduced the style to Boston with the Brattle Square Church on Commonwealth Avenue in 1869–73. Bryant's reaction to this fertile period of American architecture is not known, but the few large projects of his that have been identified suggest that he worked hard to maintain his practice in the face of increasingly strong competition from the new generation of architects.

Louis Rogers was not the only architect Bryant had trained who left him in 1877. For a brief period, roughly 1874–76, Henry Nelson Black worked as a draftsman in the Pemberton Square office. Like Rogers and James G. Hill, Black was from Malden. Born in 1850, he was twenty-four in 1874, the first year the city directory provides a listing for him. Presumably he was a student in the Bryant and Rogers office before that. On June 20, 1877, there occurred a devastating fire in St. John, New Brunswick. Hoping to repeat the success he had enjoyed in Hartford, in late July Bryant took his draftsman to St. John, where they established an office under the firm name of G. J. F. Bryant and Black. This firm lasted only a few months, until January 1878, at which time Black continued on his own in New Brunswick. Two buildings, a commercial block and a hotel, have been identified as having been designed by this short-lived Canadian branch office.[1]

During the closing years of the 1870s, Bryant worked with at least one more architect of exceptional ability, Clarence Luce. Born in Chicopee Falls, Massachusetts, in 1854, the son of a mill manger, Luce grew up outside Northampton and attended the Williston Seminary from 1867 to 1870. As a student in the "Scientific Department," Luce had the opportunity to take courses in linear and perspective drawing, surveying and engineering, and designing plans and models. He entered the Bryant and Rogers office on May 1, 1870, and after eighteen months was promoted to head draftsman. On March 1, 1874, Luce established his own practice in Boston, but spent a good deal of time in Northampton during the rebuilding after the Mill River Valley flood of that year. He returned to Boston in 1875 to work as an architect in Bryant's Pemberton Square office. Soon after, Luce designed the Massachusetts Building at the 1876 Centennial Exposition in Philadelphia. The city directories record his sharing an office with Bryant until 1879. As with so many architects who worked with Bryant, however, we have only fragmentary information to interpret shared projects. In Luce's case there is only one building, the Maplewood Congregational Church in Malden (1877–78), for which there is an account of the two men working together.[2] Luce continued to practice on his own in Boston until 1884, when he relocated to New York City. There he joined two other Bryant alumni, Edward H. Kendall and Francis H. Kimball; all three became quite successful as New York architects.

The association between Bryant and Clarence Luce is particularly intriguing, as the young architect became one of the leading early exponents in Boston of the Queen Anne style as first developed in England by Richard Norman Shaw. Before the style evolved into a variation of the Colonial Revival in this country, the early examples followed the precedents of English vernacular architecture during the reign of Queen Anne (1702–14). Two houses by Luce are perhaps the most outstanding surviving examples of Shavian Queen Anne design in the Boston area. These are the remodeled carriage barn at Mt. Vernon and Brimmer streets on Beacon Hill for Frank Hill Smith (1878), and the Edward Stanwood House on High Street in Brookline (1879).[3] Although these projects were undertaken at the time when Luce and Bryant shared an office, there is no evidence that

Bryant was involved in either. By 1880, Luce had moved to an office in the Herald Building.

Although their association was tenuous, it is almost inconceivable that Bryant's design for a major early example of the Queen Anne style in New England does not reflect Luce's influence. That building was the Cony High School in Augusta, Maine. The financing for this school came through a private trust which transferred the funds acquired from a defunct school for girls. This independent source of financing may explain why the city of Augusta did not insist on a more architecturally conventional, and therefore less costly, building. Authorization by the trustees of the girls' school to procure plans took place in August 1878, while Clarence Luce was still sharing Bryant's office. Unfortunately, also because of the private source of funding, construction records for the project have been lost.

The remarkable design for this school was featured in the new Boston architectural journal *The American Architect and Building News* in April 1880 (fig. 8.1). Ever interested in advancing his practice through publication of designs, Bryant submitted a perspective view of a design that is truly distinctive in its sophisticated embrace of Queen Anne–style motifs. Although the published rendering suggests a large and complex building, the plan was in fact rather straightforward. On the first floor was an open classroom measuring thirty by fifty feet. Above it on the second floor was another room of the same size designed as an assembly and exhibition hall. Two recitation rooms, measuring eighteen by twenty-eight feet, were located on each floor of the flanking wings. The central tower contained the staircases and large belfry. Materials used were brick with sandstone trim for the basement, the first story, and the shaft of the tower. Upper sections of the building were constructed of wood finished in wood shingles and medieval half-timbering. Vergeboard in the gable ends, corbelled brick chimneys, and "Queen Anne sash" were all characteristic of early examples of the style as it derived from England. The building was prominently sited on a hill overlooking the central business district of Augusta, stretching along the Kennebec River.[4] The high school is unique among all of Bryant's known commissions. It demonstrates that, above all, Gridley Bryant was a quick learner, able to absorb new trends in architectural design.

Two other public buildings from the late 1870s are more in the Bryant architectural tradition. These are Lyon Hall at Wheaton College in Norton, Massachusetts (1878), and Wilder Memorial Hall in Hingham, Massachusetts (1879) (figs. 8.2, 8.3). As originally built in 1849, the seminary

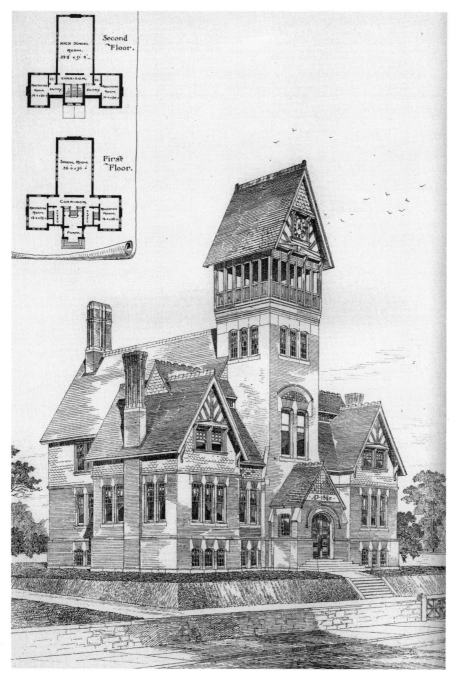

Figure 8.1. Cony High School, Augusta, Maine, 1879–80, Gridley J. F. Bryant, architect. Published in *The American Architect and Building News,* April 10, 1880, Bryant was probably assisted in this design by his former chief draftsman, Clarence Luce. (Courtesy Trustees of the Brookline Public Library)

Figure 8.2. Additions and alterations to Lyon Hall, Wheaton College, Norton, Massachusetts, 1878, Gridley J. F. Bryant, architect. Photograph from *New England Magazine* 24 (1898). (Courtesy Trustees of the Brookline Public Library)

building was a freestanding classical temple with pilasters instead of columns separating two floors of windows on each elevation. As was characteristic of that transitional period, the basic form of a Greek Revival–style temple was given Italianate embellishments such as segmental arched windows and cornice modillions. At the same time, the unknown designer of the original building created unique pilasters decorated with acanthus leaves and acorns.

The trustees could not have found a more perfect choice than Bryant to enlarge the building in a way that would retain the original exterior design. Having already been a practicing architect in 1849, Bryant understood the form and construction of the original building and was completely comfortable in making sympathetic enlargements. His solution was to extend the structure into a Greek cross and add a neoclassical cupola at the intersection. The two wings forming the arms of the cross duplicated the original design in size and ornamentation.[5] At the point where all four wings intersected, Bryant created a grand biaxial staircase leading to a second-floor gallery with a cove ceiling. A complete remodeling of the interior spaces included new oak architrave moldings stained in a natural finish.

An opportunity to call upon his long experience as an architect also came into play for Wilder Memorial Hall in Hingham in 1879, where

Bryant returned, perhaps for the last time, to French Renaissance motifs (fig. 8.3). There are aspects of this building, with its pavilion roof, ornamental dormers, and superimposed orders of wood pilasters, that call to mind the architect's work from the 1850s. Indeed, this building has little in common with what are presumed to have been Louis P. Rogers's unusual interpretations of the Second Empire style in the early 1870s. Rather, it is similar to more conservative treatments, such as the firm's 1871 Lexington Town Hall, in resembling Bryant's earlier work. For that reason it seems likely that both buildings represent Bryant's own traditional approach to design. Wilder Hall, like Cony High School, derived funding from a long-inactive family endowment. The building is situated in a residential

Figure 8.3. Wilder Memorial Hall, Hingham, Massachusetts, 1879, Gridley J. F. Bryant, architect. Designed in the same year as the Cony High School, this building was Bryant's last homage to French Renaissance design. (Courtesy Wilder Charitable & Education Fund, Inc.)

neighborhood that forms a distinct community within the town of Hingham. Bryant's design for Wilder Hall cannot be considered artistically progressive for 1879. Nonetheless, there is something appealing about a public hall dedicated to the advancement of the arts being situated in a building derived from French Renaissance architecture that stands in the middle of a neighborhood of traditional single-family homes.[6]

DURING THE 1880s, the name of Bryant's firm quickly drops from any list that could be assembled of major Boston architects. According to Henry Bailey, the death of Bryant's wife affected him deeply. Gridley Bryant had married Louisa Braid, the daughter of a housewright named John Braid, on September 9, 1839.[7] The couple had no children. Bailey stresses Bryant's utter devotion to his wife. In keeping with the architect's restless personality, they resided in a variety of locations. Early in their marriage, they lived with her parents in South Boston, then for about fourteen years they made their home on Harrison Avenue in the near South End. By 1857 they had moved into the Tremont House hotel, where they remained throughout Bryant's most productive period. The couple also summered in places as varied as Newport and Lynn, though never far from Bryant's work. In 1870, apparently at his wife's urging, Bryant purchased a house at 66 Marlborough Street in the Back Bay. This marked his only effort to acquire a fashionable address. A new house, it had been built on speculation by the architect-developer Charles K. Kirby. During the closing years of the decade, as Louisa Bryant's health declined, the couple lived in a variety of places, including the family home in North Scituate, a house that had been acquired by his father and was renovated by Bryant in 1877. It was there that Louisa Bryant died on October 13, 1883.[8]

By the mid-1880s, architectural critics were ready to condemn much of what had been built by Gridley Bryant and his early contemporaries. The *Boston Evening Transcript,* which for so many years had been unstinting in its praise of Bryant's work, featured a piece titled "Architectural Ages on Commonwealth Avenue." Written by an anonymous observer, this item dismissed the great work of Bryant and Gilman dating from the first years of the development of the Back Bay: "We enter without warning into the era of brown-stone fronts, Corinthian columns, French roofs, and pediments to the windows, and for the first block [Arlington to Berkeley] these sumptuous monuments reign supreme; very florid all of them, of course, very gorgeous, very vulgar French Renaissance applied indiscriminately to everything." In the same year that newspaper (and perhaps the same columnist) wrote in great praise of the new Romanesque-style buildings of H. H. Richardson.[9]

It was within a year of his wife's death that Gridley Bryant won his last major commission, the enlargement of the Parker House hotel (fig. 8.4). Harvey Parker had erected the original hotel on School Street in 1855. He expanded up School Street with more additions in 1860 and 1866, all the work of William Washburn. After Parker died in May 1884, his two partners, Edward O. Punchard and Joseph H. Beckman, hired Bryant to design a major expansion that continued the march of that hotel toward Tremont Street.[10] Bryant's original design called for enlarging the Tremont Street façade to six bays to incorporate an adjoining commercial block. This is documented in a photograph of the firm's original rendering. The building, constructed in 1885–86, did not include the adjacent structure, and the Tremont Street façade as built extended only three bays. Bryant's design was very characteristic of the early 1880s in the sense that that period, like the 1850s, was one of restless creativity and an extravagant striving for larger and more picturesque creations that would make an architectural statement. The Parker House extension is in the spirit of contemporary structures such as the famous Dakota Apartments by Henry J. Hardenburgh in New York City (completed in 1884). A pavilion roof with ornate dormers and paneled chimneys surmounts Bryant's narrow eight-story structure, and the design vaguely suggests the chateauesque style then fashionable for the homes of millionaires.

Regardless of the stylistic antecedents, Bryant's Parker House extension was a remarkable tour de force. Working with a very constricted site, and expanding the facilities of an existing building that had to be kept in operation, must have made heavy demands on the architect's skills in construction supervision. The exterior was sheathed in marble, but no record has survived of the structural system, which most certainly involved fireproofing measures. The Parker House extension, completed in January 1886, proved to be the last major work by Bryant. Though replaced by a more sedately designed structure in 1927, for over forty years Bryant's last great contribution to the architecture of Boston stood opposite his city hall.

From 1880 until he finally give up architectural design, Bryant worked with one last architect, John F. Eaton. Eaton was born in Ireland and raised in Everett, Massachusetts, apparently one of a family of carpenters. He worked as an architect for ten years before joining Bryant in the same office on Pemberton Square. One important early project by Eaton is

Figure 8.4. Parker House Hotel, School Street, Boston, 1884–85, Gridley J. F. Bryant, architect. Photograph of lost rendering by Bryant's office. To the left are the older sections of the hotel designed by William Washburn. This drawing shows the design as originally conceived extending farther down Tremont Street to the right than what was actually built. (Courtesy Omni Parker House, Boston)

Memorial Hall in Andover, erected in 1873.[11] A few shared commissions mark the end of Bryant's career, which certainly had come by 1894, when he entered a retirement home. Bryant and Eaton were associate architects for suburban houses and summer homes built in 1889–90. One late design survives, the house for Thomas Wigglesworth in Manchester, with original drawings by Bryant alone (fig. 8.5).

Designed for the family of a longtime acquaintance, the Wigglesworth Cottage is solidly over-built, even for its exposed site. Bryant's traditional training is evident in the multiple sheets of framing plans he prepared. By 1889 most new wooden houses in America consisted of light framing

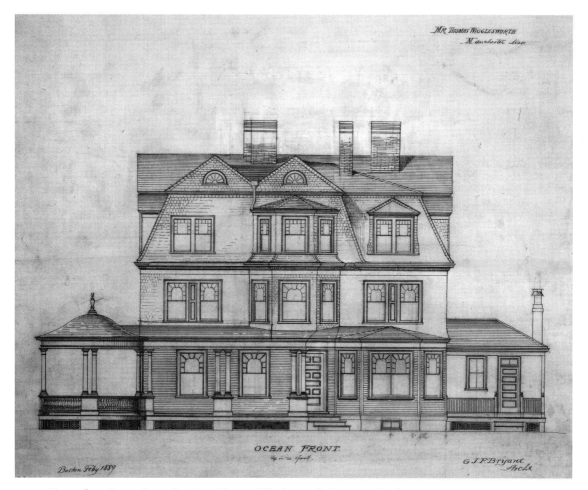

Figure 8.5. Ocean-front elevation, Thomas Wigglesworth Cottage, Manchester, Massachusetts, 1889, Gridley J. F. Bryant, architect. In practice for over fifty years, Bryant was still adapting to new styles, allbeit without great conviction. (Courtesy Historic New England)

systems with dimensionally sawn lumber (such as 2x4s) nailed and formed into a rigid frame through exterior sheathing. Called balloon framing, this type of construction was cheaper and quicker to build than traditional braced frames with mortise and tenon joints. The evolution from medieval timber framing to a lighter braced framing to balloon framing in American architecture is more gradual and complex than is generally assumed in historical accounts. Bryant's design is an example of this. The house for Wigglesworth has a system of 5x8 posts and girts joined by mortise and tenon with 5x8 bracing. Studs are 3x5 and rafters are 3x6. Although lighter than what would typically have been built in the 1850s, this is a long way from the balloon frame consisting of nailed 2x4s.

Stylistically, the house combines Queen Anne and Colonial Revival–style features that had become so popular in the late nineteenth century. Although the Colonial Revival–style gambrel roof dormers dominate the complex roof treatment, there are elements of a mansard roof (labeled "French Roof" by Bryant in his framing plans). This vestigial evidence of a mansard is visible to the right of the third-story bay window in the Ocean Front elevation drawing. In a sense, the gambrel roof motifs are applied as a concession to the new style. Not surprisingly, this design conveys a sense that Bryant, who had, after all, trained under Alexander Parris, Boston's greatest practitioner of the Greek Revival style, had no special affinity for the asymmetrical, picturesque character typical of late-nineteenth-century summer houses.

Bryant's views on the state of architecture at the end of the nineteenth century were expressed in a letter published by his friend Henry Bailey:

> There are many points in the exterior architecture of your new home that are attractive and pleasant to the professional critic. The building is also quite imposing in effect, from its comparatively large size. I hope to see the interior sooner or later, possibly before winter sets in.
>
> The rage in house designing for oddity is being carried to the verge of ridiculousness if not vulgarity. There will be a turn by and by, and Heaven knows what vagaries may be fastened on us when the change takes place.
>
> Certain novices in architecture are inaugurating the tumble-down, dilapidated, broken up, and demoralized styles, as witness one little drawing I have at hand and beg to enclose herewith.
>
> To induce a client to erect such a bit of masonry around the entrance corner of the house, as shown by the sketch, should invite quick wrath upon the architect responsible for such an uncouth, heterogeneous mass of confusion. The ponderosity of the chimney top is something fearful.

Such a top would indicate fireplaces, ovens, etc., within the house fully in keeping with the eight feet open backlog accommodation of the "Jenkins-Otis-Newcomb" homestead recently remodeled and rebuilt— home to our friend "Edgar." I am not attempting a homily in what has been herein written so far as you are concerned, but rather a warning to the rising generation of professionals not to carry "confusion worse confounded" to a point that shall become unbearable.[12]

It is not clear if the letter was addressed to Bailey, but the "Jenkins-Otis-Newcomb homestead" to which Bryant refers was the home of Dr. George L. Newcomb, remodeled by his nephew, architect Edgar Allen Poe Newcomb. Newcomb, like most fashionable Boston architects, was working in a variation of the Colonial Revival style which drew inspiration from the rambling vernacular farmhouses built in New England before the Revolution. In a sense, Bryant, whom Bailey rightly described as "decidedly classic in his architectural ideals,"[13] viewed the innovative and freely interpreted Shingle Style architecture of the late nineteenth century in much the same way that architects of the mid-twentieth century would criticize many of the products of that period.

HENRY BAILEY recorded the decline in Bryant's wealth and health during the last decade of his life. Like a devoted friend, Bailey ascribes the loss of wealth to Bryant's excessive generosity. Bryant's personal fortune rose dramatically in his first ten years of independent practice. Bailey, who had access to Bryant's account books, confirms the increase in actual income from $1,000 in 1840 to $25,000 in 1865. If we are to believe Bailey, Mrs. Bryant, who had only her peripatetic husband and pets to care for, spent a large sum for her amusement, or allowed her husband to spend it on her. Five servants ran the household at 66 Marlborough Street. Traditional domestic arrangements, however, did not suit Bryant. "He was too active and too irregular in his hours," writes Bailey. "He needed hotel conveniences— a place where he could drop in day or night and find everything ready at hand." Once Louisa Bryant's health began to decline in the 1870s, they divided their time between hotels and the house in North Scituate. Bryant, again according to Bailey, was overly generous. He not only satisfied his wife's every whim, but helped friends and acquaintances as well. His suffering late in life, says Bailey, "was almost wholly on account of the faithlessness, the greed, and the cruel cunning of others to whom he was bound by close ties." While we have no way of documenting that, if Bryant did lose all his money, there is no evidence that it was through poor investments.[14]

It is also worth noting that one characteristic of Gridley J. F. Bryant singled out in an obituary published in *The American Architect and Building News* was his exceptional honesty. While such characterizations might be expected in obituary notices, this particular praise should not be too readily dismissed. Given that he handled considerable funds in the construction of many public buildings at a time in the Gilded Age when graft was a chronic problem, a tribute to his honesty is worth noting. If true, the combination of honesty and excessive generosity offers a convincing explanation of why he ended up without money and had to rely on the support of friends.[15]

With his professional work ending, in 1893 Bryant finally moved into the Old Men's Home on Springfield Street (fig. 8.6). Remarkably, he had designed this building in 1855 as the Lying-In Hospital. He was proud of the fact that he had designed the building for unfortunate women, providing features he ended up enjoying himself: "I knew they would want large airy corridors and broad staircases to walk about in, and bright sunny rooms."[16] There is, of course, a nice irony in an architect's spending his last years in a building of his own design. However, shortly before entering the Old Men's Home, Bryant expressed what must have been a great frustration in no longer having an active life. "When I look back over my life of more than 75 years, my memory cherishes as the happiest period those years in which I labored with the greatest industry. I should say that from the time I was 35 years old until I was 55 years old I found less leisure than in any other period of my life. I had greater cares, more responsibilities and harder duties during those years than I ever had felt before or have felt since. My time was completely occupied, and I devoted to sleep in those days less than half a dozen hours in each 24. How much I accomplished in those years must be left to the appreciation of my biographers, but certainly I accomplished all of which I was capable."[17]

At the same time, as Bryant was fully aware, there is a bittersweet aspect to living long enough to see much of your life's work being replaced. "What is fame in architecture in these latter days?" Gridley Bryant wrote toward the end of his life. "Is it to witness the demolition or radical remodeling of an architect's work, with less than a third of a century of its real usefulness about it?" If Bryant lived to see much of his work undone, since then a great many more of his buildings have been demolished or heavily altered. It is hard to know what he would have thought of his jail in Dedham converted for condominiums and his Charles Street Jail renovated for use as a hotel. In one sense he was born too soon. As a "Great Builder" (to quote

Figure 8.6. Gridley J. F. Bryant, taken in the Old Men's Home. *New England Magazine* 25 (1901). (Courtesy Trustees of the Brookline Public Library)

from one of his obituaries), he would have been happier to have been one of the early-twentieth-century generation of men like Chicago architect Daniel Burnham, who famously said, "Make no little plans." In his own words, Gridley Bryant would be remembered "not as a man of remarkable genius, but rather as a hard and constant professional worker; fortunate enough to secure employment from individuals of more or less prominence in wealth and influence not less than from many of the towns, cities, counties and states of the United States and as well from the general government itself."[18] In an age when there were no standards for determining who could call himself an architect, Bryant rose to the head of his profession by establishing a reputation as a man who, in the best tradition of the nineteenth century, could get the job done. Not a bad epitaph for an architect in any age.

APPENDIX 1

List of Architectural Drawings and Lithographic Renderings of Buildings and Projects by Gridley J. F. Bryant

Rostrum, Faneuil Hall, Boston, 1840 [Boston Public Library]

Mount Auburn Cemetery Chapel Project, 1843 [Historic New England]

House for Jonathan Preston (unlabeled, previously identified as Gardner Brewer), Boston, 1844 [Bostonian Society]

Suffolk County Jail Project, South Boston, 1845, color lithograph [Historic New England]

House for Henry Williams, Salem, 1846 [Peabody-Essex Museum]

Second floor plan (unidentified house), 1846 [Library of Congress]

Art Building Project, Harvard College, 1847 [Harvard University Archives]

Lawrence Scientific School and Residence Project, 1847 [Harvard University Archives]

Suffolk County Jail, Boston, 1848, color lithograph [Historic New England]

Deer Island Almshouse, Boston, 1849, color lithograph [Historic New England]

House for John Tucker Daland, Salem, 1851 [Peabody-Essex Museum]

United State Custom House, San Francisco, 1851 [National Archives]

Alterations to House of James Beal, Boston, 1852 [Historic New England]

Pacific Mills, Lawrence, 1852 [American Textile History Museum]

Addition to Massachusetts State House, Boston, 1853 [Winterthur Library]

Interior alterations, Faneuil Hall, Boston, 1853 [Boston Public Library]

Nahant House Additions, Nahant, 1853, color lithograph [Historic New England]

House for Joseph Titcomb, Kennebunk, Maine, 1854 [Brick Store Museum]

Mercantile Building for Emery Fay, Boston, 1855, color lithograph [Historic New England]

Baltimore City Jail, Baltimore, 1856 [Baltimore City Museum]

Dormitory Project, Harvard College, 1856 [Harvard University Archives]

Parker Hall, Bates College, Lewiston, 1856 [Coram Library, Bates College]

Building for Moses Grant, Boston, 1857 [Boston Public Library]

Additions to Kennebec County Courthouse, Project, Augusta, Maine, 1857 [Maine Historic Preservation Commission]

State Street Block, Boston, 1857, color lithograph [Historic New England]

Additions to Maine State Prison, Project, Thomaston, Maine, 1858 [Maine State Library]

Washington County Jail, Machias, Maine, 1858 [Washington County Commissioners]

Cast-iron Storefront, 65–67 Franklin Street, Boston, 1858 [Boston Athenaeum]

Federal Street Church, pew plans, Boston, 1859 [American Antiquarian Society]

Probate Building, Boston, 1859 [Bostonian Society]

Agassiz Museum Project, Harvard College, c.1860 [Historic New England]

School, Alfred, Maine, 1862 [Parsons Memorial Library, Alfred]

Town Hall, Alfred, Maine, 1862 [Parsons Memorial Library, Alfred]

Double House for Brewer and Beebe, Boston, 1864, color lithograph [Historic New England]

City Hall, Boston, 1865, color lithograph [Historic New England]

Auburn Town Hall, Auburn, 1865 [Maine Historic Preservation Commission]

Massachusetts State House, remodeling, Boston, 1866 [Massachusetts State Library]

View of remodeling State Capitol, Boston, 1867, lithograph [Massachusetts State Library

View of new state capitol, Boston, 1867, lithograph [Massachusetts State Library]

Measured Plans of Brattle Street Church, Boston, 1866/1871 [Historic New England]

House for Benjamin Stark, New London, Connecticut, 1868 [Avery Library, Columbia University]

Gate Keepers Lodge, Forest Hills Cemetery, Boston, 1868, color rendering [Forest Hills Cemetery Archives]

Massachusetts State Library, alterations, Boston, 1869 [Massachusetts State Library]

Penoboscot County Jail, Bangor, Maine, 1869 [Maine Historic Preservation Commission]

House for Jonas French, Gloucester, 1871 [Mrs. Harriet Myers]

Passenger Station, Maine Central Railroad, Waterville, Maine, 1872 [Maine Historic Preservation Commission]

Knox County Courthouse, Rockland, Maine, 1874 [Knox County Commissioners]

House for Thomas Wigglesworth, Manchester-by-the-Sea, 1889 [Historic New England]

APPENDIX 2

List of Buildings and Projects by Gridley J. F. Bryant

The following list of projects is organized by year with the date given being the estimated year that design work began. Although most large projects have several sources to document Bryant's involvement, I have provided only one for each commission. Where possible, I have cited original drawings, specifications, published renderings, or long newspaper descriptions. In only a few instances have I relied on the 1890 list of Bryant's drawings assembled by his friend Henry Bailey. Since, in many cases, that list includes projects not designed by Bryant, or not built, I have generally not referred to it unless the building survives and there is reason to make a stylistic attribution. As with any list deriving from such varied sources, many attributions are subject to corrections or refinements.

GRIDLEY J. F. BRYANT

1838

Cottage for Abbott, not located [Bailey, "An Architect of the Old School" (1901)]
Boarding school for Noah Brooks, not located [Ibid.]
Mechanics' Hall for George Darracott, not located [Ibid.]
Passenger station for George Dexter, not located [Ibid.]
House for Abbott Lawrence, 8 Park Street, Boston, extant [Ibid.]
Ship house for Alexander Parris, Charlestown Navy Yard? [Ibid.]
Market house for J. W. Pinckney, not located [Ibid.]

1840

City Hall, renovations (with Jonathan Preston), School Street, Boston, destroyed
　　[*Boston Transcript*, March 19, 1841]
Faneuil Hall, rostrum, Boston, destroyed [drawings, Boston Public Library]

1841

Three houses for Abijah Johnson, Essex Street, Boston, destroyed [Suffolk Deeds
　　474/217]
Two stores for John Simmons, Milk Street, Boston, destroyed [Suffolk Deeds
　　481/110–12]

1842

Store for Bates, Turner & Co., Milk Street, Boston, destroyed [Suffolk Deeds 481/108–10]

House for Madison Beal, Boston, not located [Suffolk Deeds 481/14–15]

Two houses for Moses Clark, Boston, not located [Suffolk Deeds 485/197–200]

Three stores for William Evans, Eliot and Utica streets, Boston, destroyed [Suffolk Deeds 485/8–9]

House for Samuel R. Hart, Charles Street, Boston, destroyed [Suffolk Deeds 490/85–86]

Thirty-six houses for Abijah Johnson, Beech, Essex, Oxford, and Harrison streets, Boston, 48–56 Beech Street, extant [Suffolk Deeds 480/236]

Twelve houses for Abijah Johnson, Oxford Place, Boston, eight extant [Suffolk Deeds 480/236]

Two houses for James Marble, Washington Street, Boston, not located [Suffolk Deeds 484/29–30]

Store for James K. Mills & Co., Milk Street, Boston, destroyed [Suffolk Deeds 481/106–8]

Store for Phineas Upham, Milk Street, Boston, destroyed [Suffolk Deeds 481/105–6]

House for Sarah Vose, Bowdoin Street, Dorchester, probably destroyed [Norfolk Deeds 135/98]

Three houses for Arnold F. Wells, Bussey Place, Boston, destroyed [Suffolk Deeds 494/78–80]

Four houses for Oliver Woods, off Morton Place, Boston, destroyed [Suffolk Deeds 491/48]

1843

Building for Benjamin B. Appleton, Sudbury and Court streets, Boston, not located [Suffolk Deeds 509/13–15]

House for Demeritt and Rollins, Carver Street, Boston, destroyed [Suffolk Deeds 496/270–71]

Eleven stores for Russell and Standish, Eastern Avenue, Boston, destroyed [Suffolk Deeds 506/27–33]

Seven houses for Oliver Downing, Bowdoin and Cambridge streets, Boston, destroyed [Suffolk Deeds 501/215–16]

Seven houses for Eli Fernald, 12–14 Tyler Street, Boston, partially extant [Suffolk Deeds 505/127–29]

Seven houses for Eli Fernald, 11–23 Hudson Street, Boston, extant [Suffolk Deeds 505/127–29]

Five houses for Adin Hall, Allen Street, Boston, destroyed [Suffolk Deeds 505/43–45]

House for Warren A. Hersey, Summer Street, Boston, destroyed [Suffolk Deeds 506/168–70]

House for Jeremiah Hill, 25 Kennard Road, Brookline, extant [Webster, *Thirty-Five Brookline Residences* (1888)]

House for Ann Lavery, A and Silver streets, South Boston, destroyed [Suffolk Deeds 504/41]

Two houses for Luther Gilbert, 320 Tremont Street and 82 Pleasant Street, Boston, destroyed [Suffolk Deeds 500/154–55]

Mount Auburn Cemetery Chapel, Cambridge, competition design not executed [drawings, Historic New England]

House for Albert Sanderson, Lyman Place, Boston, destroyed [Suffolk Deeds 513/223–25]

Sts. Peter and Paul Church, Broadway, South Boston, rebuilt in 1848, extant [Suffolk Deeds 498/172–73]

Fourteen houses for Oliver Woods, Bussey Place, Boston, destroyed [Suffolk Deeds 508/1–4]

1844

Twelve houses for Adams and Kimball, Washington Street, Boston (with Isaiah Rogers), not located [Suffolk Deeds 531/104]

Four houses for Adams and Kimball, Washington Street, Boston (with Isaiah Rogers), not located [Suffolk Deeds 536/295–96]

House for Jonathan Preston, 21 Beacon Street, Boston, destroyed [drawings, Bostonian Society]

Sixteen houses for Samuel Caswell, Washington Street, Boston, not located [Suffolk Deeds 527/105–6]

House for Theodore Chase, 27 Beacon Street, Boston, destroyed [specifications, Massachusetts Historical Society]

House for Chilson and Goodnow, Clay Place, Boston, destroyed [Suffolk Deeds 517/259–60]

House for Joseph W. Clark, Harrison Avenue, Boston, destroyed [Suffolk Deeds 544/161–63]

Four houses for Crooker and Matson, 1–7 Decatur Street?, Boston, probably destroyed [Suffolk Deeds 523/30]

House for Charles Davis, Billerica Street, Boston, destroyed [Suffolk Deeds 467/79–80]

Four houses for Moses R. Denning, Eastern Avenue, Boston, destroyed [Suffolk Deeds 536/197–99]

House for Charles C. Foster, 31 Harrison Avenue, Boston, destroyed [Suffolk Deeds 529/206]

Two houses for Charles C. Foster, 33–35 Harrison Avenue, Boston, destroyed [Suffolk Deeds 520/123–25]

Twelve houses for Hall and Valentine & Co., Boston, not located [Suffolk Deeds 527/587]

Two houses for Jenkins and Bailey, 4–6 Garden Court, Boston, no. 6 extant [Suffolk Deeds 523/303–4]

House for Alvah Kimball, Allen and Chambers streets, Boston, destroyed [Suffolk Deeds 528/43]

Store for Samuel Leeds, Charlestown Street, Boston, destroyed [Suffolk Deeds 522/223–24]

House for George A. Parish, Avery Street, Boston, destroyed [Suffolk Deeds 529/30–31]

Four houses for Albert Richardson, Auburn Street, Boston, destroyed [Suffolk Deeds 524/11–12]

Four stores for Standish and Russell, Eastern Avenue, Boston, destroyed [Suffolk Deeds 528/193–96]

Six houses for William Valentine & Co., Boston not located [Suffolk Deeds 540/120]

House for Oliver Woods, Chambers and Allen Streets, Boston, destroyed [Suffolk Deeds 526/218–19]

Two houses for Oliver Woods, Allen Street, Boston, destroyed [Suffolk Deeds 518/281–83]

1845

Boston Athenaeum, competition entry not built [Slautterback, *Designing the Boston Athenaeum*]

Store for Albert Bettely, Hanover Street, Boston, not located [Suffolk Deeds 554/293–94]

Two houses for Gardner Brewer, Harrison Avenue and Indiana Street, Boston, destroyed [Suffolk Deeds 567/33–38]

Five houses for Gardner Brewer, 5–11 Indiana Street, Boston, destroyed [Suffolk Deeds 567/33–35]

Morton Block for Cutler, Pliny, and Simmons, Milk Street, Boston, destroyed [*Boston Advertiser*, September 30, 1845]

Eastern Exchange Hotel, Commercial Street, Boston, destroyed [*Boston Advertiser*, September 30, 1845]

Four houses for George Higgins, Broadway, South Boston, not located [Suffolk Deeds 552/167–68]

Goddard Block for William Goddard, Milk Street, Boston, destroyed [*Boston Advertiser*, September 30, 1845]

Old South Block for Old South Society, Milk Street, Boston, destroyed [*Boston Advertiser*, September 30, 1845]

Suffolk County Jail, South Boston, unexecuted design [*Boston Advertiser*, October 14, 1845]

Dalton Block for William Wigglesworth, Milk Street, Boston, destroyed [*Boston Advertiser*, September 30, 1845]

1846

Mariners House for the Boston Port Society, 11 North Square, Boston, extant [*Boston Journal,* April 16, 1847]

Block of stores for Peter C. Brooks, Pearl Street, Boston, destroyed [*Boston Transcript,* October 24, 1846]

House for Edward P. Deacon, (with Jean Lemoulnier) ,Washington Street, Boston, destroyed [Suffolk Deeds 566/11–12]

Commercial block for Dennison Heirs, Washington Street, Boston, no. 429 extant [*Boston Courier,* March 12, 1846]

Passenger depot, Eastern Railroad, Salem, destroyed [*Salem Register,* July 12, 1847]

Federal Theater, interior alterations, Federal Street, Boston, destroyed [*Boston Advertiser,* March 3, 1846]

Harvard Medical College, Grove Street, Boston, destroyed [*Boston Advertiser,* August 21, 1846]

Three stores for Warren A. Hersey, Pearl Street, Boston, destroyed [Suffolk Deeds 561/104–6]

Mount Auburn Chapel (with Jacob Bigelow), Cambridge, demolished [Linden-Ward, *Landscapes of Memory* (1989)]

House for Gilbert Newhall, 78 Washington Street, Salem, extant [specifications, Peabody Essex Museum]

William S. Skinner Monument, Mount Auburn Cemetery, not located [*Boston Courier,* June 11, 1846]

House for Henry Williams, 342 Essex Street, Salem, extant [drawings, Peabody Essex Museum]

1847

Boynton High School, Eastport, Maine, extant [*Eastport Sentinel,* June 16, 1897]

Naumkeag Block for Benjamin Creamer, 185–89 Essex Street, Salem, extant [*Salem Register,* December 6, 1847]

First Parish Church, Framingham, destroyed [Wharton Diaries, New York Public Library]

Art Building, Harvard College, unexecuted design [drawings, Harvard University Archives]

Lawrence Scientific School and Residence, unexecuted design [drawings, Harvard University Archives]

Building for C. M. Parker, Milk Street, Boston, destroyed [*Boston Daily Advertiser,* November 5, 1847]

Quincy Grammar School, Tyler Street, Boston, rebuilt in 1859, extant ["Specifications of Public Buildings," no. 24]

House for William R. Rodman, 79 Beacon Street, Boston, extant [Suffolk Deeds 581/10–12]

1848

Three stores for Noah Blanchard, Court Street, Boston, destroyed [Suffolk Deeds 589/4–5]

Bowdoin Grammar School, Myrtle Street, Boston, destroyed ["Specifications of Public Buildings," no. 26]

House for Elbridge Bramhall, 11 Temple Street, Boston, extant [Suffolk Deeds 592/270–71]

Engine House, Meridian Street, East Boston, demolished ["Specifications of Public Buildings," no. 39]

Hawes School, enlargement, Broadway, South Boston, destroyed ["Specifications of Public Buildings," no. 37]

Primary School, Boylston Street, Boston, destroyed ["Specifications of Public Buildings," no. 50]

Putnam Free School, Newburyport, destroyed [Barnard, *School Architecture* (1854)]

Smith School, remodeling, Joy Street, Boston, extant ["Specifications of Public Buildings," no. 38]

Sts. Peter and Paul Church, rebuilding, Broadway, South Boston, extant [Suffolk Deeds 599/283–84]

Suffolk County Jail, Charles Street, Boston, extant [*The Builder* (London), May 5, 1849]

House addition for James Wiggin, Franklin Square, Boston, destroyed [Suffolk Deeds 591/266–67]

1849

Almshouse for City of Boston, Deer Island, destroyed [*The Builder* (London), June 22, 1850]

Austin Primary School, Paris Street, East Boston, destroyed ["Specifications of Public Buildings," no. 47]

Baptist Church (with Alexander Esty), Haverhill, destroyed [*Haverhill Gazette*, November 11, 1849]

Bigelow Grammar School, 4th and E streets, South Boston, destroyed ["Specifications of Public Buildings," no. 28]

Chapman Grammar School, Eutaw Street, Boston, destroyed ["Specifications of Public Buildings," no. 22]

Tuckerman Primary School, East Fourth Street, South Boston, destroyed ["Specifications of Public Buildings," no. 41]

United States Custom House, Eastport, Maine, destroyed [correspondence, National Archives]

1850

Almshouse, Providence, Rhode Island, not built (MacKay, *Charles Street Jail* (1980)]

Bank of Commerce, 83–85 State Street, Boston, destroyed [*Saturday Evening Gazette,* May 18, 1850]

City workhouse, Blackwell's Island, New York, not built [MacKay, *Charles Street Jail* (1980)]

City almshouse, 45 Matignon Road, Cambridge, extant [MacKay, *Charles Street Jail* (1980)]

Gore Library, tower reconstruction, Harvard College, destroyed [correspondence, Harvard University Archives]

High school building, 50 High Street, Lynn, extant ["Specifications of Public Buildings," no. 56]

Holden Chapel, alterations, Harvard College, extant [Harvard University Archives]

House of Reform, Kingston, New Jersey, not built [MacKay, *Charles Street Jail* (1980)]

Maine State Reform School, Cape Elizabeth (now South Portland), extant [*Portland Advertiser,* July 16, 1853]

Massachusetts State Prison, additions, Charlestown, destroyed [MacKay, *Charles Street Jail* (1980)]

Primary school, East Orange Street, Boston, destroyed ["Specifications of Public Buildings," no. 43]

Primary school, Rutland Street, Boston, destroyed ["Specifications of Public Buildings," no. 46]

Rhode Island State Prison, additions, Providence, Rhode Island, destroyed? ["Specifications of Public Buildings," no. 15]

Block for Mary Ward, Congress and Lindall streets, Boston, destroyed [Suffolk Deeds 618/108–9]

1851

Almshouse, New Haven, Connecticut, not built [MacKay, *Charles Street Jail* (1980)]

House for John Tucker Daland, 120 Essex Street, Salem, extant [drawings, Peabody Essex Museum]

Block for William Gould, School Street and Chapman Place, Boston, destroyed [Suffolk Deeds 617/292–94]

Hampshire County Jail, Northampton, extant [MacKay, *Charles Street Jail* (1980)]

High School, Dover, New Hampshire, destroyed [*Granite Monthly* 43 (1911)]

House of Refuge, Randall's Island, New York, not built [MacKay, *Charles Street Jail* (1980)]

Massachusetts State House, alterations, Boston, not built [House Document 192 (1851)]

Norfolk County Jail, Dedham, extant ["Specifications of Public Buildings,"
    no. 13]
Phillips Grammar School, Southac Street, Boston, destroyed ["Specifications of
    Public Buildings," no. 44]
Primary school, Washington Square, Boston, destroyed ["Specifications of Public
    Buildings," no. 42]
Schoolhouse, rear Hanover Street, Boston, destroyed ["Specifications of Public
    Buildings," no. 51]
Schoolhouse, Webster Street, East Boston, destroyed ["Specifications of Public
    Buildings," no. 49]
Stable and riding school for Walter Bryant, Washington Street, Boston, destroyed
    [Suffolk Deeds 627/141–43]
United States Custom House, San Francisco, destroyed [drawings, National
    Archives]

1852

Building for Amos Baker, Chapman Place, destroyed [Suffolk Deeds
    633/263–64]
Ballou Hall, Tufts College, Medford, extant [*Ballou's Pictorial*, October 11,
    1856]
House for James Beal, alterations, Rowe Street and Essex Place, Boston, destroyed
    [drawings, Historic New England]
Boylston Grammar School, rebuilding, Fort Hill vicinity, Boston, destroyed
    ["Specifications of Public Buildings," no. 30]
Brimmer School, remodeling, Common Street, Boston, destroyed
    ["Specifications of Public Buildings," no. 34]
Fryeburg Academy, Fryeburg, Maine, extant [Fryeburg Academy Archives]
George Washington Tower, Mount Auburn Cemetery (with Jacob Bigelow),
    extant [Linden-Ward, *Landscapes of Memory* (1989)]
Lighthouse for United States Lighthouse Board, Pacific coast, not located
    [National Archives]
Missouri State Prison, Jefferson City, Missouri, not built [MacKay, *Charles Street Jail*
    (1980)]
Mayhew School alterations, Hawkins Street, Boston, destroyed ["Specifications of
    Public Buildings," no. 36]
Pacific Mills for John Lowell, Lawrence, extant [drawing fragment, American
    Textile History Museum]
Schoolhouse, Wall Street, Boston, destroyed ["Specifications of Public Buildings,"
    no. 53]
Schoolhouse, Porter Street, East Boston, destroyed ["Specifications of Public
    Buildings," no. 45]
Second District School, Natick, not located ["Specifications of Public Buildings,"
    no. 55]

1853

House for Jeffrey Brackett, 148 Presidents Lane, Quincy, extensively altered
[*Gleason's Pictorial,* November 5, 1853]
Essex County Jail, Lawrence, destroyed ["Specifications of Public Buildings," no.
16]
Faneuil Hall, Boston, interior alterations, unknown [drawings, Boston Public
Library]
First Congregational Church, Natick, destroyed [*History of Natick* (1856)]
Block for R. M. Hodges, Winter Street, Boston, destroyed [*Saturday Evening
Gazette,* November 12, 1853]
Massachusetts State House, west wing, Boston, destroyed [*The Builder* (London),
April 5, 1856]
Nahant House hotel, additions, Nahant, destroyed [Wharton Diaries, New York
Public Library]
Building for Israel and William Rice, Market and Chatham streets, Boston,
destroyed [Suffolk Deeds 655/210–11]
Building for Oliver Tenney, Atkinson Street, Boston, destroyed [Suffolk Deeds
646/135–36]
United States Mint, San Francisco, not built [correspondence, National Archives]

1854

Congregational church, additions, Eastport, Maine, destroyed [*Eastport Sentinel,*
July 19, 1854]
House and barn for Aaron Hobart Jr., 175 Central Street, East Bridgewater, extant
(Bailey list of drawings (1890) and stylistic attribution]
Building for F. O. Prince, 52–54 Devonshire Street, Boston, destroyed [Suffolk
Deeds 673/66]
House for Joseph Titcomb, Summer Street, Kennebunk, Maine, extant [drawings,
Brick Store Museum, Kennebunk]
York County Courthouse, additions, Alfred, Maine, destroyed [Bailey list (1890),
Maine Historic Preservation Commission]

1855

Androscoggin County Courthouse and Jail, Auburn, Maine, extant [*Ballou's
Pictorial,* March 28, 1857]
Boston Lying-In Hospital, Springfield Street, Boston, destroyed [Bailey, "An
Architect of the Old School" (1901)]
Building for Mrs. Hannah Mason Estate, Dover and Washington streets, Boston,
destroyed [Suffolk Deeds 678/277–79]
Mercantile Building for Emery Fay, Summer Street, Boston, destroyed [*Ballou's
Pictorial,* March 6, 1856]

1856

Baltimore City Jail, Baltimore, not executed [*Ballou's Pictorial,* August 8, 1857]

Building for Ebenezer Dyer, Congress Street, Boston, destroyed [Suffolk Deeds 701/265–66]

Dormitory for Harvard College, Cambridge, not built [drawings, Harvard University Archives]

House of Reformation, Manchester, New Hampshire, destroyed [New Hampshire State Archives]

Maine State Seminary (Bates College), Lewiston, Maine, extant [*Ballou's Pictorial,* March 28, 1857]

Mercantile Wharf Block, various clients, 75–117 Commercial Street, Boston, extant [*Ballou's Pictorial,* January 3, 1857]

Merchants Bank Building, additions (with George Snell), 28 State Street, Boston, destroyed [*Boston Transcript,* May 24, 1856]

Building for Minns Heirs, Congress Street, destroyed [*Boston Transcript,* March 11, 1856]

Two houses for Dr. C. A. Phelps, Warren Street, Boston, not located [Suffolk Deeds 692/268–69]

Building for Robbins and Monks, Summer Street, Boston, destroyed [*Boston Transcript,* May 24, 1856]

Building for Spooner and Nutting, Congress Street, Boston, destroyed [*Boston Transcript,* August 5, 1856]

1857

Building for Fifty Associates (with Charles E. Parker), Friend Street, Boston, destroyed [*Boston Transcript,* June 22, 1857]

Building for Moses Grant, Friend and Union streets, Boston, destroyed [drawings, Boston Public Library]

House for Thomas Powers, South Framingham, destroyed [*Boston Transcript,* June 5, 1866]

Building for Ropes and Codman, Hanover Street, Boston, destroyed [*Boston Transcript,* June 22, 1857]

State House reconstruction, Montpelier, Vermont., not built [rendering, Vermont State Archives]

Building for Dr. Henry Gardner, Fulton and North streets, Boston, not located [*Boston Transcript,* June 22, 1857]

Gibson School, School Street, Dorchester, destroyed [Sammarco, *Images of America: Dorchester* (1995)

Kennebec County Jail, Augusta, Maine, extant [North, *History of Augusta* (1870)]

Kennebec County Courthouse, jail addition, Augusta, Maine, not built [drawing, Maine Historic Preservation Commission]

Massachusetts Charitable Mechanics Association Building (with Hammatt Billings

and Nathaniel Bradlee), Bedford and Chauncey streets, Boston, destroyed
[O'Gorman, *Accomplished in All Departments of Art* (1988)]

Post Office Block, Chauncey and Summer streets, Boston, destroyed [*Ballou's
Pictorial,* July 31, 1857]

Building for Joshua Sears Estate (with Hammatt Billings), 74–76 Franklin Street,
Boston, destroyed [*Boston Transcript,* February 8, 1858]

State Street Block, various clients, 177–99 State Street, Boston, partially extant
[*Boston Transcript,* December 27, 1857]

Building for Phineas Upham, 30–42 Franklin Street, Boston, destroyed [*Saturday
Evening Gazette,* April 10, 1857]

Tomb for J. B. Whall (with Hammatt Billings), Mount Auburn Cemetery,
destroyed [O'Gorman, *Accomplished in All Departments of Art* (1998)]

1858

House for Peter C. Brooks, Mt. Vernon Street, Boston, probably not executed
[*Boston Transcript,* June 30, 1858]

Cheshire County Courthouse, Keene, New Hampshire, extant [*Ballou's Pictorial,*
February 12, 1859]

House for James M. Codman, Sargent Road, Brookline, destroyed [Wolcott,
"Random Recollections" (1934)]

Eliot Grammar School, Bennett Street, Boston, destroyed [specifications, Boston
Athenaeum]

Building for Horner Heirs, Hanover and Union streets, Boston, destroyed
[Suffolk County Deeds 743/218–19]

Iowa Sate Penitentiary, additions, Fort Madison, Iowa, unknown [MacKay, *Charles
Street Jail* (1980)]

Building for Abbott Lawrence Estate, Milk and Devonshire streets, destroyed
[*Boston Transcript,* June 14, 1858]

Lincoln School, South Broadway, Boston, destroyed [*Boston Transcript.* September
21, 1858]

Little Blue School for Abbott, Farmington, Maine, destroyed [*Farmington
Chronicle,* March 4, 1858]

Maine State Prison, Maine, not executed [published drawings, Maine State
Archives]

Maine State Prison, additions, Thomaston, Maine, not built [drawings, Maine
State Library]

Seven houses for Marble and Barker, 150–62 Concord Street, Boston, extant
[Suffolk County Deeds 774/262]

Building for William Ropes et al., Sudbury Street, Boston, destroyed [*Boston
Transcript,* April 26, 1858]

Building for Shattuck Estate, Hanover Street, Boston, destroyed [*Boston Transcript,*
April 26, 1858]

Building for John Simmons et al., 31–55 Franklin Street, Boston, destroyed
[*Boston Transcript,* February 10, 1858]

St. Vincent Orphan Asylum, Camden Street and Shawmut Avenue, Boston,
  destroyed [*Ballou's Pictorial,* July 10, 1858]
Washington County Jail, Machias, Maine, extant [drawings, Washington County
  Commissioners]

1859

Arlington Street Church (with Arthur Gilman), Arlington Street, Boston, extant
  [*Boston Transcript,* December 6, 1861]
Aroostook County Courthouse, Houlton, Maine, extant [Aroostook County
  Archives]
Building for Bradlee et al., Franklin Street, Boston, destroyed [*Sketches of Boston
  and Vicinity* (1859)]
Monument for Gardner Brewer (with Hammatt Billings), Mount Auburn
  Cemetery, extant [*Boston Transcript,* August 31, 1859]
Building for Bussey Estate, Bussey Place and Arch Street, Boston, destroyed
  [*Boston Transcript,* April 15, 1859]
Building for Fifty Associates, Court Square, Court Street, Cornhill, Boston, not
  located [*Boston Transcript,* July 29, 1859]
Minute Man Monument (with Hammatt Billings and Thomas Ball), Lexington,
  not built [*Boston Transcript,* September 25, 1860]
Probate Building, Suffolk County, Court Square, Boston, destroyed [drawings,
  Bostonian Society]
Building for Isaac Rich (with Hammatt Billings), Franklin Street, Boston,
  destroyed [*Boston Transcript,* September 26, 1859]
Building for Society of Natural History and Horticultural Society (with Hammatt
  Billings), unexecuted project [O'Gorman, *Accomplished in All Departments of Art*
  (1998)]
Building for Thomas Wigglesworth Estate, Franklin Street, Boston, destroyed
  [*Sketches of Boston and Vicinity* (1859)]
Building, client unknown, 141 Washington Street, Boston, destroyed [*Boston
  Journal,* February 23, 1859]
Building, client unknown, 27 Winter Street, Boston, destroyed [*Boston Journal,*
  February 23, 1859]
Building, client unknown, 27 Myrtle Street, Boston, destroyed [*Boston Journal,*
  February 23, 1859]

1860

Aggasiz Museum Project, Harvard College, not built [drawing, Harvard University
  Archives]
Building for Beebe and Weld, Winthrop Square, Boston, destroyed [*Boston
  Transcript,* April 2, 1862]
Block of six houses, various clients, 104–16 Beacon Street, Boston, extant [*Boston
  Transcript,* May 28, 1860]

City Hall, additions, School Street, competition design [Boston City Documents no. 44 (1860)]

City stables, North Grove Street, Boston, destroyed [*Architects and Mechanics Journal,* February 3, 1861]

Everett Grammar School, Northampton Street, Boston, destroyed [*Architects and Mechanics Journal,* February 23, 1861]

Building for Haven and Stephenson, Arch Street, Boston, destroyed [*Boston Transcript,* April 11, 1860]

Double house for Samuel Hooper (with Arthur Gilman), 25–27 Commonwealth Avenue, Boston, extant [*Saturday Evening Gazette,* July 14, 1860]

Building on Kent Estate, Hanover Street, Boston, not located [*Architects and Mechanics Journal,* April 21, 1860]

Norfolk County Courthouse, additions, Dedham, destroyed [*Boston Courier,* January 18, 1861]

Block for Parker Estate (with Arthur Gilman), 156–62 Washington Street, Boston, destroyed [*Architects and Mechanics Journal,* September 8, 1860]

Monument for Jonathan Phillips (with Hammatt Billings), Mount Auburn Cemetery, extant [O'Gorman, *Accomplished in All Departments of Art* (1998)]

Building for Pratt Heirs, 108 State Street, Boston, destroyed [*Boston Transcript,* February 18, 1860]

Primary school, Poplar Street, Boston, destroyed [*Architects and Mechanics Journal,* February 23, 1861]

Receiving Tomb, Mount Auburn Cemetery, Cambridge, not located (*Boston Transcript,* February 18, 1860]

School building, Middlesex and Suffolk streets, Boston, destroyed [*Boston Transcript,* March 15, 1860]

Three houses for John Simmons (with Arthur Gilman), 1–3 Arlington Street, Boston, extant [*Boston Transcript,* May 25, 1860]

Block of nine houses, various clients (with Arthur Gilman), 20–36 Commonwealth Avenue, Boston, extant [*Boston Transcript,* May 25, 1860]

Building for Thomas Wigglesworth, State Street, Boston, destroyed [*Architects and Mechanics Journal,* October 1859]

1861

Building for Minot Heirs, Sudbury Street, Boston, destroyed [*Boston Transcript,* March 7, 1861]

School building, Poplar Street, Boston, destroyed [*Architects and Mechanics Journal,* February 23, 1861]

Building for Shepard Estate, Hanover Street, Boston, destroyed [*Saturday Evening Gazette,* February 2, 1861]

1862

Boston City Hall (with Arthur Gilman), School Street, Boston, extant [*Boston Transcript,* September 8, 1865]

Boston City Hospital, Harrison Avenue, Boston, partially extant [Boston City Document no. 34 (1861)]

House for George R. Drowne, 119 Benefit Street, Providence, extant [Jordy, *Buildings of Rhode Island* (2004); Bailey list (1890)]

Police Station no. 3, 74 Joy Street, Boston, extant [*Boston Courier,* April 21, 1862]

Post Office Block, Chestnut Street, Philadelphia, destroyed [*Saturday Evening Gazette,* February 22, 1863]

School building, Alfred, Maine, destroyed [drawings, Parsons Memorial Library, Alfred]

Town Hall, Alfred, Maine, extant [drawings, Parsons Memorial Library, Alfred]

1863

House for Charles H. Dalton (with Arthur Gilman), 33 Commonwealth Avenue, Boston, extant [*Boston Transcript,* May 15, 1863]

Normal school, Farmington, Maine, destroyed [*Farmington Chronicle,* November 19, 1863]

John Hancock House, reconstruction (with Arthur Gilman), Boston, not built [*Boston Transcript,* February 13, 1863]

House for Joseph Sawyer (with Arthur Gilman), 31 Commonwealth Avenue, Boston, extant [*Boston Transcript,* February 13, 1863]

House for Joshua Stetson (with Arthur Gilman), 29 Commonwealth Avenue, Boston, destroyed [*Boston Transcript,* May 15, 1863]

Union Club, additions (with John H. Sturgis), 8 Park Street, Boston, extant [*Boston Transcript,* April 8, 1863]

1864

Double house for Brewer and Beebe (with Arthur Gilman), Beacon Street, Boston, destroyed [*Boston Transcript,* July 6, 1864]

Horticultural Hall (with Arthur Gilman), Tremont Street, Boston, destroyed [*Boston Transcript,* April 14, 1864]

New Hampshire State House, additions (with Arthur Gilman?), Concord, extant [*Concord Daily Monitor* June 6, 1866]

Double house for William F. Parrott, 132–34 Middle Street, Portsmouth, New Hampshire, extant [Bailey list (1890) and stylistic attribution]

1865

City Hall (with Arthur Gilman), Lynn, destroyed [*The City Hall of Lynn* (1869)]

Auburn Hall, Court Street, Auburn, Maine, extant [*Lewiston Evening Journal,* December 30, 1865]

Block for James Beebe (with Arthur Gilman), 156–64 Devonshire Street, Boston, destroyed [*Boston Transcript*, September 8, 1865]

Building for Boston Screw Company, South Boston, not located [*Boston Transcript*, May 23, 1865]

House for Joseph Davis (with Arthur Gilman), Ocean Street, Lynn, destroyed [*Boston Transcript*, September 8, 1865]

Building for Benjamin Doak et al. (with Arthur Gilman), 10–14 Exchange Street, Lynn, destroyed [Boston Transcript September 8, 1865]

House for Benjamin Doak (with Arthur Gilman), Ocean Street and Atlantic Avenue, Lynn, destroyed [*Boston Transcript*, September 8, 1865]

Gardner's Lodge, Hunnewell Estate (with Arthur Gilman?), 849 Washington Street, Wellesley, extant [Hunnewell Family Diaries]

Factory for Hallett, Davis & Co. (with Arthur Gilman), Harrison Avenue, Boston, destroyed [*Boston Transcript*, September 8, 1865]

Minot Building, alterations, Court and Sudbury streets, Boston, destroyed [*Boston Transcript*, May 23, 1865]

Passenger Station, Freight House, Car House, for Old Colony Railroad (with John H. Sturgis), Kneeland Street, destroyed [*Boston Transcript*, March 12, 1866]

House for Benjamn T. Reed (with Arthur Gilman), 25 Ocean Street, Lynn, destroyed [*Boston Transcript*, September 8, 1865]

House for Philo Shelton (with Arthur Gilman), Phillips Point, Swampscot, not located [*Boston Transcript*, September 9, 1865]

1866

Barristers Hall for Fifty Associates, 7–11 Court Square, Boston, destroyed [*Boston Transcript*, March 12, 1866]

Building for Thomas Burnham, School Street, Boston, destroyed [*Boston Transcript*, May 9, 1866]

Building for A. N. Cook Co. (with Arthur Gilman), 215–17 Washington Street, Boston, destroyed [*Boston Transcript*, April 18, 1866]

Congregational church (with Arthur Gilman), Georgetown, destroyed [*Boston Transcript*, July 6, 1866]

House for Josiah Coldwell (with Arthur Gilman), Lynn, not located [*Boston Transcript*, May 7, 1868]

Hotel for Hiram Cranston, Fifth Avenue and Fifty-ninth Street, New York, not built [*The Builder* (London), August 3, 1867]

Building for Hallett and Davis (with Arthur Gilman), Washington Street, Boston, destroyed [*Boston Transcript*, November 27, 1866]

House for Francis M. Lousada, Ocean Street, Lynn, not located [*Boston Transcript*, March 12, 1866]

Lower Lodge for Hunnewell Estate (with John Sturgis?), 811 Washington Street, Wellesley, extant [Hunnewell family diaries]

House for Robert Treat Paine Jr., Waltham, partially extant [Paine diaries, Paine Estate]

Building for C. A. Parker (with Arthur Gilman), 106 State Street, Boston,
destroyed [*Boston Transcript*, November 27, 1866]

Building for Charles M. Parker (with Arthur Gilman), 213–17 Washington Street,
Boston, destroyed [*Boston Transcript*, April 18, 1866]

Passenger Station for Boston & Maine Railroad, Exeter, New Hampshire,
destroyed [*Boston Transcript*, August 30, 1866]

Passenger Station for Boston & Maine Railroad, Haverhill, destroyed [*Boston
Transcript*, August 30, 1866]

Soldier's Monument (with Hammatt Billings), Boston Common, competition
entry, not executed [*Boston Transcript*, September 10, 1866]

House for Benjamin Stark (with Arthur Gilman), New London, Connecticut, not
built? [drawings, Avery Library, Columbia University]

Thayer Library (with Arthur Gilman), Braintree, competition design, not built
[*Boston Transcript*, March 12, 1866]

1867

Cushman School, Parmenter Street, Boston, destroyed ["Descriptive Schedule of
Permanent School Buildings February 1, 1925," copy of unidentified school
report in files of Boston Landmarks Commission]

Massachusetts State House, additions (with Alexander Esty), Boston, not built
["Report of Commissioners . . . Remodeling or Rebuilding the State House"
(1867)]

Peabody Institute Library, Danvers, destroyed [*Danvers Monitor*, July 29, 1869]

BRYANT & ROGERS

1867

Maine State House, additions and alterations, not built [*Maine Farmer*, October
24, 1867]

1868

Coburn Hall, Skowhegan, Maine, destroyed [*Skowhegan on the Kennebec* (1941)]

Building for Charter Oak Life Insurance Company (with Francis Kimball),
Hartford, destroyed [*Technologist* (New York), June 1871]

Building for Connecticut Mutual Life Insurance Co. (with Francis H. Kimball),
Hartford, destroyed [*Technologist* (New York), October 1870]

Freeman School, Charter Street, Boston, destroyed [*Boston Transcript*, January 1,
1870]

Gate Keeper's Lodge, Forest Hills Cemetery, Boston, extant [drawing, Forest Hill
Cemetery Archives]

Tenement block for James Parker, 792–804 Washington Street, Boston, destroyed
  [*Boston Transcript*, May 1, 1868]
Penny Savings Bank Building, Washington Street and Union Park, Boston,
  destroyed [*Boston Transcript*, November 23, 1868]
House for Henry Souther, 546 East Broadway, South Boston, extant [Bailey list
  (1890) and stylistic attribution]

1869

Apothecary store for Williams & House (with Francis H. Kimball), Main Street,
  Hartford, destroyed [Kimball Scrapbook]
Building for Bissell, Hurlburt, and Goodrich (with Francis H. Kimball), Asylum
  and Ford streets, Hartford, destroyed [Kimball Scrapbook]
Freight house for Boston & Providence Railroad, Columbus Avenue, Boston,
  destroyed [*Boston Transcript*, August 23, 1869]
House for Oliver Brewster, 9 Arlington Street, Boston, extant [Bailey list (1890)
  and stylistic attribution compared to 8 Arlington Street]
House for Barney Corey, 8 Arlington Street, Boston, extant [*Boston Transcript*,
  August 25, 1869]
House for Mrs. S. E. Casenove, 10 Arlington Street, Boston, extant [Bailey list
  (1890) and stylistic attribution compared to 8 Arlington Street]
Catholic Orphan Asylum (with Francis H. Kimball), 89–91 Church Street,
  Hartford, destroyed [Kimball Scrapbook]
House for Francis B. Cooley (with Francis H. Kimball), 29 Farmington Avenue,
  Hartford, destroyed [Kimball Scrapbook]
Block for Dow and Thompson, High Street, Boston, destroyed [*Boston Transcript*,
  January 1, 1870]
Drake School, Third Street, Boston, destroyed [*Boston Transcript*, January 1, 1870]
House for Francis Fellows (with Francis H. Kimball), additions, 135 Washington
  Street, Hartford, destroyed [Kimball Scrapbook]
Fire Station No. 5, 456 West Fourth Street, South Boston, extant [*Boston
  Transcript*, January 1, 1870]
Fire Station No. 6, remodeled, Broadway, South Boston, destroyed [*Boston
  Transcript*, January 1, 1870]
Fire Station No. 9, Paris Street, East Boston, destroyed [*Boston Transcript*, January
  1, 1870]
Fire Station, North Grove Street, Boston, destroyed [*Boston Transcript*, January 1,
  1870]
Fire Station, East Street and East Place, Boston, destroyed [*Boston Transcript*,
  January 1, 1870]
Fire Station, Church Street, Boston, destroyed [*Boston Transcript*, January 1, 1870]
Fire station, Summer Street, Boston, destroyed [*Boston Transcript*, January 1,
  1870]
Block for Jones and Tucker, 23–29 High Street, Boston, destroyed [*Boston
  Transcript*, March 1, 1869]

Building for S. W. Gregory (with Francis H. Kimball), State Street, Hartford, destroyed [Kimball Scrapbook]

Lyman School, Paris Street, East Boston, extant [*Boston Transcript,* January 1, 1870]

National Exchange Bank (with Francis H. Kimball), alterations, 76 State Street, Hartford, destroyed. [Kimball Scrapbook]

Penobscot County Jail, Bangor, Maine, extant [drawings, Maine Historic Preservation Commission]

Police Station No. 10, Washington Street, Boston, destroyed [*Boston Transcript,* January 1, 1870]

Primary school, Charter Street, Boston, destroyed [*Boston Transcript,* January 1, 1870]

Rialto Building for John Simmons, Devonshire Street, Boston, destroyed [*Boston Transcript,* January 1, 1870]

Rice School, Appleton Street, Boston, destroyed [*Boston Transcript,* January 1, 1870]

School, Berlin Street, Boston, destroyed [*Boston Transcript,* January 1, 1870]

Block for Seward and Foy, High Street, Boston, destroyed [*Boston Transcript,* January 1, 1870]

Shurtleff School, Dorchester Street, South Boston, destroyed [*Boston Transcript,* November 6, 1869]

Warehouse, client unknown, High Street, Boston, destroyed [*Boston Transcript,* March 1, 1869]

1870

Warehouse for J. F. and N. Brown, High, Federal, and Summer streets, Boston, destroyed [*Boston Transcript,* August 24, 1870]

Connecticut State Prison, Wethersfield, competition, not built [MacKay, *Charles Street Jail* (1980)]

House for Samuel H. Gookin, 12 Commonwealth Avenue, Boston, extant [*Boston Transcript,* August 27, 1870]

House for Frederick Hart (with Francis H. Kimball), Main and Elm Streets, Hartford, destroyed [Kimball Scrapbook]

Town Hall, Lexington, destroyed [*Boston Transcript,* April 18, 1870]

Town Hall, Milford, New Hampshire, extant [*Boston Transcript,* April 18, 1870]

Norfolk County Jail, addition, Dedham, extant [MacKay, *Charles Street Jail* (1980)]

School, Yoeman Street, Boston, destroyed [*Boston Transcript,* January 1, 1870]

State Reformatory, Elmira, New York, not built [*Boston Transcript,* August 27, 1870]

Town Hall (city hall), Gloucester, extant [specifications, Gloucester City Archives]

Rockingham Hotel, additions, State Street, Portsmouth, New Hampshire, destroyed [*Boston Transcript,* April 18, 1870]

House for Samuel H. White (with Francis H. Kimball), Fairfield Avenue, Hartford, not located [Kimball Scrapbook]

1871

Passenger station for Boston & Albany Railroad, Boston, competition entry, not built [*Boston Transcript,* November 29, 1872]

Cobbet School, Franklin Street, Lynn, destroyed [*Lynn Transcript,* September 7, 1872]

Connecticut State House, Hartford, competition entry, not built [*Boston Transcript,* January 8, 1872]

Orange Judd Hall of Natural Science (with Francis H. Kimball), Wesleyan University, Middletown, Connecticut, extant [*The College Courant.* August 6, 1870]

1872

Passenger Station for Eastern Railroad, Lynn, destroyed [*Boston Transcript,* January 25, 1872]

Summer house for Jonas French, 4 Cardinal Lane, Gloucester, extant [drawings, Cardinal Lane Trust]

Ingalls School, Lynn, demolished [*Lynn Transcript,* September 7, 1872]

House for George W. Keene, 11 Atlantic Street, Lynn, extant [stylistic attribution with client connection]

Passenger station for Maine Central Railroad, Waterville, Maine, destroyed [drawings, Maine Historic Preservation Commission]

Merchants Bank Building, Boston, remodel interior, not located [*Boston Transcript,* May 15, 1872]

Michigan State House, Lansing, competition entry, not executed [*Boston Transcript,* January 8, 1872]

Reconstruction of State Prison, Jackson, Michigan, unknown [*Boston Transcript,* April 15, 1872]

Addition to Rialto Building for John Simmons, Devonshire Street, Boston, destroyed [*Boston Transcript,* February 8, 1872]

Building, client unknown, Kingston near Summer Street, Boston, not located [*Boston Transcript,* June 8, 1872]

1873

Atherton School, Columbia Street, Boston, destroyed [Boston City Document no. 22 (1874)]

Boston Transcript Building, 322–28 Washington Street, Boston, extant [*Boston Transcript,* February 9, 1874]

Building for John F. Mills, 6–10 Lindell Street, Boston, destroyed [*Boston Transcript,* January 13, 1873]

Warehouse for National Dock and Wharf Co., Lewis Street, East Boston, not located [*Boston Transcript,* August 18, 1873]

Building for James Parker Estate, 34–40 Pearl Street, Boston, destroyed [*Boston Advertiser,* October 8, 1873]

Rialto Building, Devonshire Street, Boston, destroyed [*Boston Transcript,* November 14, 1873]

Building for Simmons et al., 41–71 Franklin Street, extant [*Boston Advertiser,* February 26, 1873]

Building for Amasa Whiting, 162–64 Washington Street, Boston, destroyed [*Boston Transcript,* April 19, 1873]

1874

Blackstone Bank Block, Hanover and Union streets, Boston, destroyed [*Boston Transcript,* January 3, 1874]

Building for Burnham Estate, Tremont Street, Boston, destroyed [*Boston Transcript,* November 23, 1874]

Building for T. P. Burnham, Lewis Park and Highland Avenue, Boston, not located [*Boston Transcript,* April 21, 1874]

Building for Michael Doherty, Wendell and Hamilton streets, not located [*Boston Globe,* March 28, 1874]

Knox County Courthouse, Rockland, Maine, extant [drawings, Knox County Commissioners]

1875

Chapel, St. Paul's Church, Dedham, extant [specifications, St. Paul's Church]

GRIDLEY J. F. BRYANT

1877

Maplewood Congregational Church (with Clarence Luce), Salem Street, Malden, destroyed [*Malden Mirror,* July 7, 1877]

Hotel for John McCoskery (with Henry N. Black), Prince William Street, St. John, New Brunswick, not located [*St. John Daily Telegraph,* April 4, 1878]

Building for Stewart and White (with Henry N. Black), Charlotte Street, St. John, New Brunswick, not located [*St. John Daily Telegraph,* August 27, 1877]

1878

Merchants' National Bank, additions (with George Snell), 28 State Street, Boston, demolished [drawings, *American Architect and Building News,* February 14, 1880]

North Wheaton Female Seminary, additions, Norton, extant [Wheaton College Archives]

1879

Wilder Memorial Hall, 666 Main Street, Hingham, extant [Robinson, *Two Hundred Years,* (1980)]

Building, client unknown, 6–12 Haymarket Place, Boston, destroyed [permit files, Boston Public Library]

1880

Cony High School, Augusta, Maine, destroyed [rendering, *American Architect and Building News,* April 10, 1880]

1881

Liberty Building for Moses Williams, 30 Kilby Street, Boston, destroyed [*Boston Daily* Globe, June 18, 1882]

Norfolk County Jail, keeper's house, Dedham, extant [*Brookline Chronicle,* April 9, 1881]

1884

Essex County Jail, additions and alterations, Salem, extant [Stahl Associates Architects, "Feasibility Study for Essex County Correctional Facility" (1991)]

Parker House hotel, additions, 60 School Street, Boston, destroyed [photo of architect's rendering, Parker Omni House]

1886

Building for J. Amory Codman, 177 Tremont Street, Boston, destroyed [permit file, Boston Public Library]

1889

Armory building (with John F. Eaton), Boston, not located [*Sanitary Engineer,* May 25, 1889]

House for Howard Greenleaf (with John F. Eaton), Melrose, not located [*American Architect and Building News,* April 20, 1889]

House for Thomas Wigglesworth, 9 Old Neck Road, Manchester-by-the-Sea, extant [drawings, Historic New England]

1890

Cottage for F. A. Folson (with John F. Eaton), Rockport, not located [*American Architect and Building News,* March 8, 1890]

House for A. F. Haywood, 161 Allerton Street, Newton Highlands, extant [*Newton Graphic,* September 16, 1890]

Cottage and stable for Thatcher Estate (with John F. Eaton), Rockport, not located [*American Architect and Building News,* March 8, 1890]

UNITED STATES GOVERNMENT PROJECTS AS SUPERINTENDING ARCHITECT

United States Custom House, Boston, superintendent of repairs, 1863, unknown [National Archives]

United States Courthouse, Boston, remodel, 1866, unknown [*Boston Transcript,* June 27, 1866]

United States Post Office and Sub-Treasury Building, Boston, superintendent of construction, 1869–1875, destroyed [National Archives]

United States Custom House, Bristol, Rhode Island, alterations, ca.1872, unknown [*Boston Transcript,* October 12, 1872]

United States Custom House, New Bedford, alterations, ca.1872, unknown [*Boston Transcript,* October 12, 1872]

United States Custom House, Newport, Rhode Island, alterations, ca.1872, unknown [*Boston Transcript,* October 12, 1872]

United States Custom House, Providence, alterations, ca.1872, unknown [*Boston Transcript,* October 12, 1872]

United States Post Office and Custom House, Hartford, superintendent of construction?, 1873, destroyed [*Boston Transcript,* October 12, 1872]

United States Custom House, Boston, interior alterations, 1873, unknown [*Boston Transcript,* June 19, 1873]

DATES UNKNOWN

Cliff Cottage, client unknown, Maple Street, Longwood, Boston, destroyed [*Boston Transcript,* May 14, 1870]

Interior finishes for Steamer Bristol, Old Colony Railroad, presumably destroyed [Bailey, "Architect of the Old School"]

Interior finishes for Steamer Providence, Old Colony Railroad, presumably destroyed [Bailey, "Architect of the Old School"]

Storefront for Kramer, Federal Street, Boston, not located [Badger, *Illustrations of Iron Architecture* (1865)]

Thornburgh Plantation House for H. K. Burgwyn, Northampton County, N.C. (ca. 1842?), not built? [Burgwyn Family Papers, University of North Carolina, Chapel Hill]

Storefront for L. Ware, Congress Street, Boston, not located [Badger, *Badger's Illustrated Catalogue* (1981)

NOTES

Introduction

1. Henry Turner Bailey, "An Architect of the Old School," *New England Magazine* 25.3 (November 1901): 326–49. This biographical account by Bryant's friend is the only good source on the architect's life. Bailey had access to Bryant's account books and letters (now lost), as well as his reminiscing in the final years of his life.

2. Obituary accounts appeared in the *Boston Daily Advertiser,* June 19, 1899, p. 4; *Boston Globe,* June 9, 1899, p. 12; *Boston Herald,* June 9, 1899, p. 1; *Boston Morning Journal,* June 9, 1899, p. 1; *Boston Post,* June 9, 1899, p. 4; and *Boston Traveler,* June 9, 1899, pp. 13, 14. All of these accounts drew from the same source, that is, information supplied by Henry Bailey.

3. Bainbridge Bunting was the first to make this observation, although he assumed that meant Bryant had a large office of draftsmen. Bainbridge Bunting, *Houses of Boston's Back Bay* (Cambridge: Belknap Press, 1967), pp. 162–63.

4. John Hubbard Sturgis to Gridley J. F. Bryant, December 5, 1868, John H. Sturgis Papers, Boston Athenaeum.

5. Walter H. Kilham, *Boston after Bulfinch* (Cambridge: Harvard University Press, 1946), p. 67.

1. Granite Bred in the Bone

1. There are several accounts of the life of the elder Gridley Bryant. See, for example, Charles Stuart, *Lives and Works of Civil and Military Engineers of America* (New York: D. van Nostrand, 1871), pp. 119–31; Justin Winsor, ed., *The Memorial History of Boston,* vol. 4 (Boston: James R. Osgood & Co., 1881), 116–21. For an account by G. J. F. Bryant himself, see *Boston Evening Courier,* February 2, 1859, p. 4. Twentieth-century biographical dictionary entries build on these sources.

2. Gridley J. F. Bryant to Henry T. Bailey, undated letter cited in Bailey, "An Architect of the Old School," p. 329. Young Bryant was also involved in the construction of this building. Alexander Parris, the architect responsible for preparing drawings for Solomon Willard's design, was assisted by Bryant, then a student in his office. George M. Dexter to Loammi Baldwin, December 16, 1833, Loammi Baldwin Papers, Harvard University. Thanks to Sara Wermiel for this information.

3. Bulfinch has several biographers, but the best complete record of his work remains Harold Kirker, *The Architecture of Charles Bulfinch* (Cambridge: Harvard University Press, 1969).

4. George L. Vose, *A Sketch of the Life and Work of Loammi Baldwin* (Boston: Press of George H. Ellis, 1885).

5. Edward F. Zimmer, "The Architectural Career of Alexander Parris

(1780–1852)" (Ph.D. diss., Boston University, 1984); Denys Peter Myers, "Isaiah Rogers, 1800–1869," in *A Biographical Dictionary of Architects in Maine*, vol. 3, no. 2 (Augusta: Maine Historic Preservation Commission, 1986; this was a series of articles, printed separately and not paginated); William W. Wheildon, *Memoir of Solomon Willard* (Boston: Monument Association, 1865). Scholars interested in Alexander Parris should not fail to consult the "Alexander Parris Digital Poject" webpage featuring the architect's drawings and other documents from various collections established by the State Library of Massachusetts: www.parrisproject.org.

6. The three brothers were George A., Charles H., and Edward W. Bryant. It is known that George worked in a shoe factory. Charles first worked as a farmer in Scituate, but later evidently became a mason. Nothing is known about Edward. Even less information is available on the six sisters, Eliza B., Frances E., Marcia J., Mary L., Eunice B., and Priscilla C. Bryant. Mary married Henry Merritt, a fisherman, and Priscilla married Edwin Studley, who also worked in a shoe factory.

7. Charles B. Stuart, *Lives and Works of Civil and Military Engineers of America* (New York: D. Van Nostrand, 1871), pp. 119–181. For a somewhat more critical view of Bryant's involvement, see William H. Wheildon, *Memoir of Solomon Willard: Architect and Superintendent of the Bunker Hill Monument* (Boston: Bunker Hill Monument Association, 1865), pp. 107–12.

8. Stuart, *Lives*. See also Justin Winsor, *The Memorial History of Boston*, vol. 4 (Boston: James R. Osgood and Company, 1881), pp. 116–21.

9. *Portsmouth Journal*, October 9, 1841, p. 1.

10. E. C. Wines, "A Trip to Boston, In A Series of Letters to the Editor of the United States Gazette" (Boston: Charles C. Little and James Brown, 1838), pp. 207–8; Henry R. Cleveland, "American Architecture," *North American Review*, no. 93 (October 1836): 363.

11. Kirker, *Architecture of Charles Bulfinch*.

12. The house, enlarged by Sears and later owners, now stands as part of a row of nineteenth-century buildings on Beacon Street. It is difficult today to appreciate fully the imposing elegance of the freestanding house as originally built.

13. Cleveland, "American Architecture," p. 367.

14. Arthur Gilman, "Architecture in the United States," *North American Review* 123 (April 1844): 447.

15. Ibid., pp. 364–65.

16. Bulfinch's Federal Street Church of 1809 was an earlier example of the Gothic Revival, though of brick construction.

17. William Washburn (1808–1890) is treated in Rochelle S. Ellstein, "William Washburn and the Egyptian Revival in Boston," *Old Time New England* 70 (1980): 63–80.

18. Two of the houses still stand. The granite for the houses may have been shipped in to a point close to Brookline Village on the Worcester Turnpike before the dam shut off direct access to the Charles River.

19. John M. Bryan, "Boston's Granite Architecture, c. 1810–1860" (Ph.D. diss., Boston University, 1972).

20. Earle G. Shettleworth, Jr., director of the Maine Historic Preservation Com-

mission, has compiled extensive records of school reports and contemporary newspaper accounts of the Gardiner Lyceum.

21. Bailey, "Architect of the Old School," pp. 331–33.

22. Sara E. Wermeil, *The Fireproof Building: Technology and Public Safety in the Nineteenth-Century American City* (Baltimore: Johns Hopkins University Press, 2000), p. 47.

23. The Parris correspondence from the National Archives is cited by Edwin C. Bearss in *Historic Resources Study,* vol. 2, *Charlestown Navy Yard, 1800–1842* (Boston: United State Department of the Interior, National Park Service, 1984).

24. For a complete account of Boston's long history of landfill projects, see Nancy S. Seasholes, *Gaining Ground: A History of Landmaking in Boston* (Cambridge: MIT Press, 2003).

25. *Boston Daily Transcript,* May 13, 1837.

26. Parris to Loammi Baldwin, January 8, 1833, in Alexander Parris Papers, Massachusetts Historical Society, Boston; Upjohn to Robert H. Gardiner, October 4, 1837, cited in Everard M. Upjohn, *Richard Upjohn: Architect and Churchman* (New York: Da Capo Press, 1968), p. 41.

27. Bailey, "An Architect of the Old School," p. 333. This is one of many examples in which Bailey refers to account books that would have been of inestimable help in documenting Bryant's career.

28. Richard B. Johnson, *Seven and Eight Park Street: A Brief History of the Home of the Union Club* (Boston: Union Club, ca. 1976). This building is one of the most fascinating multilayered historic structures in Boston and deserves an in-depth architectural and social history.

29. *Boston Evening Transcript,* June 25, 1839, July 11, 1840, and March 19, 1841.

30. Bailey, "An Architect of the Old School," p. 327.

31. Ibid., pp. 341–42.

2. Mastering His Profession

1. *Boston Daily Advertiser,* April 28, 1845; Upjohn, *Richard Upjohn,* pp. 57–58. Richard Upjohn (1802–1878) was born in England and came to Boston in 1833. He left for New York around 1839 and quickly became one of the most admired architects in the country. There is evidence that Bryant did some work for Upjohn, though it is not specified. Judith Hull, "The School of Upjohn: Richard Upjohn's Office," *Journal of the Society of Architectural Historians* 52, no. 3 (September 1993): 282 n. 15.

2. Burgwyn Family Papers, Collection no. 1687, Southern History Collection, University of North Carolina, Chapel Hill. The house no longer survives, and I was unable to locate a photograph. Based on the family papers, the house is believed to have been built around 1843–45. For this reason, the undated specifications are estimated to date from around 1842.

3. In 1994 Earle G. Shettleworth Jr. began a project of indexing the building contracts in the Suffolk County Registry of Deeds. The first volume, privately

printed by him in a limited number of copies, was issued in 1995 and covered the years 1820–29. Subsequent volumes included "Suffolk County, 1830–39," "Suffolk County, 1840–44," Suffolk County, 1845–49," "Norfolk County, 1790–1849" (compiled by Roger G. Reed), "Middlesex County, 1820–25" (compiled by Laura B. Driemeyer), and "Middlesex County, 1830–39" (compiled by Roger G. Reed). In preparation at the time of writing were the final volumes for Suffolk and Norfolk counties.

4. Suffolk County Registry of Deeds, book 505, pp. 127–29, 142–44; book 508, pp. 41–46; book 515, pp. 107–8. Although there were exceptions, the men engaged in this speculative construction who used Bryant as an architect were predominantly in the building trades.

5. Suffolk County Registry of Deeds, book 523, pp. 303–4; book 525, pp. 35–36.

6. The drawings, dated September 2, 1844, are located in the collections of the Bostonian Society. Bryant's authorship of these drawings has not been clearly established. The bottom portion of the elevation drawing with the architect's name has been lost, but an unknown person has penciled in Bryant's name as architect. It is logical to assume this was done in reponse to information given by the donor, who may have trimmed the drawing for display. The elevation drawing identifies the owners of houses on either side. With that information, and the date, deed research clearly establishes that Jonthan Preston was original owner. Preston began his career as a mason and was chiefly known as a builder rather than an architect. Late in his career he collaborated first with William Ralph Emerson, then with his son William Gibbons Preston. He first collaborated with Bryant in remodeling the Boston City Hall in 1840. For Jonathan Preston, see Jean Follett-Thompson, "The Business of Architecture: William Gibbons Preston and Architectural Professionalism in Boston during the second half of the nineteenth century," Ph.D. diss., Boston University, 1986.

7. Theodore Chase Papers, Massachusetts Historical Society.

8. See 21 Beacon Street, Gardner Brewer House, Bostonian Society; "Plan of a Dwelling House for A. W. Thaxter, Jr., Boston, 1836," Fine Arts Library, Fogg Art Museum, Harvard University. For an account of Shaw's career, see Earle G. Shettleworth Jr., "Edward Shaw, Architect and Author," in a reprint of Shaw's 1854 publication *The Modern Architect* (New York: Dover Publications, 1995), v–xiv.

9. These drawings are in the collections of the Peabody Essex Museum.

10. "Specifications of Public Buildings of which Gridley J. F. Bryant Furnished Plans and Instructions," no. 60, Massachusetts State Library, Boston, printed in two volumes, 1847–53, including three specifications by Joseph E. Billings and one each by Richard Bond and Charles Roath.

11. Ibid., no. 24.

12. The Kennard House, at 25 Kennard Road, is the earliest surviving intact example of Bryant's work. Although the kitchen ell was demolished, the main body of the house was sensitively renovated for the Brookline Music School.

13. *Boston Daily Advertiser,* November 17 and 28, 1843. Charles Sullivan and

Susan Maycock of the Cambridge Historical Commission made their best effort to identify that project.

14. Lemoulnier published an announcement of his practice in the *Boston Daily Advertiser*, January 7, 1846. The contract for the Deacon House with Bryant listed as architect is in the Suffolk County Registry of Deeds, book 566, pp. 11–12. A retrospective description of the house appeared in the *Boston Daily Advertiser*, December 30, 1870. For an account of what little is known about Lemoulnier, see Harold Kirker and David van Zanten, "Jean Lemoulnier in Boston, 1846–1852," *Journal of the Society of Architects* 3, no. 3 (October 1972): 204–8.

15. Nathaniel Dearborn, *Boston Notions: Being an Authentic and Concise Account of that Village from 1630 to 1847* (Boston: Nathaniel Dearborn, 1848); *Boston Daily Advertiser*, September 30, 1845.

16. James F. O'Gorman, *Accomplished in All Departments of Art: Hammatt Billings of Boston, 1818–1874* (Amherst: University of Massachusetts Press, 1998); Catharina Slautterback, *Designing the Boston Athenaeum: 10 1/2 at 150* (Boston: Boston Athenaeum, 1999). Bryant was paid one hundred dollars for his design, which is believed to be a transitional Greek Revival/Italian Renaissance design that can be found in the Athenaeum collections. See Slautterback, *Athenaeum*, p. 24.

17. *Boston Weekly Courier*, March 12, 1846.

18. *Salem Register*, July 12, 1847; Francis B. C. Bradlee, *The Eastern Railroad* (Salem: Essex Institute, 1922), pp. 40–41. The Leipzig station is illustrated in Carroll L. V. Meeks, *The Railroad Station: An Architectural History* (New York: Dover Publications, 1995), fig. 22.

19. Record Group 56, entry no. 273, National Archives, College Park, Md.

3. Architecture and Reform

1. *Boston Daily Evening Journal*, April 16, 1847.

2. Lawrence A. Cremin, *The Republic and School: Horace Mann on the Education of Free Men* (New York: Teachers College, 1957).

3. S. V. Dickinson, *The Boston Almanac for the Year 1849* (Boston: B. B. Mussey & Co., 1849), pp. 83–89.

4. Joseph W. Ingraham obituary, *Boston Daily Transcript*, August 29, 1848; *Boston Globe*, June 28, 1897.

5. The Quincy School burned almost to the ground and was rebuilt in 1859. It is not known if Bryant was involved in the rebuilding, or if the design was changed in any significant way. Subsequent alterations included removing the pitched roof. *Boston Courier*, December 28, 1859.

6. Henry Barnard, *School Architecture, or Contributions to the Improvement of Schoolhouses in the United States* (Cincinnati: H. W. Derby & Co., 1854), pp. 198–203, 211; Kathleen Curron, *The Romanesque Revival: Religion, Politics, and Transnational Exchange* (University Park: Pennsylvania State University Press, 2003).

7. A Gloucester Web site for a nonprofit organization that uses the two surviving schools lists Bryant as the architect for the town-wide school building program

in 1850–51. There were a total of eight schools in the building program. After a search of the city archives, I have been unable to confirm that attribution.

8. Robert B. McKay, "The Charles Street Jail: Hegemony of a Design" (Ph.D. diss., Boston University, 1980). I have made extensive use of this outstanding study. Also helpful is an unpublished paper by a student at Wesleyan University, Nils S. Vaule, "The Creators of the Charles Street Jail: The Boston City Government, Louis Dwight, and Gridley J. F. Bryant," January 17, 1998. Numerous city reports trace the development of the jail from 1845. A good summary is "Final Report of the Committee on the Erection of the New Jail for Suffolk County," Boston City Document no. 61, November 10, 1851. Views and descriptions of the jail were published in *Boston Daily Transcript,* June 10, 1849; *Puritan Recorder,* May 31, 1849; and *The Builder* (London), May 5, 1849.

9. O'Gorman, *Accomplished in All Departments of Art.* With Billings's artistic talents and Bryant's skills in construction, the two would have made an extraordinary partnership. For whatever reason, however, Billings went into partnership with his brother, a not very successful combination.

10. *Boston Courier* (semiweekly), July 3, 1845. The published view of the jail and keeper's house identifies only Bryant as the architect. In September, Bryant reported to Alexander Parris that the Common Council was not happy with changes in the plan that increased expenses. They nonetheless agreed to authorize having the plan lithographed. Therefore, it is not clear if the keeper's house shown in the Billings rendering is the Bryant or the Bond design. Bryant to Alexander Parris, September 19, 1845, Alexander Parris Papers, Special Collections, Massachusetts State Library.

11. MacKay, "The Charles Street Jail," pp. 34–35.

12. *Boston Daily Advertiser,* September 8, 1848 (contains a long description of jail design); November 8, 1848 (RFP for pile drivers); December 4, 1848 (RFPs for masons, granite cutters, stone contractors, wharf builders, and blacksmiths).

13. *Boston Courier,* December 26, 1848.

14. *Boston Daily Advertiser,* October 5, 1848; March 14, 1849.

15. The Beacon Hill Reservoir was dedicated in November 1849. I have been unable to identify an architect for this structure. Mostly forgotten today, it was admired by architects in the nineteenth century. For example, in a lecture before the Charitable Mechanics Association in 1862, Arthur Gilman singled out the reservoir for its design. *Boston Evening Journal,* January 30, 1862. See also, James F. O'Gorman, *H. H. Richardson: Architectural Forms for an American Society* (Chicago: University of Chicago Press, 1987), pp. 83–84.

16. MacKay, "The Charles Street Jail," pp. 155–57; *Ballou's Pictorial,* August 18, 1857. Bryant's drawings survive in the Baltimore City Historical Society.

17. "Annual Report of the Directors of the Houses of Industry and Reformation, April 1, 1849," Boston City Document no. 25 (Boston: J. H. Eastburn, 1849), p. 6.

18. *Boston Daily Evening Journal,* June 27, 1849 (competition announced); *Saturday Evening Gazette,* March 23, 1850 (lithographed print of design on public view).

19. *The Builder* (London), June 22, 1850, pp. 290–91.

20. See *Portland Advertiser,* November 11, 1850, and July 16, 1853; *Rural Intelligencer* (Augusta), February 17, 1855. According to MacKay, "The Charles Street Jail," pp. 150–53, Bryant and Dwight entered into competition for four out-of-state almshouses in 1850–51. These were the Kingston, N.J., House of Refuge; the New Haven, Conn., Almshouse; the Blackwell's Island Almshouse and the Randall's Island House of Refuge, both in New York City.

21. Roger G. Reed, "To Exist for Centuries: Gridley Bryant and the Boston City Hospital," *Old Time New England* 77, no. 266 (Spring–Summer 1999): 65–89.

22. Henry G. Clark, M.D., "Outlines of a Plan for a Free City Hospital," p. 11.

23. "The Free City Hospital," *Evening Gazette* (Boston), March 6, 1858.

24. "Report of the Committee on a Free City Hospital," Boston City Document no. 34 (1861).

25. "Second Report of the Committee on the Free City Hospital," Boston City Document no. 69, December 16, 1861.

4. Transforming Boston

1. "Report of the Commissioners for the Enlargement of the State House," Senate Document no. 76, March 1, 1854; *Ballou's Pictorial Drawing-Room Companion,* April 26 and May 31, 1856; Ann Beha Associates, "The State House Historic Structure Report," vol. 1, March 1985. John D. Towle and Francis Foster had only a brief partnership, and it is unlikely that they could have demonstrated particular expertise in such a large-scale public project.

2. This is not to suggest, however, that he did not recognize that architects should be compensated for their ideas. In 1859 his friend Arthur Gilman sued architect Nathaniel Bradlee in a case in which Bryant was involved in mediation. Gilman had been approached by a client to design a commercial block. The client ended up hiring Bradlee but incorporated some of Gilman's ideas into his project. In the mediation ordered by the court, George Dexter spoke for Bradlee and Edward C. Cabot acted as a neutral party. This court case confirmed the value of an architect's ideas even when they had not been put to paper. *Boston Evening Transcript,* July 30, 1859.

3. Sara E. Wermiel, *The Fireproof Building: Technology and Public Safety in the Nineteenth-Century American City* (Baltimore: Johns Hopkins University Press, 2000).

4. *The Builder,* April 5, 1856, pp. 190–91.

5. Bailey, "Architect of the Old School," p. 334.

6. City of Boston, Tax Assessment Records, Boston City Archives. William Sparrell (1806–1879) began as a housewright around 1828 and was active until his death. Nathaniel Bradlee (1829–1888) trained in the office of George M. Dexter and, like his mentor, had a talent for engineering projects. O'Gorman, *Accomplished in All Departments of Art.*

7. Bryant to Parris, January 5, 1846, Alexander Parris Papers, Massachusetts State Library, Boston.

8. J. Eliot Cabot to Eliza Follen, March 11, 1851, Cabot Papers, Schlesinger Library, Harvard University. J. Eliot Cabot was then in partnership with his brother Edward. He was writing to Eliza Follen, his aunt, to offer advice for her son regarding a decision to pursue a career in architecture or engineering. Richard Upjohn's office in New York was probably one of the most desirable places for a student to be engaged. In 1851 Upjohn charged his pupils on a sliding scale ranging from $200 for six months to $500 for two years. Hull, "The School of Upjohn," 304. The same article reproduces a standard contract for students.

9. Bryant to Sturgis, November 17, 1868; Sturgis to Bryant, December 5, 1868, John Hubbard Sturgis Papers, Boston Athenaeum.

10. Joseph R. Richards (1828–1900) attempted to secure the commission to rebuild the Vermont State House (as did Bryant). "Testimony and Defense of the Superintendent of Construction for the October Session of the Legislature of Vermont, 1858," Online Research Center. The Denman Ross House (1868) at 26 Craigie Street, Cambridge, is perhaps the most substantial Richards design that is still standing and is certainly comparable with Bryant's domestic work for that period. For Briggs, see Edward F. Zimmer, "Luther Briggs and the Picturesque Pattern Books," *Old Time New England* 67, nos. 3–4 (Winter–Spring 1977): 36–55. Little is known about Charles Parker, although three important surviving examples of his work are masonry structures, the Brookline Reservoir Gate House (1848), the current headquarters of the Boston Society of Architects at 50–52 Broad Street (1853), and a row of houses on Blackstone Square (1853). Some of Alexander Esty's important surviving work is also stone construction, including Emmanuel Episcopal Church on Newbury Street in Boston (1861–62), Colby Hall at Andover-Newton Theological Seminary in Newton (1865), and Grace Episcopal Church in Newton (1872–73). The most extensive account of Esty's career, including his work for Bryant, is found in a series of articles by architect Frank A. Kendall published in a Framingham, Massachusetts, newspaper. Earle G. Shettleworth Jr. obtained copies of these undated articles from a scrapbook and shared them with me. See also Nina Harkrader's article for the Winchester Historical Society, "Alexander Esty: A Romanesque Church Design: Image and Meaning," published in *The Architects of Winchester, Massachusetts* series, no. 4 (1998).

11. Charles A. Cummings and Willard T. Sears later formed a partnership that would become one of the premier Boston firms. They became known chiefly for work in the High Victorian Gothic style, which they most certainly did not learn from Bryant. Park married the sister of Joseph and Samuel Richards (and was briefly a partner of the latter) but died young. He trained as a marble mason and traveled in Europe, and therefore may have made an interesting contribution to Bryant's practice, as he was a draftsman throughout the 1850s. Little is known about Samuel Richards (1833–?) and Rheimunt Sayer (1834–?). Sayer married a relative of Bryant's wife and later moved to New York.

12. Francis R. Kowsky, *Country, Park, and City: The Architecture and Life of Calvert Vaux* (New York: Oxford University Press, 1998), pp. 43–45. Curiously, the building contract in the Suffolk County Registry of Deeds, book 633, pp. 67–68, references Vaux's partner, landscape architect and author Alexander Jackson Downing,

as the architect. The *Boston Evening Journal* on September 1, 1857, also credited Downing: "Every one who has noticed the progress of architecture in this city during the last five years, must have been struck with the great improvement in the appearance of the rough granite buildings, following in great measure, the style inaugurated in the Commercial Block, which was designed by the lamented Downing."

13. *Boston Daily Evening Journal,* May 29, 1857; *Ballou's Pictorial Drawing-Room Companion,* January 3, 1857, p. 12; "Plan of Mercantile Wharf Property," Suffolk County Deeds, book 679, p. 243; for a typical building contract for one of the warehouses, see book 699, p. 174.

14. All quotations in this discussion are from a description of the completed building in the *Boston Evening Transcript,* December 27, 1857. For a typical building contract for one of the warehouses, see Suffolk County Deeds, book 724, pp. 3–5.

15. "Catalogue and terms and conditions of sale of lots of land, situated between Long and Central Wharves in the City of Boston belonging to the Long Wharf Corporation and the Central Wharf Corporation," Suffolk County Deeds, book 724, pp. 300–304.

16. *Saturday Evening Gazette,* December 25, 1858; *The Builder,* January 15, 1859.

17. The drawings in the Bradlee Collection provide rare documentation of the internal arrangements of these great palatial wholesale houses. The architect of the tall building that did not conform to Bryant's design has not been identified. A view of the entire block as Bryant envisioned it appeared in *Sketches and Business Directory of Boston and its Vicinity for 1860 and 1861* (Boston: Damrell & Moore and George Coolidge, 1860), p. 159.

18. *Saturday Evening Gazette,* February 13, 1858. The same newspaper, commenting on the demolition of the old cathedral, stated "We hope to see a magnificent Catholic Cathedral erected in some central part of the city that shall do credit to Boston. We should not expect a St. Peter's erected here, but believe that if our friend Bryant were to have a carte blanche permission to draw the plans, we might have a structure to remind us of some of the old world magnificence." Ibid, May 1, 1858. For historical background on the building on the site of the Franklin Street development, see *Boston Evening Transcript,* August 19, 1857.

19. H. H. Richardson's great Marshall Field Warehouse in Chicago, built in 1885–87, was also a wholesale store.

20. Extensive collections of drawings survive for Briggs (Historic New England) and Bradlee (Boston Athenaeum), allowing scholars opportunities to study their work.

21. Bryant F. Tolles Jr., *The John Tucker Daland House: Historic House Booklet Number Seven* (Salem: Essex Institute, 1978). The Peabody Essex Museum now uses the house for offices.

5. From Down East to San Francisco Bay

1. *Portland Advertiser,* November 11, 1850, and July 16, 1853; *Portland Pleasure Boat,* September 1, 1853.

2. *Portland Advertiser,* July 16, 1853.

3. Archives, Fryeburg Academy, Fryeburg, Maine.

4. The Joseph Titcomb House is documented through a set of drawings by Bryant dated October and November 1854. Collection of the Brick Store Museum, Kennebunk, Maine.

5. The Hobart House is attributed through Henry Bailey's catalogue of Bryant's drawings, prepared in 1890. The house has been altered for use as the East Bridgewater town hall.

6. *Ballou's Pictorial Drawing-Room Companion,* March 28, 1857, p. 200. This issue featured both the Maine State Seminary and the new Androscoggin County Courthouse complex. For an account of Ballou Hall at Tufts College, see Bryant Tolles Jr., "Gridley J. F. Bryant and the First Building at Tufts College," *Old Time New England* 63, no. 4 (April–June 1973): 89–99; idem, "Maine State Seminary: Gridley J. F. Bryant and Antebellum Architectural Master Planning," *Old Time New England* 78, no. 268 (Spring–Summer 2000): 41–55.

7. *Lewiston Falls Journal,* November 26, 1856.

8. Ibid., December 1, 1855; January 5, March 8, and April 19, 1856; *Democrat Advocate* (Lewiston), December 6, 1855.

9. McKay, "Charles Street Jail," pp. 178–83. See also by the same author "Gridley J. F. Bryant, 1816–1899," in *A Biographical Dictionary of Architects in Maine,* vol. 3, no. 9 (Augusta: Maine Historic Preservation Commission, 1986). This was a series of articles, printed separately and not paginated.

10. Cited in MacKay, "The Charles Street Jail," pp. 165–66.

11. The drawins and specifications are in the Washington County Archives.

12. *Machias Union,* December 21, 1858; Washington County Archives, Machias, Maine. Unfortunately, the windows have all been replaced and the brick corbelling encased in a false cornice. Thanks to the efforts of local attorney and historian Lyman Holmes, the cupola survives.

13. Bryant to the Washington County Commissioners, January 4, 1858, Washington County Archives.

14. Records of the Aroostook County Commissioners, cited in Nancy L. Yarborough, "Gridley J. F. Bryant and the Aroostook County Courthouse," unpublished paper, December 1985.

15. James G. Blaine, "Report on the system of disbursements, labor and discipline in the Maine State Prison" (Augusta: Stevens & Sayward, 1859), pp. 81–94.

16. *Lewiston Daily Evening Journal,* December 30, 1865.

17. Theodore Chase to Gridley J. F. Bryant, January 26, 1844, Chase Papers, Massachusetts Historical Society.

18. Harvard University Archives, vol. 17, p. 382; Boston Documents, "Specifications of public buildings of which Gridley J. F. Bryant furnished plans & instructions," no. 8, Massachusetss State Library.

19. There is a letter from Bryant to Richard Upjohn in the Upjohn Papers at the New York Public Library that suggests the pitfalls when there was a close relationship between contractor and architect. The correspondence, dated May 5, 1845, is a letter of introduction for a contractor who had submitted his bid on providing sandstone for a school in Newburyport based on information Bryant had supplied about a stone dealer in New York. Bryant's information proved inaccurate, and he was now looking for help for his contractor friend in obtaining a break in the price of the stone in return for a commitment to use that source on future projects.

20. Antoinette J. Lee, *Architects to the Nation: The Rise and Decline of the Supervising Architect's Office* (New York: Oxford University Press, 2000).

21. The records in the National Archives relating to construction projects during this period appear to be very incomplete. I was unable to find any record of the Eastport Custom House, for example, except for reference made in a letter written several years later.

22. *Eastport Sentinel,* June 9, 1897.

23. Eliot to Treasury Secretary Thomas Corwin, December 1, 1851, Record Group 56, Records of the Division of Appointments," National Archives, Washington, D.C.

24. Eliot to Sparks, May 14 and 15, 1852, Harvard College Papers, vol. 18, pp. 443–44, Harvard University Archives.

25. Record Group 56, entry 37, Records of the Division of Appointments, National Archives; *Gleason's Pictorial Drawing-Room Companion,* May 29, 1852, p. 345; diaries of Thomas U. Walter, 1851, Thomas Ustick Walter Collection, Athenaeum of Philadelphia.

26. First Auditor's Certificate no. 109.743, April 15, 1853, Record Group 56, National Archives. Bryant was paid $131.60 for a trip to Washington to consult with the secretary of the treasury on plans for "Light Houses etc." on the Pacific Coast. Payment was authorized on August 28, 1852. I was unable to locate any drawings for lighthouses that identify Bryant as the architect. The Lighthouse Board constructed sixteen lighthouses between 1852 and 1858. Bryant's role may have been to consult the Corps of Engineers, which typically was responsible for the construction of lighthouses during this period.

27. Montgomery Blair to Bryant, April 21, 1862, Record Group 121, National Archives. Unlike the Eastport Custom House, this project is well documented in terms of appointments and bills for Bryant's involvement.

6. Bryant and Gilman

1. Roger G. Reed, "Paris in the New World: Arthur Gilman's Vision of American Architecture," *Nineteenth Century* 23, no. 1 (Spring 2003): 19–29. Gilman attended Topsfield Academy and entered Trinity College in Hartford but left because of illness.

2. Arthur Gilman, "Rural Architecture in America," *North American Review,* no. 56 (January 1843): 4; Boston *Daily Advertiser,* November 17 and 24, 1843. The

author of the two articles on the Mt. Vernon Street Church is not identified. The style and substance, however, and the fact that Gilman is identified in a third letter, published on November 28, make him the likely author. The Reverend Kirk supplied a spirited defense of his new church in a letter published on December 4, 1843.

3. Gilman, "Architecture in the United States."

4. Gilman's lectures for the Lowell Institute ignited public comment. The exchange between Gilman and a trustee of Mt. Auburn Cemetery appeared in the *Boston Daily Advertiser* on October 29, October 31, November 1, and November 5, 1844. Two letters on Gilman's lectures also appeared in the *Boston Courier* on November 5, 1844. William Wheildon published an (unsigned) rebuttal to Gilman: "The New Custom House. Strictures on an article in The North American Review for April, 1844, titled 'Architecture in the United States' " (Boston: W. D. Ticknor & Co., 1844). The copy owned by the Boston Public Library includes a letter from Wheilden written in 1870 in which he identifies himself as the author and indicates that Young requested that the defense be written.

5. Wheildon, "The New Custom House," p. 22.

6. The Dedham Historical Society owns Gilman's specifications for the Dedham church. The Maine Maritime Museum in Bath owns the original drawings for the Bath church. Although the drawings have been misplaced, photographs are in the archives of the Maine Historic Prservation Commission.

7. Gilman rarely named living architects. An important exception is Richard Upjohn, whom Gilman clearly held in the highest regard. Gilman also designed two small board and batten Gothic churches in the late 1840s, St. Mary's in Dorchester and St. James in Amesbury, Massachusetts, both no longer standing.

8. *Boston Daily Advertiser*, November 17, 1843. This is the first of several instances in which Gilman praised Upjohn.

9. Copy in the collection of Earle G. Shettleworth Jr.

10. Bailey, "An Architect of the Old School," p. 332.

11. Mrs. Fanny Winchester Hotchkiss, *Winchester Notes* (New Haven: Tuttle, Morehouse & Taylor Co., 1912).

12. The Hunnewell family still owns the house, and the family records are the primary source for Gilman's and Bryant's involvement.

13. Archives, Exeter Historical Society, Exeter, N.H. Interestingly, the town hall was built on the site of a Gilman family home.

14. "Thomas K. Wharton, Diaries and Sketchbooks," New York Public Library, vol. 1, p. 197. My thanks to James O'Gorman for bringing these diaries to my attention.

15. *Sketches of Men of Mark: Written by the Best Talent of the East* (New York: New York and Hartford Publishing Co., 1871), pp. 817–21.

16. The plan by Gilman for the Back Bay design has not been located. There are several allusions to his prominent involvement in the planning process. The most compelling connection is an article written by Alfred Stone, his former draftsman, in 1903. Stone recalled that in 1856 he prepared plans for the development under Gilman's direction; *The American Architect* 20 (June 20, 1903): 94–95. An

interesting coincidence is that Samuel Hooper, for whom Gilman designed a major house on Commonwealth Avenue, traveled to Europe in 1853 after serving as one of the first commissioners charged by the state to develop plans for filling the Back Bay. See *The Boston Almanac for the Year 1859* (Boston: Brown, Taggard & Chase), p. 62; and for a comprehensive history of the development of the Back Bay neighborhood, see Bainbridge Bunting, *Houses of Boston's Back Bay* (Cambridge: Belknap Press, 1967).

17. *Boston Evening Transcript*, June 11, 1857. This newspaper item documents that Gilman design the Hotel Pelham, but that his former draftsman, Alfred Stone, supervised construction and carried out changes to the interior plan. For an article on this building, see Jean A. Follett, "The Hotel Pelham: A New Building Type for America," *American Art Journal* (Autumn 1983): 58–73.

18. Edward H. Kendall (1842–1901) was born in Boston. Prior to working for Bryant and Gilman, he studied art and architecture in Europe in 1858–59. He became prominent in New York and was elected president of the American Institute of Architects in 1891–93. See *New York the Metropolis*, pt. 1 (New York: The New York Recorder, 1893), p. 10; *National Cyclopedia*, vol. 12 (New York: James White & Co., 1904), p. 247. James G. Hill (1841–1913) was from Malden, Massachusetts, where Louis P. Rogers grew up and resided. He entered Bryant's office as a student in 1857, eventually becoming a draftsman. Moving to Washington to work for the government in 1862, Hill was appointed by Supervising Architect Alfred Mullett in 1867. Treasury Secretary John Sherman appointed James Hill supervising architect in 1876. Lee, *Architects to the Nation*, pp. 123–35.

19. Actually Bryant had worked with Gilman many years earlier in the conversion of several townhouses for the Winthrop Hotel in 1849. Bryant was a contractor on that project. Suffolk County Registry of Deeds, book 562, pp. 85–86.

20. For Gilman's position on Christ Church, see *Boston Evening Transcript*, August 22, 1857.

21. *Boston Evening Transcript*, December 6, 1861. This four-column article describing the church was probably largely written by Gilman. The same paper had announced, on August 20, 1859, that Gilman's plan had been accepted, and that he was to be "assisted" by Bryant.

22. Paul R. Baker, *Richard Morris Hunt* (Cambridge: MIT Press, 1980), pp. 118–19. Sadly no longer standing, this block for Dr. H. H. Williams raises the issue of Hunt's influence as an École des Beaux-Arts–trained designer on the early development of the Back Bay neighborhood.

23. George L. Wrenn III, "The Boston City Hall, Bryant and Gilman architects, 1862–1865," *Journal of the Society of Architectural Historians* 21, no. 4 (December 1962): 188–92.

24. A color lithograph of the building was prepared by Carl Fehmer, a German-born architect who had replaced James G. Hill in the firm in 1864–65. Boston City Documents, "The City Hall, Boston" (Boston: Alfred Mudge & Son, 1866), p. 2. Carl Fehmer (1838–?) was born in Germany and came to this country in 1852. He trained under George Snell. In 1866 he established his own practice. He worked for a few years in partnership with William R. Emerson.

25. Bailey, "An Architect of the Old School," p. 338.

26. City of Lynn, *The City Hall of Lynn: being A history of the Events leading to its Erection, and An Account of the Ceremonies at the Dedication of the Building, November 30, 1867* (Lynn: Thomas P. Nichols, 1869).

27. Bryant and Gilman designed a large number of projects in Lynn in 1865–66, most of which are no longer extant. Bryant's connections with that city may have coincided with the period when he summered there. Letter to author from Arthur Krim, September 30, 1996.

28. *Sketches of Men of Mark*, p. 819.

29. "Enlargement of the State Capitol. Report of the Architect Appointed by His Excellency the Governor" (Concord: Amos Hadley, 1864); see *Concord Daily Monitor*, May 28, June 9 and 23, 1864, July 14, and August 9, 1864.

30. "Enlargement of the State Capitol," p. 13.

31. Gilman to Andrew Dickson White, January 27, 1867, Gilman Papers, American Institute of Architects, New York.

32. His obituary in the *New York Times* on August 6, 1882, barely mentioned his professional career, recounting only examples of his humor which do not resonate with twenty-first-century ears.

33. *Boston Evening Transcript*, July 17, 1882.

7. Bryant and Rogers

1. According to the *Boston Courier* of February 14, 1863, Bryant and Gilman were preparing estimates to dismantle the Hancock House for its reconstruction on a new site. Margaret Henderson Floyd completed a manuscript on the career of John Hubbard Sturgis (1834–1888). Her papers are in the collections of Historic New England, Boston (formerly Society for the Preservation of New England Antiquities).

2. Gillman's call for the AIA to serve as a final court of appeals on professional matters was in keeping with his opinions: "Nobody knows enough to contradict us on our ground, if only we are united, nor could they find a leg to stand on in the way of argument if they did." Henry H. Saylor, "The A.I.A.'s First Hundred Years" (Washington, D.C.: The Octagon, 1957), p. 133.

3. Marvin E. Goody and Robert P. Walsh, eds., *Boston Society of Architects: The First Hundred Years, 1867–1967* (Boston: Boston Society of Architects, 1967).

4. Ibid., pp. 34–38.

5. How else can one explain the change in Gilman's attitude from his 1867 address to the convention? See note 2.

6. Louis B. Rogers, obituary, *Andover (Massachusetts) Townsman*, April 28, 1905. I am indebted to Donald H. Morrow for filling in information on Rogers and his family. See also the February 1890 edition of *Architectural Era* (Syracuse, New York).

7. John Hubbard Sturgis to Bryant, December 5, 1868, John H. Sturgis Papers, Boston Athenaeum. Robert Peabody "studied architecture" with Bryant and

took courses in the new School of Architecture at M.I.T. from 1866 to 1867. *Harvard College Class of 1866 Class Report* (Boston: Rand, Avery & Frye, 1869), p. 28.

8. Mullett to Treasury Secretary George S. Boutwell, March 12, 1869, Record Group 56, National Archives, Washington, D.C.

9. For photos and descriptions of all of the Boston public schools still in use in 1900, including many buildings designed by Bryant that are now long gone, see "Annual Reports of the School Committee of the City of Boston" for 1900 and 1901, Special Collections, Massachusetts State Library, Boston.

10. *Boston Evening Transcript,* January 1, 1870.

11. The Maine Historic Preservation Commission has the drawings for the railroad station. The jail and courthouse drawings are owned by Penobscot and Knox counties, respectively.

12. *The Technologist* (October 1870): 242–43, 245; ibid. (June 1871): 146–49, 153.

13. Francis H. Kimball (1845–1919) was yet another architect who trained with Bryant and rose to prominence in New York City. David F. Ransom, "Biographical Dictionary of Hartford Architects," *Connecticut Historical Society Bulletin* 54, nos. 1–2 (Winter–Spring 1989): 66–68. My thanks to Darrin Von Stein, an architectural historian working on a monograph on Kimball, who supplied me with extensive documentation derived from the Francis Kimball Scrapbook, in his possession.

14. Henry Russell Hitchcock and William Seale, *Temples of Democracy: The State Capitols of the USA* (New York: Harcourt Brace Jovanovich, 1976), pp. 159–65; David F. Ransom, *George Keller: Architect* (Hartford: Stowe-Day Foundation, 1978); Francis Kimball Scrapbook.

15. Archives, City of Gloucester, Massachusetts; *Gloucester Telegraph,* May 29 and October 2, 1869; January 12 and November 19, 1870.

16. *Boston Evening Transcript,* January 8, 1872. The newspaper published the entire description submitted by the architects for their proposal, but no illustrations have been located.

17. James F. O'Gorman, "Two Granite Tents at Bay View on Cape Ann: An Architectural Note on the B. F. Butler and J. H. French Houses," *Essex Institute Historical Collections* 118, no. 4 (October 1982): 241–47. The portfolio of original drawings includes floor plans, elevations, and framing plans. As with so many of these small projects, Bryant and Rogers may not have provided construction supervision, nor may they have designed the granite carriage barn on the site. Jonas French, an experienced builder, probably supervised the work.

18. Conversation with the owner, Mrs. Harriet Myers, August 2005. The entrance hall also retains surviving wall paintings, but this work, in the Pompeiian style, may have been added later.

19. McKay, "Charles Street Jail," pp. 169–72, 202–3.

20. "Carlton An eye-witness," "The Story of the Great Fire, Boston, November 9–10, 1872" (Boston: Shepard and Gill, 1872), p. 10.

21. City of Boston, "Report of the Commissioners to Investigate the Fire" (Boston, 1873), pp. 542–47

22. As with any individual who lived in several locations and returned to his hometown late in life, information on Louis Rogers is difficult to come by. In addition to sources already cited, there are partial records of his employment in the office of the supervising architect of the Treasury Department in Record Group 56, National Archives, Washington, D.C. Thanks to Earle G. Shettleworth Jr. for recovering a small selection of letters from Rogers to Albert G. Eaton of Maine written at the end of his career in 1892. For an unfavorable description of Rogers in Rochester, see Claude Bragdon, *More Lives Than One* (New York: Alfred A. Knopf, 1938), pp. 29–30.

8. An Architect of the Nineteenth Century

1. The historian C. A. Hale identified the two St. John projects through newspaper research. Little is known about Black's career. In 1884 he was married in Woodstock, New Brunswick, where he then lived. When a fire destroyed most of the commercial district of Eastport, Maine, in October 1886, Black became the principal designer of the new downtown. Plans and specifications survive for several projects.

2. *Malden Mirror,* July 7, 1877. Luce (1852–1924) moved to New York City in 1884. Thanks to Rick Teller, archivist and librarian at the Williston Northampton School in Easthampton, Mass. See also Cotle Reynolds, *Genealogical and Family History of Southern New York and the Hudson River Valley,* vol. 3 (New York, 1914), pp. 1427–29.

3. Known as the "Sunflower House" for its characteristic Queen Anne–style motif, the Smith House still stands at 130 Mt. Vernon Street. The Stanwood House, also still standing, is located at 76 High Street in Brookline.

4. *American Architect and Building News,* April 8, 1880.

5. Marion B. Gebbie Archives and Special Collections, Wheaton College, Norton, Mass. The original name was Seminary Hall.

6. L. Howard, "Wilder Memorial Hall," unpublished paper for Radcliffe Seminars, September 1981. Thanks to Monique Lehner for sharing this paper and other documentation.

7. "Old Boston Families, Number Six: The Bryant Family," *New England Historical and Geneaolgical Register* 97 (January 1943): 43–45.

8. With only an uncritical obituary to provide an alternate view *(Saturday Evening Gazette,* October 13, 1883), we are forced to rely on Henry Bailey for a personal account of Mrs. Bryant. Bailey blamed her for squandering Bryant's money and described her as a "born aristocrat" and "imperious." If we are to believe Bailey, she probably had no use for her husband's siblings, all of whom remained in the working class. Bailey, "An Architect of the Old School," pp. 327–28. There is, however, a diary account by one acquaintance from 1853, who writes: "Mrs. Bryant is a lady of refined and cultivated taste and very engaging manners. The [Bryants'] drawing rooms were brilliantly lighted and well stored with objects of 'virtue'—and the conversation very animated until we withdrew to the Tea-rooms." Thomas K.

Wharton Diaries and Sketchbooks, entry for November 14, 1853, New York Public Library.

9. *Boston Evening Transcript,* August 22, 1885.

10. *Boston Evening Transcript,* January 18, 1886; Susan Wilson, "The Omni Parker House: A Brief History of America's Longest Continuously Operated Hotel," privately printed booklet, 2001.

11. John F. Eaton (1842–1905) died in Newton. I have not been able to locate any information on his training. For Memorial Hall, see *Boston Transcript,* May 31, 1873. The first documentation I have been able to locate of Eaton's working with Bryant concerns the construction of the Liberty Building in Boston in 1882. This was perhaps Bryant's last opportunity to design a richly embellished commercial block. Eaton served as clerk of the works for the construction. *Boston Globe,* June 18, 1882.

12. Bailey, "An Architect of the Old School," pp. 347–48.

13. Ibid., p. 347.

14. Ibid., pp. 342, 348. For example, he had no credit rating through R. C. Dunn & Co. (unlike Arthur Gilman, for whom credit ratings are given).

15. *American Architect and Building News,* June 24, 1899, p. 97. His funeral was attended by a few friends, his sister Mrs. Maria Coburn, John F. Eaton, and a delegation from the Boston Society of Architects. *Boston Globe,* June 11, 1899.

16. Bailey, "An Architect of the Old School," p. 347.

17. *Boston Daily Globe,* February 21, 1894, p. 20.

18. Ibid., p. 347.

BIBLIOGRAPHY

Bacon, Oliver N. *A History of Natick.* Boston: Damrell & Moore, 1856.

Badger, Daniel D. *Badger's Illustrated catalogue of cast-iron architecture.* New York: Dover Publications, c.1981.

Bailey, Henry T. "An Architect of the Old School." *New England Magazine* 25.3 (November 1901): 326–49.

Barnard, Henry. *School Architecture, or Contributing to the Improvement of School-houses in the United States.* Cincinnati: H. W. Derby & Co., 1854.

Bryan, John Morrill. "Boston's Granite Architecture." Ph.D. diss., Boston University, 1972.

Bryant, Gridley J.F. *Specifications of Public Buildings of which Gridley J.F. Bryant Furnished Plans and Instructions.* Two volumns. Massachusetts State Library, 1850–1853.

Bunting, Bainbridge. *Houses of Boston's Back Bay.* Cambridge: Belknap Press, 1967.

Cleveland, Henry R. "American Architecture." *North American Review* 93 (October 1836): 356–84.

City Council. *The City Hall of Lynn.* Lynn: Thomas P. Nichols, 1869.

City of Boston. *City Document no. 21: Report of the Superintendent of Public Buildings.* Boston, 1851.

———. *City Document no. 61: Final Report of the Committee on the Erection of the New Jail.* Boston, 1851.

———. *City Document no. 98: Concerning the Publication of a History of the City Hall.* Boston, 1866.

———. *Report of the Committee on Public Buildings in Relation to a New City Hall.* Boston: J. F. Farwell & Co., 1862.

Coburn, Louise Helen. *Skowhegan on the Kennebec.* Skowegan: Indpendent Press Reporter, 1941.

Committee on Public Buildings. *The City Hall, Boston. Corner Stone Laid Monday, December 22, 1862. Dedicated September 17, 1865.* Boston: Alfred Mudge & Son, 1866.

Curron, Kathleen. *The Romanesque Revival: Religion, Politics, and Transitional Exchange.* University Park: Pennsylvania State University Press, 2003.

Davis, Helen W., Edward M. Hatch, and David G. Wright. "Alexander Parris, Innovator in Naval Facility Architecture." *Industrial Archaeology* 2.1 (1976): 3–22.

Dearborn, Nathaniel. *Boston Notions: Being an Authentic and Concise Account of that Village from 1630 to 1847.* Boston: Nathaniel Dearborn, 1848.

Ellstein, Rochelle S. "William Washburn and the Egyptian Revival in Boston." *Old Time New England* 70 (1980): 63–81.

Floyd, Margaret Henderson. *Architectural Education in Boston.* Boston: Boston Architectural Center, 1989.

Follett, Jean A. "The Hotel Pelham: A New Building Type for America." *American Art Journal* 30 (Autumn 1983): 58–73.

Gilman, Arthur. "Architecture in the United States." *North American Review* 58 (April 1844): 436–80.

———. "Landscape Gardening." *North American Review* 59 (October 1844): 302–29.

———. "Rural Architecture in America." *North American Review* 68 (January 1843): 1–17.

Goody, Marvin E., and Robert P. Walsh, eds. *Boston Society of Architects: The First Hundred Years, 1867–1967.* Boston: Boston Society of Architects, 1967.

Hitchcock, Henry Russell, and William Seale. *Temples of Democracy: The State Captiols of the United States of America.* New York: Harcourt Brace Jovanovich, 1976.

Holly, H. Hobart. "The Granite Railway." *Quincy (Mass.) History,* no. 26 (Fall 1991): 1–4.

Huxtable, Ada Louise. "Commercial Buildings, c.1850–1870, Gridley James Fox Bryant, Architect." *Progressive Architecture in America* 39 (August 1958): 105–6.

———. "Granite Wharf, Warehouse, Office Buildings, c. 1923–1872, Boston, Massachuestts, Alexander Parris, G.J.F. Bryant, Others, Architects." *Progressive Architecture in America.* 39 (June, 1958): 117–18.

Johnson, Richard B. *Seven and Eight Park Street: A Brief History of the Home of the Union Club.* Boston: Union Club, ca. 1976).

Jordy, William H. *Buildings of Rhode Island.* Oxford: Oxford University Press, 2004.

Kilham, Walter H. *Boston after Bulfinch.* Cambridge: Harvard University Press, 1946.

Kirker, Harold. *The Architecture of Charles Bulfinch.* Cambridge: Harvard University Press, 1978.

Kirker, Harold, and James Kirker. *Bulfinch's Boston, 1787–1817.* New York: Oxford University Press, 1964.

Kirker, Harold, and Van Zantan, David. "Jean Lemoulnier in Boston, 1846–1852." *Journal of the Society of Architectural Historians* 3 (October 1972): 204–8.

Lee, Antoinette J. *Architects to the Nation: The Rise and Decline of the Supervising Architect's Office.* New York: Oxford University Press, 2000.

Linden-Ward, Blanche. *Silent City on a Hill: Landscapes of Memory and Boston's Mount Auburn Cemetery.* Columbus: Ohio University Press, 1989. Rev. and expanded edition to be published as Blanche Linden, *Silent City on a Hill: Picturesque Landscapes of Memory and Boston's Mount Auburn Cemetery* (Amherst: University of Massachusetts Press / Library of American Landscape History, 2007).

MacKay, Robert B. "The Charles Street Jail: Hegemony of a Design." Ph.D. diss., Boston University, 1980.

Meeks, Carroll L. V. *The Railroad Station: An Architectural History.* New Haven: Yale University Press, 1956.

Myers, Denys Peter. "Isaiah Rogers, 1800–1869." In *A Biographical Dictionary of Architects in Maine,* vol. 3, no. 2. Augusta: Maine Historic Preservation Commission, 1986.

North, James W. *The History of Augusta, Maine.* Augusta, Me.: Clapp & North, 1870.

O'Gorman, James F. *Accomplished in All Departments of Art: Hammatt Billings of Boston, 1818–1874.* Amherst: University of Massachusetts Press, 1998.

————. *On the Boards: Drawings by Nineteenth-Century Boston Architects.* Philadelphia: University of Pennsylvania Press, 1989.

————. *This Other Gloucester.* Boston: privately printed, 1976.

————. "Two Granite Tents at Bay View on Cape Ann: Architectural Notes on the B. F. Butler and J. H. French Houses." *Essex Institute Historical Collections* 118.4 (October 1982): 241–47.

Ransom, David F. "Biographical Dictionary of Hartford Architects." *Connecticut Historical Society Bulletin* 54.1–2 (1989): 13–160.

Reed, Roger G. "Paris in the New World: Arthur Gilman's Vision of American Architecture." *Nineteenth Century* 23.1 (Spring 2003): 19–29.

————. "To Exist for Centuries: Gridley Bryant and the Boston City Hospital." *Old Time New England* 77.266 (Spring–Summer 1999): 65–89.

Robinson, Donald F. *Two Hundred Years in South Hingham, 1746–1946.* Hingham, Mass.: Hingham Historical Society, 1980.

Sammarco, Anthony Mitchell. *Images of America Dorchester.* Dover, N.H.: Arcadia Press, 1995.

Saylor, Henry H. *The A.I.A.'s First Hundred Years.* Washington, D.C.: The Octagon, 1957.

Shand Tucci, Douglas. *Built in Boston: City and Suburb, 1800–2000.* Amherst: University of Massachusetts Press, 1999.

Sketches and Business Directory of Boston and its Vicinity for 1860 and 1861. Boston: Damrell & Moore and George Coolidge, 1860.

Sketches of Men of Mark: Written by the Best Talent of the East. New York: New York and Hartford Publishing Co., 1871.

Slauterback, Catharina. *Designing the Boston Athenaeum: 101/2 at 150.* Boston: Boston Athenaeum, 1999.

Stuart, Charles. *Lives and Works of Civil and Military Engineers of America.* New York: D. Van Nostrand, 1871.

Tolles, Bryant F., Jr. "Gridley J. F. Bryant and the First Building at Tufts College." *Old Time New England* 63.4 (Spring 1973): 89–99.

————. "The John Tucker Daland House." *Historic House Booklet No. 7.* Salem: Essex Institute, 1978.

————. "Maine State Seminary: Gridley J. F. Bryant and Antebellum Architectural Master Planning." *Old Time New England* 78.268 (Spring–Summer 2000): 41–55.

————. *New Hampshire Architecture: An Illustrated Guide.* Hanover, N.H.: University Press of New England for the New Hampshire Historical Society, 1979.

Upjohn, Everard M. *Richard Upjohn: Architect and Churchman.* New York: Da Capo Press, 1968.

Vose, George L. *A Sketch of the Life and Work of Loammi Baldwin.* Boston: Press of George H. Ellis, 1885.

Webster, W. B. *Brookline: A Collection of Thirty-Five Promiment Residences, Public Build-ings and Churches.* Boston: W. H. Couillard, 1888.

Welch, Kathryn. "Boston's Old City Hall." *Antiques* 107 (June 1975):110–15.

Wermiel, Sara E. *The Fireproof Building: Technology and Public Safety in the Nineteenth-Century American City.* Baltimore: Johns Hopkins University Press, 2000.

Wheildon, William W. *Memoir of Solomon Willard.* Boston: Monument Association, 1865.

Whitehall, Walter Muir. *Boston: A Topographical History.* Cambridge,: Belknap Press, 1968.

Winsor, Justin, ed. *The Memorial History of Boston.* Boston: James R. Osgood & Co., 1881.

Wolcott, Cora Codman. *Random Recollections, or, Much Ado about Nothing.* Brookline: Twin Pine Farm, 1934.

Wrenn, George L., III. "The Boston City Hall, Bryant and Gilman Architects, 1862–1865." *Journal of the Society of Architectural Historians.* 21.4 (December 1962): 188–92.

Zimmer, Edward F. "The Architectural Career of Alexander Parris (1780–1852)." Ph.D. diss., Boston University, 1984.

———. "Luther Briggs and the Picturesque Pattern Books." *Old Time New England* 67.3–4 (Winter–Spring 1977): 36–56.

INDEX

ROGER G. REED has been researching and writing about the architecture of New England since 1983. A graduate in Preservation Planning from Cornell University, Mr. Reed worked as an architectural historian for the Maine Historic Preservation Commission for over ten years. In Maine he wrote several books and articles, including *A Delight to All Who Know It: The Maine Summer Architecture of William R. Emerson* and *Summering on the Thoroughfare: The Architecture of North Haven*. Since moving to Newton Highlands, Massachusetts, Mr. Reed has been working as a preservation planner for the Town of Brookline. He is married with two children.